HOLISTIC MYSTICISM

The Integrated Spiritual Path of the Quakers

HOLISTIC MYSTICISM

The Integrated Spiritual Path of the Quakers

AMOS SMITH

ANAMCHARA
BOOKS

Anamchara Books
Vestal, New York 13850
www.anamcharabooks.com

With gratitude to Harper Collins Publishers for permission to quote extensively from Thomas Kelly's classic, *A Testament of Devotion.*

Except as noted, Bible translations are from New Revised Standard Version Bible (NRSV), copyright © 1989 National Council of the Churches of Christ in the United States of America. Used by permission. All rights reserved worldwide.

Scripture quotations marked NIV are taken from the Holy Bible, New International Version®, NIV®. Copyright © 1973, 1978, 1984, 2011 by Biblica, Inc.™ Used by permission of Zondervan. All rights reserved worldwide, www.zondervan.com. The "NIV" and "New International Version" are trademarks registered in the United States Patent and Trademark Office by Biblica, Inc.™

Scripture quotations marked YLT are from the 1898 Young's Literal Translation of the Holy Bible by J.N. Young, public domain.

All the boxed short biographies in this book were written by Anamchara Books editors. At the author's request, we are stating that he was not responsible for their content.

IngramSpark paperback ISBN: 978-1-62524-902-9
eBook ISBN: 978-1-62524-901-2

Dedicated to Elders Herb and Ellie Foster,
founders of Santa Cruz Friends Meeting,
who taught me the meaning of spiritual marriage
and applied mysticism.

CONTENTS

Forewords

by Margery Post Abbott and Max Carter

T o fall into the transforming power of the Light can be a painful and joyous thing. For some of us, it opens another dimension of the universe far removed from rationality, strict rules, and even words. A simple moment tastes of eternity as our being recenters in a nameless space that many call Christ, the Word that existed before the beginning (John 1:1).

When my life was broken open, I was overwhelmed and somewhat lost, seeking for guides to help me sort through this astonishing call to renewal. Fortunately, I was in a Quaker community where individuals walked alongside me, and a cloud of witnesses from across generations affirmed and sustained me in the hard work required to realize the changed life to which I was called (Ephesians 4:22).

In *Holistic Mysticism*, Amos Smith makes available to a broader audience some of those Quaker voices and wisdom. My parents loved the Down-East humor of mystic Rufus Jones; the stories of his Quaker childhood in Maine were favorites of my dad. I was introduced to Thomas Kelly's writings as a young adult, and I was delighted to find in Caroline Stephen a woman who spoke with authority of the mystical way of Friends (Quakers). George Fox, widely accepted as the organizer of Quakers (along with Margaret Fell Fox), left us a journal documenting his lifelong encounters with the one, Christ Jesus, who could speak to his condition and to every soul who listens for the Inward Guide (Luke 17:21). I am grateful to Amos Smith for bringing alive these voices from Quaker tradition

Quakerism is at times called "group mysticism," and Quakers are sometimes called a society of mystics, for we can experience the Spirit moving among the congregation during worship or as we settle into the worshipful Meetings for business. One Sunday in the silence of worship, I was made startlingly aware of this group mysticism when I was given a clear message to stand and speak. In my shyness, I was not able to share the words I was given, but soon after, someone behind me stood and gave that same message word for word.

Often, when I share my experience of corporate mysticism, others share similar stories. Many of us also have stories of major disagreements in Business Meetings, which turned into surprising agreements on new ways forward. This happened when the community let go of trying to find a yes/no answer. They became open to creative tension and the Presence of God, rather than caught up in personal fears or demands of the ego.

Amos Smith's words shine light on these individual and communal encounters with the Inward Teacher who sets us on a path of integrity, humility, and justice, which is at the core of Friends' practice and identity. He makes clear that mysticism is not confined to monasteries or otherwise isolated from the problems of the world. Mysticism broadly defined is very much needed in our world today and will help us navigate the colossal challenges of our times.

— *Margery Post Abbott*
  Author of *To Be Broken and Tender, a Quaker Theology for Today*

When people see or hear the word *Quaker*, their first association is often, mistakenly, oats, motor oil, or the Amish. The more informed might think of peace work, women's rights, antislavery work, prison reform, or the business acumen of the Lloyds, Barclays, Macys, and Cadburys. When thinking of Quakers, few people, however, immediately think of "mysticism." Yet without what Amos Smith carefully describes as the mystical DNA of Quakerism, Quaker contributions in the realm of peace, the arts, the sciences, justice, human rights, and even business integrity would be much less significant.

Many contemporary Friends (as Quakers are officially called) do not use the term mysticism themselves in describing Quakerism. Large numbers of Quakers have assimilated into a Protestant understanding of Christianity, and many Quakers today are probably more likely to associate mysticism with crystals, Tarot cards, and astrology rather than the deep mystical roots of their own faith tradition. Those Friends who do embrace the importance of mysticism in Quaker understanding and experience often characterize its essence as conscience, reason, or "bits" and "sparks" of the Divine.

As this book helpfully describes, the source of Quaker mysticism is a direct encounter, without broker or mediator, with the Divine—in its fullness—as the Real Presence of God, an Inward Light of Christ, a Seed. The many terms by which Quakers historically described that Real Presence indicate the experiential nature of the encounter. This Presence is not a "spark" that only insiders can experience; not a "bit," either, for God cannot be divided up into what one of my students humorously described as "God chunks."

Once Quakers encountered the illuminating power of this Real Presence, they harmonized their practice with this principle and its nature. Out of this experiential encounter arose Friends' "testimony" to the importance of integrity, peace, equality, simplicity, and community. Margaret Fell Fox (1614–1702) wrote of "women's speaking justified;" Benjamin Lay (1682–1759) kicked the door open for later Quaker abolitionists. Lucretia Mott (1793–1880) and Susan B. Anthony (1820–1906) agitated for women's rights—and Alice Paul (1885–1977) saw it come to fruition.

Once they encountered the illuminating power of this Real Presence, Adam Curle (1916–2006), Ham Seok-heon (1901–1989), Bayard Rustin (1912–1987), Elise Boulding (1920–2010), and David Niyonzima worked for peace, justice, and civil rights. Artist James Turrell (born 1943) illustrated it in light. Quaker scientists such as Luke Howard (1772–1864), Kathleen Lonsdale (1903–1971), Maria Mitchell (1818–1889), Jocelyn Burnell (born 1943), and Arthur Eddington (1882–1944), believing that God could be encountered in the natural world as well as in a book, made abundant discoveries.

Oats, oil, and avoiding electricity were not central to any of this! What *was* central was the Divine Center, an inner sanctuary where the very Presence of God dwelt. The Divine Center's power leads, guides, directs, and enables the obedient to overcome great obstacles. As Rufus Jones stated, "The kingdom of God is not a place where we go, but a state of being we can live in." And we don't need to take the journey by horse and buggy!

— *Max Carter, PhD*
   William R. Rogers Director of Friends Center and Quaker Studies (Emeritus), Guilford College

Author's Disclaimers

F irst, this book chronicles my personal faith journey and integrates elements from Quakerism and beyond. I identify as a contemplative Christian, and my primary influences are Quakerism and contemplative Christianity. In brief, I am a contemplative Quaker. Implied in the word *Quaker* is that I am ecologically minded.

Second, since this book is personal, I don't consider it to be authoritative; it describes my own understandings and experiences only. Anyway, authorities are something Friends usually manage to do without.

Third, I realize many people are uncomfortable with religious language, including the word *God*. The word has baggage. So, when someone says to me they don't believe in God, I ask them about the God they don't believe in. When they describe a judgmental anthropocentric God (as they often do), I say, "I don't believe in that God either." Then other words or phrases can be used, which can open minds to *Real Presence* (a term coined by Thomas Kelly that I'll discuss in chapter 7). Also, people who are okay with the concept of God may still be uncomfortable with the term *Christ*. I am comfortable with this term, and you will see it throughout this book, but my understanding of Christ is inclusive and expansive.

I also realize many people have given up on organized religion of any kind because of historic baggage and dysfunction. Within any faith tradition, however, lies a broad spectrum of adherents. Christianity has a span that includes Dorothy Day and Albert Schweitzer on one end of the spectrum and the Conquistadors and Inquisitors on the other. It is up to us to choose the life-giving saints and their teachings while avoiding the demons. In this book, I focus on wisdom I have learned specifically from the Quakers, as well as from contemplative Christians who practice centering prayer. The common ground for both Quakers and contemplative Christians is holy silence.

Our language for the Divine and for spiritual matters is always approximate. We can never pigeonhole or define the Great Mystery. Quakers use various phrases to refer to God, such as *Inward Light, Light of Christ, That of God in All People,* and *Real Presence.*[1] If you're uncomfortable with "God language"—or if you want to expand your understanding of the Divine—you may find these Quaker terms helpful.

Fourth, I use inclusive language, which is appropriate for a book about Quakers, whose leadership was egalitarian from the beginning. Along these lines, where appropriate, I change quotations throughout the book to be inclusive and indicate the changes with brackets.

Fifth, in this book, I include many quotations and biographical information about historical Quakers. However, I do not speak for all Quakers, past or present. Quakers like me have in common a history of membership and regular Quaker Meeting attendance, but we each have independent thoughts. My words will resonate with a broad spectrum of Quakers, but some thoughts are unique to me and my experiences and cannot be tagged "Quaker." I include these independent thoughts because they are relevant to the text and to contemporary Quakerism, which values the individualism of its members.

Sixth, you will notice that throughout this book I reference numerous strong female Quaker leaders. This is intentional. A unique quality of Quakerism is its strong female leaders from the beginning to the present day. This three-hundred-and-fifty-year-old egalitarian legacy is appropriate for a book titled *Holistic Mysticism*. The balance of mature female and male leadership will best lead our spiritual communities toward equilibrium and wholeness.

Seventh, you'll find in each chapter a short biography of a Quaker individual. Anamchara Books' editors added these biographies to give a sense of the diversity, depth, and breadth of Quaker tradition through the ages.

Finally, *you don't need to be a Quaker to learn from this book.* Instead, I hope this book will serve as an entryway, opening up new perspectives and possibilities in your own spiritual journey.

Introduction

What Is Mysticism?

Do not let the word "mystic" scare you off.
It simply means one who has moved
from belief systems or belonging systems
to actual inner experience.

—Richard Rohr[2]

In this book, we will talk about mysticism and meditative practices. I realize some readers may find these terms intimidating—but remember, meditative practices cover a wide range. Anything we engage in with awareness and mindfulness (for example, walking, washing dishes, knitting and other fabric arts, hiking, fishing, and almost any other activity you can think of) can become a contemplative practice when we intentionally slow down with full presence of mind.

Today, mysticism, defined as "the direct and immediate experience of the Absolute,"[3] is no longer relegated to the Middle Ages or to dreamy, self-deluded practitioners. While church attendance has decreased significantly in past decades,[4] a Pew study found that an interest in mysticism has more than doubled since the 1960s.[5] "The Christian of the future will be a mystic or will not exist at all,"[6] said Karl Rahner.

Rahner understood that the mystic's faith is anchored in experience, not in academic doctrines, a charismatic pastor, generational peer pressure, or warm community songfests bathed in candlelight. All these aspects of faith can be important, but they are not the anchor. They are no substitute for Christ's Real Presence. Today, people thirst for experiential spirituality and its sources, and Christianity has seen a resurgence of contemplative arts across traditions (Protestant, Catholic, and Orthodox).[7] With climate change, global terrorism, widespread political upheaval, the technological divide, and global pandemics, now more than ever, people need to reconnect with their unified and unifying Source.

While many spiritual searchers have turned for insight to the great Catholic mystics of the past, Quakerism offers a rooted and integrated form of mysticism that has often been overlooked. From the beginning, Quakers were a society of mystics. One of their founders, George Fox, didn't define himself as a theologian or Bible scholar; instead, he was someone who experienced Christ's Real Presence. He didn't know *about* Christ through secondhand knowledge; he knew Christ personally, intimately, and experientially.

In contrast to the undisciplined and wishy-washy mysticism that can lead to spiritual stagnation, Quakerism offers a stream of clear fresh water, a stream that flows out of sacred silence experienced in community. This communal mysticism, unique to Quakers,[8] is not so much about the solitary person sitting on a rock or in a hermit's cell but about sitting in the presence of others who seek obedience to the Light.[9] Quakers worship Christ's Presence revealed in collective stillness and silence.

Quaker mysticism is practical, accessible, communal, earthy, and integrated. It exemplifies the journey toward ultimate homecoming and wholeness in Christ, which then rolls up its sleeves in service.

Contemplation and Activism

Mysticism was the entry point for Jesus, who began his work as a teacher with a forty-day fast in the wilderness (Matthew 4:1–11); blinding light and mystical vision also defined the start of Paul's ministry (Acts 9:3–9). For both Jesus and Paul, their direct encounters with God provided the fuel for their busy lives of teaching and healing. Anyone who claims Christianity is not a mystical religion has simply failed to read many of the root stories of the Bible, such as Jesus' forty-day fast in the wilderness, the Transfiguration (where Jesus speaks with Elijah and Moses), and Paul's conversion experience.

Sometimes, though, people assume that mystic contemplation and engaged activism are either-or options in the spiritual life. And it's true, some contemplatives focus so much on silence and solitude that they isolate themselves from the world and its problems. They may become hooked, even addicted, to deep stillness to the exclusion of everything else. Meanwhile, activists may be so busy with projects and causes that they forego time spent alone in prayer or meditation. Quakers, however, were clear from the beginning that contemplation and activism are two sides of a single coin.

We cannot have Mary, who sat at Jesus' feet in rapt silence, without Martha, the efficient busybody with a long to-do list (Luke 10:38–42). Each tempers and complements the other. Activist Martha without contemplative Mary is a recipe for burnout—and contemplative Mary without activist Martha may become narcissistic and self-focused. Contemplation and action together form the integrated approach of Quaker spirituality. Their pattern is activism of various kinds throughout the week, followed by an hour of silence spent in waiting worship (also referred to as *expectant worship*) on Sundays at the Meeting House.[10] This is a beautiful, lived-out balance.

When an entire community harnesses mysticism in the service of activism, the energy is enormous. It starts avalanches. The Divine encounters Quakers experienced in silence were the geneses of the widespread social justice reforms that changed American and British society.[11] From their direct, communal experience of Real Presence, Quakers learned respect for the dignity and rights of others (both human and nonhuman) and the utmost importance of dialogue as an alternative to violence. (We'll discuss Quaker activism at greater length in part IV.)

Befriending the Soul

Mysticism is not only encounter with the Divine, which is then expressed in the service of others; it also requires an encounter with our own souls. It asks us to journey inward and discover our true selves.

The soul is elusive, like a wild animal hiding in the forest. It is hard to get a glimpse of it. I'm reminded of my recent experience with a squirrel in our yard. At first, it darted up the cedar tree as soon as it saw me. Now, after I've been giving him a walnut every other day, the squirrel looks at me in anticipation. We also get to know the soul in similar gradual stages, from those first glimpses to eventually befriending it. This is not some esoteric, optional process, for the soul whispers to us the origins of life and consciousness. It reveals primordial intimacy with our Source—and it tells us who we are and what we are on earth to do.

When we first encounter this level of reality, we may not know what to do with it. We may recoil in fear. But as we continue on our spiritual journeys, we take gradual risks into a deeper relationship.

Bridging Quaker Silent Prayer and Centering Prayer

In the 1970s, three monks—William Meninger, Basil Pennington, and Thomas Keating—worked together to develop a simple method of silent prayer. They pulled their ideas from ancient sources (the fourteenth-century *Cloud of Unknowing* in particular) and then made them accessible to contemporary people. The form of prayer they created is known as *centering prayer* (a reference to Thomas Merton's description of contemplative prayer as prayer that is "centered entirely on the presence of God"). Today, people all around the world practice centering prayer.

It's a very simple practice:

1. First, choose a sacred word as a symbol of your intention to consent to God's presence and action within. (One- or two-syllable words from the Bible are generally best, such as *peace, rest, Jesus, Mary,* etc.)

2. Then, sitting comfortably with eyes closed, settle briefly and silently introduce the sacred word as the symbol of your consent to God's presence and action within.

3. When engaged with your thoughts (these include body sensations, feelings, images, and reflections), return ever so gently to the sacred word.

4. At the end of the prayer period, remain in silence with eyes closed for a couple of minutes.[12]

Meanwhile, Quakers use the phrase "centering down" for Quaker silent worship.[13] The centering-down worship of Quaker communities and the silent prayer of centering prayer are united in that most significant and pervasive word: *silence.* Both see silence as sacred and a means of communing with our Higher Power, and both focus on "centering."

Centering prayer is my practice, and Quakerism is my community. I seek to build bridges between them. In this book, I focus on Quaker ideas and history, including the practice of centering down, but I will refer often to centering prayer as well. The two silent prayer forms are virtually interchangeable, and to fuel your spiritual journey, I invite you to practice either one or to synthesize the two.

Journey of Holistic Mysticism

This journey will not be separate from your ordinary life, confined to Sunday services or religious beliefs. Instead, you'll find that holistic mysticism can interweave with your entire life.

"Life is one," wrote Quaker author Dan Wilson. "There is an invisible spiritual aspect and a visible material aspect of the same life. This life includes the whole world and all there is in it. Each aspect has its peculiar function: but the spiritual and the material are inextricably one. Each is to be known in and through the other. The material is infused with the spiritual. The spiritual is intrinsic to the material."[14]

In contemplative practices, either alone or in community, we encounter our whole selves, body, mind, and spirit. We reject compartmentalization and work to live in such a way that we fully embody our spiritual journeys, making our inner life with God visible. We move out of our heads, beyond belief and doctrine, and integrate our faith with our emotions and actions. We *experience* God for ourselves.

Mystical experiences like this animated the lives and adventures of Paul the Apostle, George Fox, Thomas Keating, Caroline Stephen, and countless others. The Divine Presence found in silent prayer animates human life. It fills us with surprising resilience and zeal, giving meaning to our life journeys.

And it starts with experiences of silence.

We have here, then, a type of Christianity
which begins with experience rather than dogma.

—Rufus Jones[15]

PART I

Core Soul Skills

1

Holy Silence

Christ comes to us
when our hearts and minds are still and silent. . . .
Silence is the Quaker Sacrament.

—J. Brent Bill[16]

Our world is filled with noise. As you read these words, perhaps you hear the roar of an engine or someone shouting in the street outside; maybe you hear the quiet hum of home appliances—or an adolescent's blaring music. Before you read any further, take a moment to imagine yourself in a place where there is no noise whatsoever.

Picture yourself on a mountaintop, high above the tree line, looking out over a vista that stretches to a distant horizon. The view before you is spartan and unadorned, yet exquisite. As you sit there, resting from the climb up the mountain, the sun warm on your head, you hear nothing, not even the hum of insects or the rustle of leaves. Wrapped in this absolute silence, your mind naturally grows still. The cares and responsibilities of ordinary life fall away, and you find a place of refuge.

Silences are the most natural phenomena in the world—and yet few of us have many opportunities to seek them out in natural places. Instead, most of the time, the atmosphere around us carries constant synthetic hums, buzzes, and beeps. As we become accustomed to the background din of engines, sirens, and other noises, the racket becomes "normal." According to scientists, however, noise can be an invisible danger that contributes to high blood pressure, heart disease, stress, and sleep disturbances.[17] Silence counters the noise distortion and puts our nervous system at ease.

Transformative Power

From the very beginning of the Quakers, George Fox understood that silence is of God, a powerful catalyst for the soul's integration and unification. Amid a constant barrage of sound, silence can be radical and revolutionary. When we are quiet, we are capable of hearing whispers from our interior depths—and when we make a habit of interior silences, we may eventually experience transformation, or our personal missions may reveal themselves. Transformation may simply bring more daily calm and patience. Or, after many years of disciplined silences, radical transformation becomes possible, such as the healing of the nervous system and the release of most muscle tension. Our personal mission may be as simple as volunteering at the soup kitchen—or as radical as dropping everything and working for Habitat for Humanity in Ecuador.

Caroline Stephen's life is a shining example of this. She was born in an age when a woman's role was confined to being a wife and a mother. Since she was neither of these, people easily dismissed her as having little to offer. Caroline was loving and kind, though, and spent her time caring for her elderly mother. A biographer of her better-known niece, Virginia Wolff, described Stephen as an "intelligent woman who fell, nevertheless, into the role of the imbecile Victorian female."[18]

Then, in her late twenties, Caroline's life changed. "On one never-to-be-forgotten Sunday morning," she wrote, "I found myself one of a small company of silent worshipers, who were content to sit down together without words, that each one might feel after and draw near to the Divine Presence."[19]

In the silence of a Quaker Meeting, Caroline discovered her own worth, a worth that came from the realization that "God does indeed communicate with each one of the spirits He has made, in a direct and living in-breathing of some measure of the breath of His own Life."[20]

From then on, her life was full of meaning, with a depth that went far beyond the values of nineteenth-century society. As the years went by, her writing and friendship influenced countless people, and today, she is still considered one of the important Quaker authors. The clarity and wisdom she found in stillness continue to form Quakerism, as her writings also touch the larger world. I recall her words and feel her legacy when I join a Quaker Meeting for Worship.

My mother's experience with Quaker Meeting is also part of my personal legacy. I think many Quakers experience a similar sense of connection to the past. They feel they are part of a cloud of witnesses that exists through and beyond time.

Who Was Caroline Stephen?

Born in 1834, Caroline Stephen is today considered one of the important Quaker theologians. She was an eloquent spokesperson for Quakerism and authored several books that remain influential to Quaker spirituality. "In life, as in art," she advised in *Quaker Strongholds,* a Quaker classic, "whatever does not help, hinders. All that is superfluous to the main object of life must be cleared away,"[21]

What many people do not know about Caroline is that she was also Virginia Woolf"s aunt. Virginia's family regarded their aunt with dismissive amusement, calling her "Silly Milly," "Nun," or "the Quaker." Then, when Virginia was twenty-two, she had one of her many mental collapses and went to Caroline's house to recover. As Virginia began attending Quaker Meetings with Caroline, the silence she experienced there soothed and calmed her mind. Throughout the rest of Caroline's life, she encouraged her niece to pursue her creative work. When Caroline died, at the age of seventy-five, she left a small legacy to Virginia, which helped Virginia live independently as a creative, unmarried, and often troubled woman.[22]

Sacred Silence

As a young woman, my mother often attended a Quaker Meeting for Worship—and in her life, she emulated the Quaker integration of activism and contemplation. When I was a college student, she encouraged me to go to Quaker Meeting. My experience there was similar to Caroline Stephen's: I knew I had found something I needed, something I wanted to pursue.

"Why on earth do you get up so early on Sundays?" a dormmate asked me.

"Because I like attending the Meetings," I answered.

"How come?"

"I like the quiet I find there."

He groaned, rolled over toward the wall, and pulled the sheet over his head.

I knew many of my friends wouldn't understand the attraction Quaker Meetings held for me. Nevertheless, silent worship drew me in, and I felt a deep sense of spiritual homecoming. The pervasive, collective silence settled my mind, bathed me in ancient waters, and shaped me in ways I had not anticipated.

As the years went by, my love affair with silence and stillness led me to take numerous extended silent retreats.[23] I intuitively knew what Quakers have always known: that silence is God's primary love language. Or, as Thomas Keating and others have said, "Silence is God's first language. Everything else is a poor translation."[24]

Quakers started me on an adventure into silent prayer, one that eventually led me to both centering prayer practice and extended silent retreats. Today, the disciplined silences of Quaker Meeting and centering prayer still lead me to deep stillness and at times to a state of mind I might call primordial freedom, or what Saint Paul refers to as "a peace that passes understanding" (Philippians 4:7).

Historically, centering prayer and Quaker Worship come from different branches of Christianity—and yet, as I explained in the introduction, what Quakers call centering down and what the contemplative community calls centering prayer are very similar. Both practices see silence as sacred and a means of communing with our Higher Power. Silence brings the contemplative arts of the mystics—from the third- and fourth-century Desert Mothers and Fathers up through the fourteenth-century *Cloud of Unknowing*,[25] from the early Quakers in the seventeenth century and Thomas Keating in the twentieth—to us here today, in the twenty-first century.

A Universal Language of the Spirit

Silence is the universal language of all mystics, regardless of their religious tradition. The biblical authors, many of whom were shepherds, nomads, and hermits, also experienced a deep atmosphere of quiet where they encountered God. This was the original stillness that inspired the Bible.

Words allow us to express thoughts and feelings; they convey meaning between people. But ultimately, words are limited. They cannot express a spiritual Reality that goes far beyond what our everyday language can describe. This means that if we focus our attention on words, we limit our experience of ultimate Reality, which lies beyond thought. A few well-chosen words or a profound passage of scripture can serve as a preamble to silence—but ultimately, only silence allows us to reach past words' limitations to the Source, the Ground of consciousness.

Every word we utter can be affirmed or negated. This yes-or-no aspect of all language is often called *dualistic*. But consciousness has a deeper root—the energized, pregnant silences before words are formed. These silences are beyond affirmation or negation. They are simply the ground from which all language arises.

If we think of spiritual and religious practices as forming a staircase that leads us higher toward God, then silence is the highest rung. It allows us to step free from this world's noisy demands and enter into the vast stillness of God. Here, there are no distractions to come between us and the Source of our being. Here, we can listen for the Divine Voice, speaking to us not in words but in mysterious nudges that align us more closely with both our true selves and our Source.

Silence, by its very nature, is not showy. Sacred silence is like the leaven in dough that makes bread rise; it is also like a candle that reveals a trail through a dark thicket. We are unlikely to see stadium floodlights pointing to well-paved highways; that's seldom the way silence works. Still, silence brings clarity and discernment. Silent worship is the still small voice (1 Kings 19:12), not the big loud voice; it is the hidden footpath, not the four-lane highway; it is the candle, not the floodlight; and it is the acoustic guitar, not the electric.

The Inward Substance of Stillness

Some branches of Christianity focus on sacraments, the outward signs of spiritual realities, but for Quakers, the source of ultimate strength and resolve is the inward substance behind any symbol (Romans 2:28–29). From the Quakers' early days, they were not interested in religious terminology or in rites and ceremonies; they wanted to experience inner spiritual Reality. They wanted interior baptism of the heart, not the baptismal font. They wanted to experience the message that emerges from silence during Meeting, rather than passively listening to a message delivered from a pulpit. They yearned for the inaudible Word that is beyond all uttered human words, which probes the deepest questions of meaning and purpose.

Quakers were confident that God puts Divine wisdom into each human mind and writes it on each heart, empowering all people to know God for themselves. As Jeremiah 31:33 reads, "I will put my law within them, and I will write it on their hearts." This scripture, popular among Friends, bears witness to the interior nature of revelation, to an inward covenant, an inner Light.

And so, in silence and stillness, Quakers discovered the holy of holies, the inner sanctuary of worship and prayer. Although Quakers don't believe in the sacraments per se, they overwhelmingly agree that silence, especially collective silence, is sacramental, an experience of deep holiness from beyond our ordinary sensory perceptions. Quakers refer to the "Real Presence" of God in silent worship.[26] We'll talk about this more in chapter 7, but for now, it's enough to say that many Quakers see the Real Presence in silence as equivalent to the Catholic belief in Christ's Real Presence in the Eucharist. This communion with the Divine is not metaphorical but substantial and embodied. It's a form of mysticism that is plain and accessible—and yet sometimes, the modern mind feels confused, even repelled by it.

Discomfort with Silence

For many Westerners, stillness can be uncomfortable because it is countercultural. To become still—and better yet established in stillness—requires self-discipline. It goes against our over-caffeinated clock-ruled societal norms. The absence of noise can make us jittery. We try to fill silent space with radio, television, podcasts, anything. It's as though we are afraid of being left alone with our own thoughts.

Many people perceive disciplined silence as a threat, for silence is countercultural. In fact, the most countercultural thing a person can do might be to attend Quaker Meetings—or simply set a twenty-minute timer to sit and do nothing! We are heavily scripted to be productive; we think we need to proactively tackle the to-do list. Detractors will say, "Sitting there is not useful; get off your hindquarters and do something!"

Stillness, however, breaks through the confinement of linear minutes and hours. It reaches into an exquisite dimension outside time, where it reveals spaciousness, freedom, profound depth, and beauty.

Still, making time for silence doesn't come easily to many of us, especially not at first. I learned to be comfortable with stillness at Quaker Meeting for Worship; if not for the support of my Quaker community, I might not have stuck with it. In my experience, collective silence is an easier introduction to stillness than trying to establish an individual discipline by ourselves. In Meetings for Worship, the more experienced role models around us inspire us to keep vigil; they hold us accountable. The scaffolding of a weekly Quaker Meeting can start us on a gradual path that will deepen in time, extending out beyond Meeting into our individual prayer time.

Even then, silence is not easy. I recall Meetings for Worship when I could not still my mind no matter how I tried. Preoccupied with some weighty issue in my life—or even something as trivial as an empty stomach or an itchy toe—my mind resisted the quiet. Despite the lack of auditory sound, the interior of my mind was *noisy*.

Such experiences are both common and discouraging. The answer, however, is not to feel guilty or give up but to simply discipline ourselves to return to Meeting Sunday after Sunday.[27] In time (though not our timing), the cultivation of quiet bears fruit. We simply need to trust the process. Self-discipline brings us to silence again and again—and once there, we relax and let the Great Mystery work within us, opening the doorway of silence into an ever-deepening world of spacious calm and primordial freedom.

Silence in Practice

"Silence," said Quaker author Brent Bill, "is a form of intimacy." He goes on to explain: "When we really want to hear, and be heard by, someone we love, we do not go rushing into noisy crowds. . . . As relationships grow deeper and more intimate, we spend more and more quiet time alone with our lover. We talk in low tones about the things that matter. . . . That is why Christ comes to us when our hearts and minds are still and silent."[28]

I like to compare holy silence to the level of intimacy I find on a "heavy date" with my wife. The communion between us includes tenderness and a sense of shared essence. "Be still and know that I am God," wrote the psalmist (46:10)—and sometimes, my wife tells me something similar: "Don't fill up our silence with words." So the first requirement in the practice of silence is to quiet the rush of words that so often pours from our mouths.

Another requirement is to stop our physical movements. When our bodies are in motion, it is hard for our minds to be still, especially at the beginning of our contemplative journeys. So in the early stages of our practice, we need to be physically motionless for our minds to experience extended periods of quiet.

During Quaker worship, I've noticed that most people in the Meeting House sit with hands folded, perfectly still. A minority, however, journal, pray with the assistance of beads, or even knit or crochet. Each person is different, and Quakers value both diversity and inclusion. So start out with whatever manner of mindful silence works for you. The inner state of mind is more important than outer behaviors or noise.

You don't need to climb a mountain to experience inner stillness. The person adept at stillness can maintain interior quiet, even in a noisy lobby or on a busy street. We don't always have control over exterior noise, but we can learn to exercise control over interior distractions.

If you do begin with the simplicity of a weekly Quaker Meeting for Worship as the framework for your silence, you can then replicate it at home. The beauty of Quaker worship is that it's highly portable. Elaborate church liturgies are difficult to duplicate, but scripture reading followed by silence, with brief verbal responses when inspired, can easily be repeated in your house, office, or car. Centering prayer allows me to carry the disciplined silence of the Meeting House into my daily life. Innovative and hybrid thought and practice are Quaker institutions.

Most Quakers insisted on an unadorned, unvarnished, simple lifestyle. That intentional minimalism, in my opinion, makes Quaker silence exquisite. The pure quiet is hallowed; it needs no compliment. In fact, props of any kind (such as candles, incense, or background music) may distract us and diminish silence's singular power. When our senses are bombarded with multiple messages, diffusion, fragmentation, and confusion can be the result. Simplicity, on the other hand, creates a nurturing womb where unity and power can grow.

I have found that disciplined silences in both solitude and community are like the two wings of a bird. Individual times of silence give me a depth of personal experience and inner knowing, while community silences offer a vital container for relationships, tradition, and historical witness. The collective silence of Quaker Meetings grounds the silence I cultivate on my own, giving it deeper resonance.

Silence and Autonomy

External pressures can easily motivate and manipulate us. These pressures come in many forms, including social media, criticisms from friends or family, work responsibilities, and societal expectations. We are barely aware that we are like puppets dancing on strings; we don't realize our lives are being scripted by others.

In silence, we cut the strings, we stop listening to the scripts, and we go deep within ourselves. This is a rare and beautiful experience,[29] for only then will be free from the external voices that dictate our behaviors and beliefs. We stop doing what everyone else wants us to do, and we become inner-directed, a state of being that's a precious rarity.

At the end of a busy workday, our minds and spirits are like depleted electric toothbrushes that need to return to their bases to be energized. For those of us who have found the value of regular, disciplined times of silence, the silence becomes our home, the place to which we return again and again to be enlivened and refreshed. Silence is no longer a foreign land we visit on rare occasions; it is our homeland, the familiar habitual refuge to which we return.

Some skeptics say that when all other voices fade and then go quiet, all that's left is a void, an empty barren space. In reality, stillness is a fertile, life-giving place where we can hear God's Voice, the Word spoken before the world began (John 1:1). One way to think about this Voice is as flashes of insight that sometimes resolve complex multifaceted problems. This is the Voice that spoke to Abraham and Sarah, to Job and David, to the Apostles, and to countless saints through the centuries. And it will speak to us, if we take the time to clear away distractions and settle into the silence.

In order clearly to hear the divine voice . . .
we need to be still.

—Caroline Stephen[30]

True silence is the rest of the mind;
and is to the spirit, what sleep is to the body,
nourishment and refreshment.

—William Penn[31]

2

Settling into Silence

The silence we value . . . is a deep quietness
of heart and mind, a laying aside
of all preoccupation with passing things—
yes, even with the workings of our own minds;
a resolute fixing of the heart
upon that which is unchangeable and eternal.

—Caroline Stephen[32]

W hen I attend Quaker Meeting, I enter the silence by quieting my mind. Some Friends call this "centering down"—or "settling." Although various noises may interrupt the quiet—the rustle of someone shifting their legs, a car passing in the street outside, someone coughing—I direct my focus to my center, the silent inner space deep within me. In my individual practice of centering prayer, I do the same. When distractions arise, either externally or from my own thoughts, I ever so gently bring my mind back to that deep stillness. I settle deeper and deeper into the silence.

An Active Process

If we were to look at a person engaged in "settling," we would likely see nothing more interesting than someone sitting motionless. We might mistake this motionlessness as passivity. Unlike most church services, however, where we can be detached recipients of the words and music offered us from the front of the room, settling is an active process that requires deep engagement.

When I think about this process, what comes to mind is the image of a glass of water. The water in the glass has particles of dirt floating in it. There is so much dirt that the water is opaque rather than transparent. If I stir the water, the dirt swirls and spreads through the water, making the water so dark that no light penetrates it. But now, imagine I place the glass on a countertop and let it sit there. I don't stir it, I don't jiggle it, and after several minutes, the water becomes translucent, as the dirt settles at the bottom of the glass. When I put my eye up to the glass, the view is still cloudy but not completely opaque as it was before. If I let the glass sit for a longer time, the water in the glass eventually becomes clear, transparent to the light. All the dirt has settled at the bottom.

In a similar way, I often enter silence with many things on my mind. The turbulence of my thoughts and emotions swirls through my consciousness—but if I sit in intentional stillness, slowly my thoughts settle. The opaque quality of my mind becomes clear, transparent to Divine light. I experience what the apostle Paul called "the mind of Christ" (Philippians 2:5). When tiny thought particles sputter upward, I let them go, so that they sink back down to the bottom of my awareness. As I settle, I enter a clear and spacious state.

"Look not out, but within," wrote William Penn, quoting George Fox. "Remember it is a still voice that speaks to us . . . and that it is not to be heard in the noises and hurries of the mind; but it is distinctly understood in a retired frame."[33]

Self-Surrender

Settling requires far more self-discipline than simply attending a church service, where my thoughts often drift from one thing to another, even as my body sits motionless in a pew. Quaker settling requires a surrender of my ego-self—that noisy, busy outer shell we all wear that's constantly preoccupied with its own selfish concerns. When we let this aspect of ourselves control our thoughts, we experience what many meditation practitioners refer to as the "monkey mind."

More than two thousand years ago, the Buddha was familiar with this state of mind, which he described as similar to the constant chatter, screech, restlessness, and chaos of a bunch of monkeys. Modern-day author Elizabeth Gilbert described this same mental condition as "thoughts that swing from limb to limb, stopping only to scratch themselves, spit and howl. My mind swings wildly through time, touching on dozens of ideas a minute, unharnessed and undisciplined." Gilbert concluded that she is a slave to her thoughts.[34]

Settling sets us free. In silence, as we release our attachment to our jabbering monkey mind, we enter a period of liberty and lucidity. We let go; we surrender. We will discuss self-surrender at greater length in chapter 15, but the process of settling is a first step into this state of openness and freedom. The discipline of settling is good practice for the even deeper levels of self-surrender the spiritual journey eventually requires.

In past centuries, words like *surrender* and *self-denial* were understood to be necessary aspects of our relationship with God. In today's world, where we are careful to affirm and cherish a sense of identity, these words may, at first glance, seem psychologically unhealthy, even offensive. The Quaker perspective, however, as we shall see in greater detail in later chapters, always focuses on the true inner identity rather than the shallow outer one. We surrender what is false or empty, in order to enter the abundant selfhood we encounter in silence. In other words, we abandon the lonely, needy false self in exchange for the abundant true self, which then takes years to live into. We transform from the path of loneliness to the synergistic balance between solitude and community.

Acceptance

Settling can also act as a thermometer that indicates our spiritual health. We may have fooled ourselves into thinking we are deeply spiritual people. If we can't quiet our own thoughts, we are forced to realize something is lacking in our spirituality. As our thoughts incessantly buzz and swoop around us, we see the true chaotic state of our minds.

When our thoughts betray us in this way, something is going on that's far deeper than we may think. In effect, we are resisting life as it is; we are insisting on our own right to be in control. We often connect the need to be in control with arrogance and a lack of concern for others, qualities we may firmly reject in our outer lives. In reality, though, the desire for control is present in most of us. Our stubborn ego-selves struggle against reality, demanding that they *should* have their own way.

As I write, the world is recovering from another COVID-19 variant. Forced to step back from our "normal" lives, many of us daydream about both the past and the future. Instead of living our lives to the best of our abilities in the here and now, accepting what *is*, we regret and reminisce, we yearn and feel frustrated. We imagine that any time would be better than the time we are in now.

It takes profound humility to submit to our life as it is, not as we want it to be. Settling into silence, we let go of both our dreams and our fears. We accept the *now* that surrounds us, just as it is—and in that acceptance, we discover the sacrament of the present moment. The secret of the spiritual journey is that the Divine shows up in the details of our lives. In fact, the nitty-gritty of our lives is where real spiritual work takes place.

There's a paradox at work here, for acceptance of what *is* does not mean we resign ourselves to the world's injustice and violence. (We'll discuss this more in part IV of this book, "Outer Expressions of Inner Work.") We see the interplay between self-surrender and activism played out in the lives of many Quakers.

John Woolman, one of the early Quakers, recorded his spiritual life in his journal, and there we can catch a glimpse of how he settled into Divine Reality while also confronting the burning social issue of his day—slavery. In his journal, he describes the need he felt in Meeting to "watch diligently against the motions of self in my own mind"—and then, based on that settling into silence during Meeting, he changed his life to align his external actions with his inner conscience. His activism was so effective that by the year 1776, there were no more Quaker enslavers. This achievement added significant momentum to the fledgling abolitionist movement.

In silence, Woolman encountered "the daily instruction of Christ, the Prince of Peace." This initial surrender, this first and most basic step in his spiritual practice, was the foundation for his lifework. Woolman's settling down into self-surrender helped bring wider justice to our world.

Who Was John Woolman?

When John Woolman was born in 1720, slavery was inter-woven with daily life, so ever-present that most people took it for granted. Some individuals condemned slavery as the cruel and hideous practice it was, but at the same time, they felt helpless to do anything. Slavery was so inter-twined with America's economy and society that it seemed impossible to uproot it. Quakerism, however, gave John a different perspective.

John's guiding scripture was "be far from oppression" (Isaiah 54:14). As he strove to live the Light he had been given, he refused to lodge anywhere there were enslaved people; he also refused to purchase goods produced by slave labor. Because enslaved people made dyes, Woolman wore only undyed fabrics. At the same time, he made a practice of speaking respectfully with people who defended slavery, and often, he was able to persuade them to release their enslaved workers. He also worked to connect with Indigenous people, meeting with them as honored equals.

When he journeyed to England in 1772, the English Quakers disapproved of his undyed clothing and sloppy appearance; nevertheless, he persuaded them to change their policy on slavery. In England, he refused to travel by stagecoach because the coachmen drove the horses too hard and overworked their servants—so he walked slowly around the country, preaching everywhere. After six weeks, he caught smallpox and died. He was only fifty-two—but during his life, he had accomplished far more than most people.

Purity of Heart

We often connect purity with righteousness; in our minds, a "pure" person commits no evil. Philosopher Søren Kierkegaard, however, defined purity differently: "Purity of heart is to will one thing."[35] This is also the "single eye" that Woolman referred to—a quiet mental focus that allows all the tumultuous debris of our thoughts to fall away, leaving behind a new clarity.

Mental purity requires self-discipline—but at the same time, perhaps counterintuitively, the self-surrender that underlies the "single eye" means we simply relax into the Real Presence of God. We don't achieve anything through our own effort; instead, we let go of all effort. In his book *Christian Zen*, William Johnston encourages read-ers not to try to stop the mind during times of silent contemplation.[36] Thoughts will inevitably enter our minds; we can't stop that from happening. Instead, we simply release each thought, letting it "settle." We refuse to focus on it. Let thoughts come—and then let them go, Johnston counsels.

Quaker author Caroline Stephen, whose life we mentioned in the previous chapter, had similar advice. "True inward quietness," she wrote, cannot be achieved by violently seeking to shun all thought, "a process which, when carried out too severely, may intensify the inward ferment of the mind." In other words, if we *try* to empty our minds, we instead find our minds filled up with our striving. "It is not vacancy" we seek, wrote Stephen, "but stability—the steadfast-ness of a single purpose. . . . The one thing needful is that the heart should turn to its Maker as the needle turns to the pole. For this we must be still." [37]

As we settle into silence, we seek a single purity of purpose: we point our attention away from our own thoughts. Beyond that, there is nothing to be achieved, no prize to be won through our own strength, for that kind of thinking belongs to the ego-self. The deeper, truer self simply relaxes into the stillness with the absolute trust of a sleeping baby held in her mother's arms. As the psalmist described so long ago, "I have calmed and quieted my soul . . . like a child quieted at its mother's breast, like a child that is quieted is my soul" (Psalm 131:2).

What happens next is up to God, not us. As Caroline Stephen wrote, "No clear impressions, either from above or from without, can be received by a mind turbid with excitement and agitated by a crowd of distractions." Instead, in silence, all effort and striving are surrendered; it settles to the bottom of our minds, leaving room for clarity. "The stillness needed for the clear shining of light within is incompatible with hurry,"[38] Stephen advised.

Just as we cannot push a river or force fruit to ripen, we cannot make something happen in the silence. We cannot nudge it to go faster or fast-track its emerging dynamic. We can only settle into the pregnant quiet, waiting.

> *Hurrying makes no sense.*
> *To where am I running, you ask yourself,*
> *and why am I running so?*
> *Anguish does not exist here anymore.*
> *All is in its place.*
>
> —Davide Melodia[39]

3

Waiting and Listening

Wait for the Lord;
be strong, and let your heart take courage;
wait for the Lord!

—Psalm 27:14

Wait upon God to feel his power
to gather their minds together
to feel his presence and power. . . .

—George Fox[40]

When I entered my first Quaker Meeting back in 1989, I found a circle of about forty people sitting silently, their eyes closed and their hands folded, many with their heads bowed. As quietly as I could, I found a seat. I tried to settle into the silence.

Visually, there was nothing to distract me from the quiet. The walls were bare wood, without decorations or icons, and the windows were plain, clear glass. As I sat there, though, I found myself irritated by small noises: someone coughed; another person joined the group, and there was a brief clatter as people shifted their chairs to make room; a minute later, a dog barked outside; ten minutes into the Meeting, a man sidestepped the others in the group to get to the restroom; someone's stomach growled; a distant, intermittent siren wailed.

The silence wasn't silent.

Ben Handy described a similar scenario in an article he wrote for *Friends Journal*, and he concluded that the small noises in a Meeting House are not only normal but necessary. "I need that chaos of life to surround my meetinghouse," he wrote. "While it swirls outside, I find the peace inside amplified. The noise is a part of my life every day, and my worship is not an attempt to escape my everyday life but to understand it."[41]

On that first day in a Meeting for Worship, despite the interruption of small noises, I found that slowly but surely, my thoughts did settle. I had no control over the intermittent sounds, yet I did have control over my resolve to be still, which led eventually to inner stillness. Then, in the clear space within my mind, I had a sense I was waiting for something—but I had no idea what it would be.

When we wait for something, we often have a specific outcome we're anticipating—but as we wait for the Divine, we need to remember our concepts about God are not the Reality. Our rigid ideas about the Divine get in the way of naked experience. So, we must do what is repugnant to the ego; like Abraham and Sarah in the Hebrew scriptures

(Genesis 12:1), we must let go of what we know and wait to welcome the Unknown

Waiting for the Light

When I am part of more traditional worship services, I always know, more or less, what to expect. As a longtime churchgoer, I am familiar with the patterns of standing and sitting, singing and praying as the prelude to the preacher's sermon. At a Quaker Meeting, though, I never know quite what lies ahead. There is no set order of worship. It all depends on the Spirit. We simply wait in silence to see what will happen.

There is a place for talking to God, pouring out the yearnings of our hearts in words—but imagine if you were in a relationship where the other person never stopped talking, never paused to listen for what you had to say. The friendship would very soon feel lopsided. You might even begin to wonder how much you were actually a part of the relationship at all, since every interaction focused on the other person, leaving no room for you. In Quaker Meeting, we leave room for the Divine Presence. We wait to hear what the Spirit has to say.

Silent worship in Quaker tradition was called "waiting on the Lord" (Psalm 27:14).[42] This waiting is neither a metaphor nor an abstract concept; it is directed, focused, and real. It is the reason we first settle our thoughts, for waiting requires our full attention. Like Mary of Bethany, who waited in silence at the feet of Jesus, hanging on his every word (Luke 10:39), Quakers wait for the Spirit to lead. Their silence is filled with expectancy.

Edward Burrough, one of the early Quakers, invited all sincere seekers to attend Meetings for worship that lasted for hours. He described these Meetings as being similar to the experiences of the first Christians at Pentecost: "And while waiting upon the Lord in silence, as often we did for many hours together, with our minds and hearts toward him, being stayed in the light of Christ within us, . . . in our diligent waiting and fear of his name, and hearkening to his word, we received often the pouring down of the spirit upon us, and the gift of God's holy eternal spirit as in the days of old, and our hearts were made glad."

Quakers know that silence can plug us into our primordial Source. As prophets of old waited on the Lord in reverential and expectant silence, so can we. And as prophets received revelations when they imbibed the Word, so can we (John 1:1–5). But it takes patience.

Who Was Edward Burrough?

Born in 1634, Edward Burrough was a young man when he first heard George Fox speak. Edward immediately knew the Quakers' path was the one he wanted to travel. He began preaching throughout England, telling everyone who would listen about the Light of Christ. Edward was a powerful speaker, but he also used his written words to spread Quaker ideas, publishing many pamphlets that circulated throughout England.

When Edward heard about the persecution of Quakers in the Massachusetts Bay Colony, he went to King Charles II and persuaded him to stop the corporal and capital punishments of the Quakers in Massachusetts. Hangings did stop, but sadly, imprisonments and floggings were resumed the next year.

In 1662, Edward was arrested for preaching his Quaker faith and sent to Newgate Prison. King Charles ordered that he be released, but the local authorities ignored the king's demand. Edward remained in prison for another year, until he died there. He was only twenty-nine years old.

Like so many other heroes in the history of Quakerism's holistic mysticism, Edward Burrough had an interior anchor, a foundation on the Rock that held him and stabilized him. With the psalmist, he could say, "God alone is my rock and my salvation, my fortress; I shall never be shaken" (Psalm 62:2).

Timelessness and Patience

A sense of linear time is deeply imprinted on the Western brain. We think of our lives in terms of minutes, hours, days, months, and years. Throughout the day, we check the time often. We try to "use time" wisely, accomplishing as much as we can in the time allotted to us each day. If something or someone makes us wait, we feel frustrated, even angry.

In silent waiting worship, however, we set aside our sense of time. We resist the urge to "make" something happen. Although our brains naturally run ahead of the silence, planning and anticipating what will come next, we practice letting those thoughts go. Francis Howgill, a prominent early member of the Quakers, wrote about this: "But as there is a keeping back, and quietly waiting, and a keeping out of willing or running, and haste.... [T]hat which moves of the Lord of life will carry through, by its own operation and power, to accomplish the will of God."[43] Even back in the 1600s, waiting worship required profound patience.

When we sit in silence, the twenty minutes of centering prayer or the hour of Quaker waiting-worship can seem endless. We fight the urge to glance at our watches or phones to see how much time remains. At the same time, however, as we let these thoughts go, we sink deeper and deeper into the silence—and there we encounter a different dimension. As twentieth-century Quaker author Thomas Kelly wrote, "The world of time is no longer the sole reality of which we are aware. A second Reality hovers, quickens, quivers, stirs, energizes us, breaks in upon us and in love embraces us, together with all things." In those moments, said Kelly, we realize that "we live our lives at two levels simultaneously, the level of time and the level of the Timeless."[44] In silent waiting, we marinate in the eternal now; we hit the pause button on our urgent to-do lists. We rest in the deepest sense of the word. This is countercultural and requires discipline and extraordinary patience.

The Greek language distinguishes two types of time: *Chronos* (ordinary time) and *Kairos* (the fullness of time, an abundant dimension outside ordinary time). In silent worship, we set aside Chronos and enter Kairos. We enter into the Spirit beyond time.

John's Gospel refers to Christ as the preexistent Word (John 1:1–3), and the Book of Revelation speaks of Divinity "who was and is and is to come" (4:8). When we speak of the Word, the Christ, we use the present tense, but when we speak of the Word made incarnate in Jesus of Nazareth, we use past tense. Jesus of Nazareth was in time, but the Word is outside time. This is the Spirit, always available in the eternal present, that we encounter in silent worship. Waiting in silence, as the spaces between our thoughts lengthen, we glimpse eternity.

Each time of silent worship is a brief Advent season, where we anticipate the coming of Christ, the One who is beyond time.[45] We wait for the Word to mysteriously become flesh and dwell among us in our unique context, amid our particular challenges (John 1:14). Whether silence is cultivated alone or collectively, we wait expectantly but without an agenda. We expect to be filled but we put no demands on how this will happen. We listen for the Spirit's voice. Waiting and listening go together.

Listening

In times of silent waiting, despite the interruptions of small noises, we discover a deeper sense of prayer. As Kierkegaard observed, "A man prayed and, at first, he thought that prayer was talking. But he became more and more quiet until, in the end, he realized that prayer is listening."[46]

An older Friend I know uses the phrase "listening in tongues." This phrase is a reminder that the Spirit does not only prompt Christ's disciples to speak in tongues, as the Book of Acts described (chapter 2); the Spirit also cues us to listen on a deeper level as we are enveloped in sacred silence. We learn to hear with more than our ears, and we begin to comprehend the wordless presence and electricity of the Word.

Taking the time to listen requires patience and humility. We must nudge our noisy and demanding egos out of the centers of our consciousness. Our minds become like empty cups expectantly waiting and yearning to be filled.

The true prayer-relationship does not exist
when God is the only one listening
but rather when the person praying . . .
is the one hearing what God wills.

—Søren Kierkegaard[47]

4

Words into the Silence

Words should not break the silence,
but continue it.

—Thomas Kelly[48]

During that first Quaker Meeting I attended, the silence was inter-rupted three times when someone got to their feet and spoke. Each of the three individuals described a personal experience of the Divine, and yet their words spoke to my heart as well.

One speaker had had an intuition to seek out an old friend, another had been driven to nab a certain book, and the third described a recurring dream. They spoke of these ordinary events as persistent nudges to align their lives more fully with God and their true selves through ordinary actions as well as political involvement. Their words were gentle, inclusive, and solid; their tone measured, thoughtful. Each time, when the person was finished speaking, the silence rose and enveloped us once again.

After an hour, the circle stood and clasped hands. The Meeting's clerk announced community events, which included signup sheets for hospital visitation and volunteer work rotations at the local homeless shelter and prison. I slipped out the door, not ready yet to commit myself further.

I wandered downtown Santa Cruz as I collected my thoughts. In my mind, I compared the service I had just experienced with the church services I was more accustomed to. I realized we had not been listening for a message to come to us from "out there," from some exemplary microphoned person on a stage or behind a pulpit. Instead, we had listened *within*—and the spoken words that emerged came from that time of shared silence. The messages shared during the Meeting were not merely an individual's experience; they came from our shared Source, to enlighten and inspire us all.

Words from the Source

There's an old story about someone who was trying to show the Moon to another person by pointing at it. Instead of looking at the Moon, however, the second person kept looking at the first person's finger. They didn't understand what was important, and they settled for the lesser thing rather than the shining reality.[49]

When it comes to words, many of us are like the second person in the story. We focus on the words themselves, rather than the larger light to which they point. The squiggles and lines that spell the word

"God" or the vocal sounds we make to utter the word are not the pervasive, electric Reality we seek (Romans 8:26). Visual squiggles and sounds can engage our brains, but they distract us from a direct experience of the Divine; only in silence are we free from all symbols, concepts, words, and images.

We could not do without words for very long, of course. Words tell us where and how to drive our cars; they tell us how to make cookies or prepare Grandma's chicken stew; they inform us about events in the larger world; and perhaps most important, they allow us to express at least some of our thoughts and feelings to one another. Words have spiritual value as well. This book is built from words—and so is scripture.

According to George Fox, though, the Bible had a Source "before the Scriptures were given forth."[50] In silent Meeting, Quakers seek to connect with this Source. They speak out loud only when they feel they have a message to convey from the Spirit. In other words, they look at the gleaming orb of light in the sky—and they no longer fixate on the scrawny finger

George Fox's Experiment

As a young man, George Fox was frustrated with pretty much everything he encountered in church. Like so many of today's young people, he felt organized religion was empty, boring, and not relevant to his life. Formal liturgies left him cold; so did long sermons, and the clergy seemed out of touch with his real needs. He wrote in his journal: "I saw there was none among them all that could speak to my condition."[51]

Then, in 1647, when Fox was twenty-three, his life changed. "When all my hopes in [clergy] and in all [people] were gone," he recorded, "so that I had nothing outwardly to help me, nor could I tell what to do; then, oh! then I heard a voice which said, 'There is one, even Christ Jesus, that can speak to thy condition'; and when I heard it, my heart did leap for joy."[52] At that moment, George Fox experienced the Divine Light, directly and experientially.

George Fox was not an educated man, and he never claimed to know much about church history or doctrine. He had seen quite clearly, however, that many of the experts in these areas did not practice compassion; they did not actively express Divine love to the people around them. After his mystic encounter with the Light, he realized he did not need to depend on any person or religious structure to enlighten him. He didn't need a finger to point the way, because he could go directly to the Source of Light.

And so can every other person who seeks God.

Fox did not intend to start a new religion or denomination. Instead, he proposed an experiment: a community of people who together would seek "the living experience of Christ as the Light available for all."[53] This Light, Fox believed, is freely offered to everyone and anyone. William Penn put it like this: George Fox "saw people as thick as motes in the sun, that should in time be brought home to the Lord; that there might be but one shepherd and one sheepfold."[54]

In silence, the Spirit speaks—and then Quakers share what they hear with the rest of the group. As Quaker historian William Charles Braithwaite wrote, Fox's legacy is a community that "goes through life trying to decide every question as it arises, not by passion or prejudice, nor mainly by the conclusions of human reason, but chiefly by reference to the Light of God."[55] Fox's experiment continues each time we gather in silence, waiting and listening for Presence, speaking only as the Spirit leads.

Waiting on the Spirit is not saved for only Sunday Meetings. The same attitude is alive and well at Quaker business Meetings, where Friends are advised to "not come to a meeting with mind made."[56] In other words, don't prepare ahead of time what you will say or do. Wait and see what arises in the present moment, in the electric now. Friends also cultivate a spirit of openness to Divine leading in family interactions. The family can come together, settle into silence, and then, from this gathered place, seek discernment.

Who Was George Fox?

Born in 1624, George Fox grew up surrounded by the political tensions leading up to England's Civil War. When he was nineteen, he left home in search of "Truth." He came to believe that everyone, both women and men, could, through Jesus, directly encounter God themselves. No priests or clergy were needed.

George talked to anyone he met about his ideas. He was soon in trouble with the authorities, who threw him in prison in 1649. This was only the first of his many prison sentences. The term Quaker, George wrote in his journal, originated from a sarcastic remark the judge made during George's second trial, in 1650.

In 1652, George climbed Pendle Hill in Lancashire, England, where he had a vision of a "great people to be gathered." Quakerism's beginning is usually dated from a day soon after this, when crowds flocked to hear George speak. During this period, he spent time at the home of the Fell family, and Margaret Fell took on an important organizational role in the Society of Friends. She became as influential as George was in the building of Quakerism.

In fact, Quakerism snowballed when, in 1669, George married the upper-class and well-connected Margaret. Her eloquence and intelligence are well-documented in her collected letters titled *Undaunted Zeal*. She and George worked together to spread the Light, until George's death in 1691.

Spontaneous Words

Quaker author D. Elton Trueblood wrote: "In Quaker worship, one is not to come prepared to speak or not to speak. One is to come prepared to be obedient to the inner promptings of the Spirit."[57]

In other words, the verbal ministry that arises out of silent Meetings is spontaneous. People do not sit at home on Saturday nights reading their Bibles and taking notes in order to construct an eloquent sermon to deliver at Meeting the following morning. They simply come prepared to be silent, to settle, to wait, to listen . . . and when they hear the Spirit speak, if they do, they share it with the rest of the gathered group. They enter the silence with no plans to either speak or not speak.

Quakers value scripture (as we'll discuss in chapter 10), but unlike many ministers and priests, they do not attempt to plug into scripture in order to deliver a sermon. Instead, they plug into the

Source of scripture—and then they wait expectantly to see what will happen.

Quakers do not plan what will happen in Meeting, but they *do* come with open hearts and minds, made ready throughout the week through prayer, reading, and contemplation. This holistic spiritual practice readies the heart and mind for connection with the Light. Then, on Sunday morning, Quakers gather to enter a familiar Reality that resides within us and provides a reliable invisible stream, which we can access at any time.

Words may arise out of the silence—or they may not. Several people may speak during Meeting—or no one. It's all up to the presence and action of the Spirit within the gathered Meeting. But when words do come, they are particularly powerful because they are spoken against the backdrop of silence.

Words Powered by Silence

If we do not eat for a day or more, we notice, after our fast is done, that the first morsel we eat bursts with flavor. Something similar happens with words. When we are settled into a deep silence, a word is like a clap of thunder. Its light and heat startles us, and we hear it more sharply, with a greater clarity, than we do ordinary words.

There was an age when written words were rare and cherished. Before the age of the printing press, when only the very wealthy could afford books, people crowded into cathedrals on Sundays to hear scripture read aloud. Some of them had walked many miles for the rare privilege of listening to the spoken Word. Now, in contrast, everywhere we look, we are inundated with words. We stare at our tiny, handheld computers, and we drown in electronic text messages.

In silence, however, we let the murky soup of words drain out of our minds, leaving behind a clean, airy space. This is why we do not skip the "settling" stage of silent worship; otherwise, if we went straight to waiting, the temptation would be to sit there mentally tapping our feet, impatient for something to "happen." In settled silence, as we make a space for the Light to shine into our hearts and minds, we realize something is always happening. If spoken words arise, they have first marinated in silence, so they are timely and seasoned.

Caroline Stephen wrote: "After the long silences which had fallen like dew upon the thirsty soil, [spoken words] went far deeper, and were received in a much less thorny region than had ever been the case with the words I had listened to from the pulpit."[58]

A Life-Giving Tree

You might think that an hour of silence, practiced daily in centering-down or centering prayer or weekly in silent Meeting, would have little effect on the rest of our busy, noisy lives. Even a little silence, however, can change our lives. Think of the way leaven changes bread dough; the tiny pinch of yeast may seem inconsequential, yet without it, the dough would never turn into a loaf of bread. Likewise, a pinch of daily or weekly silence can mean the difference between centered composure at work and with our families. It takes control away from the foot-tapping monkey mind, and creates spaciousness, where insights and graces are more likely to thrive.

In silence, we enter the realm of God—and Jesus said this realm is like a mustard seed, so tiny that it could easily get lost in the folds of your pocket, and yet in time, when planted in good soil, it "becomes a tree, so that the birds come and perch in its branches" (Matthew 13:31–32). The cultivation of sacred silence is similar. A dash of blessed silence enlivens the entire day. An hour of waiting worship invigorates the week. And even a few words, when they come directly from the Spirit, can change our lives.

When we rise to offer vocal ministry in meeting for worship,
we are seeking to give voice
to the inbreaking of the Divine among us
. . . to be channels for Love's continuing birth in the world.

—Noah Baker Merrill[59]

Are you a child of Light
and have you walked in the Light,
and what you speak, is it inwardly from God?

—George Fox[60]

PART II

Foundational Beliefs

5

Built on Love

There is no other way to know God
but this way of inner love-experience.

—Rufus Jones[61]

At the most basic level, the foundation of Quaker holistic mysticism is love—love of God and love of others. For Quakers, church doctrines and organizational structures are far less important than love. Still, love is too easy on the mind as a catchall word for the Christian spiritual journey. So we need to proceed carefully, defining exactly what we mean by *love*.

The love of Jesus jumps off the pages of the Gospels. This is the vital starting point, the essential root from which our spiritual lives grow. We cannot hope to build a "house"—a spiritual practice—without first being certain it has a firm foundation. Love is holistic mysticism's paramount foundation.

The love Christ demonstrated was practical, expressed with loving hands, tired feet, gentle words, and the willingness to surrender even his life. The only law he taught is very simple: to love one another (John 13:34), in the same way that he loved us. This highest form of love, which Quakers exemplify, is not the sentimental, tear-stricken variety, and it has nothing to do with the ego's need for recognition. Instead, it expresses itself in a willingness to suffer and go the distance. Because it is both practical and persistent, it creates lasting, earth-moving change.

A Mystic's Active Love

Rufus Jones, a Quaker of the nineteenth and early twentieth centuries, believed Inner Light did not stop at the individual soul's enlightenment. As he studied the history of mysticism, he realized there are two types of mystics: "negation mystics," who focus on their personal union with the Divine, and "affirmation mystics," whose spiritual experiences empower them to active engagement with the world. The first is often referred to as *apophatic mysticism* and the second as *cataphatic*.

Mystics don't always fall into one of these neat categories. A mystic can embody aspects of both. This was Jones' take on his fellow Quakers, in whom he saw a practical, down-to-earth spirituality that combined mysticism with love-in-action. A catastrophe in Jones' own life made this clear to him:

> I found to my horror that a fearful storm in the night had blown the barn down with almost everything we possessed

in it. It was such a wreck as I had never seen. . . . The news went fast, and before the day was over men from near and far gathered in our yard. . . . The entire neighborhood went to work, and a new structure rose where the ruin had been. . . . I saw, as I had not seen before, that the religion of these [people] was not merely an affair of the meeting house; not merely a way to get to heaven. It was something which made them thoughtful of others and ready to sacrifice for others.[62]

Jones became convinced that "listening to the Spirit, being guided by the Inner Light of Christ" always leads to "an appeal to help build a better world." The Quaker mystic does not float in an ethereal reality severed from the tangible world. "Keep your feet on the ground and get something done," Jones wrote.[63]

Action and love cannot be separated, Jones believed. He described God as a force of love, "a unique type of love, a love that pours itself out regardless of merit . . . it floods out like the sun to reach the just and the unjust."[64] As mystical experience connects us with this Force of Love, we become more Divine, acting to heal and teach and change the world in ways similar to the historical Jesus' methods.

Rufus Jones's own life expressed this connection between mysticism and active love. In 1917, after the United States entered World War I, he and another Quaker, Henry Cadbury, formed a committee to help conscientious objectors (COs) serve the cause of freedom without joining the military. The American Friends Service Committee (AFSC) trained COs to work with groups like the Friends Ambulance Unit in Europe. After the war was over, Jones steered the committee into relief work in war-torn Europe. He also helped organize a wide-scale food donation that saved millions of Germans from starvation. Then, when German Jews were first attacked in 1938, Jones returned to Germany to plead for their safety; because of his earlier action on behalf of Germany's people, German leaders gave him an opening that allowed many Jews to emigrate to safety. In 1947, Jones represented the Quakers in Stockholm when they were awarded the Nobel Peace Prize. The essence of any authentic religion, Jones believed, is love.[65] He experienced this love in worship and acted upon it in service.

Who Was Rufus Jones?

When we grow up with a set of beliefs, we may take them for granted. We inherit them from our parents and grandparents, but ultimately, this is not enough. We have to claim them as our own, with our minds and with our hearts. This was the experience Rufus Jones had.

Rufus, a cradle Quaker, grew up in a family of longtime Friends. As a boy, he attended a Quaker school and then went on to study at a Quaker college. Like many of us raised in Christian homes, Rufus was not all that excited about his family's faith.

Then, as a young man, Rufus read Ralph Waldo Emerson's writings—and he viewed his family's religion from a new perspective. Emerson believed Quaker George Fox was one of the world's great mystics. After reading this, Rufus took a new and deeper look at Quaker beliefs. As he studied the writings of the early Quakers, Rufus began to write and speak about the "Inner Light"—"the doctrine that there is something Divine, 'Something of God' in the human soul."[66]

Active and Authentic Love

I saw this same active and authentic love when I first attended Quaker Meeting back in Santa Cruz during my college days. At the Santa Cruz Meeting, people looked after one another and helped each other. If a woman needed someone to clean her gutters and weed her garden, this was announced, and volunteers came forward. Elders in the group visited the sick, prisoners, and an Alzheimer's ward. They did not do these things for payment; they did them because they embodied the gospel. The Good News of Jesus had journeyed from their heads to their hearts—and from there, to their hands and feet and mouths.

Quakers not only express active love to their own members. Many Quaker Meetings also have an outside "niche" where they focus their service; examples of these niches are reading to elementary school kids, managing a subsidized low-income housing project, and staffing a soup kitchen. The AFSC, the Quaker organization Rufus Jones helped to found, continues to be based on the Quaker beliefs in both the worth of every person and the power of love to overcome violence and injustice; it offers service opportunities in the ongoing work for social justice and peace. Other Quaker organizations, including the Friends Committee on National Legislation and Friends Disaster Service, also carry out the Quaker expression of holistic mysticism. And you do not have to be a Quaker to volunteer with these organizations![67]

Faith expressed in service is not unique to Quakers, nor should it be. In one church I served, a member named Joanne had suicidal tendencies. After a suicide attempt and stint in the hospital, church members sat with Joanne around the clock. Doctors had told us that most suicide attempts happen within the first two weeks after a failed attempt, so we each took eight-hour rotations at her home for two weeks. Joanne, who had chronic depression, took me by the hand after one of my rotations and said to me, "Now I know what church is about." When love is the foundation of our spiritual communities, we look after each other, especially our struggling members. Within this shared humanity, the gospel comes alive once again in our time.

The Meaning of the Gospel

Christianity has often lost sight of the real meaning of Jesus' message. Focusing on external traditions such as pulpits, baptismal fonts, and printed scripture, it forgets about the real foundation that lies beneath these traditions.

I like to compare our relationship with Christ to the love that leads to the marriage of two individuals. The wedding cake, dress, certificate, and ceremony are secondary, outward signs of a primary, underlying love. Without the foundation of that love, all the external material props are meaningless fluff.

Holistic mystics like Rufus Jones experience Divine Union, which leads them to express the message of Christ in tangible, practical ways that go far beyond Christianity's traditional "props." These mystics build the Realm of God in the here and now, in homes and communities and nations, in hospitals, prisons, disaster sites, and schools. As their mysticism fuels their service, their service fuels their mysticism. The inner light within them grows like a living seed.

*The first stage of "entry into life" for Jesus
is learning to love.*

*To start executing a "social program"
without the creative and motive power
of a great love behind it is like building a factory
and forgetting to attach the machinery
to any driving energy that would turn the wheels.*

—Rufus Jones[68]

6

The Seed of Christ

But the seed on good soil stands
for those with a noble and good heart,
who hear the word, retain it,
and by persevering produce a crop.

—John 8:15 NIV

The Lord's everlasting Seed, Christ Jesus,
was set over all that day

—George Fox [69]

According to Quaker theology, inside each individual human being, regardless of beliefs or religious affiliation, is "something of God"—a tiny seed with the potential to grow into an immense tree of life. The Quakers call this the Seed of Christ.

This concept underlies the Quaker beliefs that we are all equal and that all humans have a "measure of Christ"[70] within them—for when this seed is nurtured and allowed to grow, it can lead to a direct experience of God's love and guidance. This experience is often referred to as the "Inward Light," a light that guides everyone—whether they know it or not—in decision-making and living a meaningful life. The Inward Light also brings comfort and solace in hard times. Through daily disciplined silences and yearly silent retreats, avid seekers of this Light sometimes have profound transformative experiences of homecoming, of being bathed in the Light of Christ.

The Seed of Christ can also be present in communities and organizations. When individuals come together with a shared commitment to the Inward Light, they can create a community that reflects God's deliverance and passion.

The Seed of Christ—and the Inward Light it brings—is not merely a point of Quaker doctrine or belief. It is essential to Quaker practice; it guides how Quakers interact with others and with each other. Just as Jesus sought out his disciples in their unique circumstances and called them to greater and more complete identities (Mark 3:16–20), the Seed of Christ calls to each of us. We are called to break open, awaken, and germinate into a new life.

The Seed of Christ to which Rufus Jones, Isaac Penington, and others referred is pristine and pure. The Seed within us is uncompounded, unadulterated, beyond words and human constructs: holy. Just a glimpse transforms. God planted this core of our nature and made it in the Divine image (Genesis 1:27). It cannot be sinful or tainted. This Seed or Light may become obscured or distorted as life unfolds because of mistreatment, degenerate cultural influences, and social scripting, yet it always starts out pure. We can recover that purity through contemplative prayer, marinating in our Source and emerging washed and whole.

Isaac Penington, one of the first Quakers, described the Seed and called us to focus on it as something *within* us, rather than looking for it in any outward circumstances or conversations. For Penington, the Seed was a "precious Truth" that he described as "the inward word of life, the inward voice of the Shepherd in the heart, the inward seed, the inward salt, the inward leaven, the inward pearl."[71] In other words, the Seed is something we must each experience for ourselves in the private recesses of our hearts and minds—in "the secret place of the Most High" (Psalm 19:1).

The Historical and Biblical Basis for the Seed of Christ

One of the Bible's foundational assumptions is that we are made in God's image (Genesis 1:27). This is also the assumption of Quakers, beginning with George Fox. Without this core understanding, every other element of holistic mysticism would unravel.

Jesus told us, "The reign of God is within you" (Luke 17:21 YLT), and he describes this realm as a treasure hidden in the field of the heart (Matthew 13:44). Each human being contains a place where the Divine dwells, a place that is already present within us and yet one we must seek to enter through prayer and silence.

Again and again, scripture describes the Reality that Quakers call the *Seed of Christ,* using verses such as these:

> Do you not know that you are God's temple and that God's Spirit dwells in you? (1 Corinthians 3:16)

> This is the Spirit of truth. . . . You know him, because he abides with you, and he will be in you. (John 14:17)

> I will put my spirit within you, and make you follow my statutes and be careful to observe my ordinances. (Ezekiel 36:27)

Quakers discovered this Light through silent worship, and monks of the Eastern church through silent prayer[72]—and it is present in each of us, waiting for us to recognize it. This Seed is none other than the preexistent Christ or the Word described in John's Gospel:

> In the beginning was the Word, and the Word was with God, and the Word was God. He was in the beginning with God. All things came into being through him, and without him not one thing came into being. What has come into being in him was life, and the life was the light of all people. The light shines in the darkness, and the darkness did not overcome it. (John 1:1–5)

Many early theologians from the Eastern church affirmed a state of intimacy and communion with God as humanity's natural, primordial condition, before any transgression or separation. They referred to this as our "pre-fallen state,"[73] and they promised we can return to primal innocence and communion with God; we can return to Adam's intimate walks with God in the Garden of Eden (Genesis 3:8). We are hardwired for this intimacy.

The experience-based Quakers and the experience-based Eastern church, both with well-developed mystical approaches, come to the same conclusion about this foundational mystical theology. For both, their faith is rooted in the weekly and daily experience of disciplined silences.

The Seed of Christ planted within us is the ultimate root that's deep enough to weather all storms. It is the Source of endless energy and resilience. It is the Light and hope of all ordinary monks and mystics. It is our birthright, the hidden treasure Jesus described (Matthew 13:44). Beneath people's inner distortions and layers of dysfunction, the Seed remains—something of Christ in all people.

I have been a skeptic all my life, and it took me a long time to affirm the Seed of Christ through actual experience. Like scientists, I ultimately trust experience, and so, after twenty years of silent prayer and extended retreats, after glimpse after glimpse of this brilliant life-giving Seed, I became a believer (actually, a *knower* more than a believer). Like many Quakers before me, after witnessing the Seed firsthand in sacred silences, I now assert knowledge of the Seed that comes from experience. For me, this knowledge and understanding is all in all.

Cultivators of the Seed

From the very beginnings of Quakerism, George Fox taught about the Seed of Christ. He grounded his teachings in the Bible and Christian tradition, particularly the Gospel of John and the Epistles of Paul, which he interpreted in in a contemplative way, long before the label "contemplative Christianity" even existed. Fox often referred to the Gospel parable of the farmer scattering seed (Luke 8:4–15).

During the spiritual vision Fox experienced as a young man, when he saw "a great people to be gathered,"[74] he realized the Seed of Christ was present in each and every one of that vast crowd. This experience gave him a profound sense of purpose and inspired him to begin preaching and spreading his message, establishing a community of believers who shared his vision. Fox believed every human being has an innate spiritual capacity, which he called the Seed of Christ; this Seed could be awakened and nurtured through direct experience of the Divine in silent prayer.

This idea was not entirely new, as it had been hinted at in earlier forms of Christian mysticism, especially in the Eastern church, although some Western theologians also wrote about it. "The real teacher is inside you," Saint Augustine wrote in the fourth century. "It is the Divine Master within who teaches you. It is Christ who teaches you."[75] Ten centuries later, Meister Eckhart, the German mystic, wrote about the "light in the soul that is uncreated and uncreatable."[76] However, Fox's radical reinterpretation of these ideas challenged the traditional Christian beliefs of his time. He rejected the institutionalized church and its hierarchical structure, emphasizing that direct communion with God was possible without the need for intermediaries such as priests or bishops.

Soon after George Fox began teaching and preaching, he met Isaac Penington. Penington was initially skeptical of Fox's ideas, but he was eventually drawn to the emphasis on the inner presence of God and the direct experience of the Divine.

During this time, the Quakers' rejection of the established church and its doctrines had led to them becoming outcasts. Both Fox and Penington were imprisoned several times because of their beliefs, but their time in prison only deepened their resolve. They saw their own suffering as a reflection of Christ's suffering. In suffering, the Seed of Christ grew.

These two men's beliefs about the Seed shaped their lives and spiritual journeys. They rejected material possessions and worldly pleasures in favor of spiritual fulfillment. Seeing a "portion"[77] of Christ in each person inspired them to advocate for social justice and equality, opposing slavery and promoting women's rights, beliefs that were radical in their time. Penington wrote: "As the seed is suffered to grow, the increase of the Spirit of life is known, and by degrees it brings forth more and more of the fruits of life and holiness."[78]

Under the leadership of individuals like George Fox and Isaac Penington, Quakers dispensed with all outward forms of Christian ministry, such as vestments, paid clergy, baptismal fonts, chalices, and stained-glass windows. They distilled ministry to its essence: Christ within us—his call on our lives and our response, which can be discovered in silent worship. This is how the transformative power of the Seed of Christ scatters throughout our world.

Who Was Isaac Penington?

Isaac Penington, born in 1616, came from a wealthy family of devout Puritan merchants. He studied law at Oxford University, where he excelled. For many years prior to his meeting with George Fox, he had been discouraged by the Puritan doctrines regarding hell and sin. Their teachings made him feel fearful and guilty, never able to rest in the peace of Christ. But then, he wrote: "The Lord opened my

spirit." He went on to say, "The Lord gave me the certain
. . . feeling of the pure Seed, which had been with me from
the beginning."[79]

After this experience, Isaac became a leading figure
in the Quaker movement, and his writings helped shape
Quaker theology and practice. Despite their close relationship, Isaac and George Fox did not always agree. Isaac
was more inclined to emphasize the inward experience
of the Seed of Christ, while George stressed the outward
manifestation of the Seed within the Quaker community.
However, their differences were expressed with respect
and love, allowing each to balance the other. They remained
close friends and collaborators until Isaac's death in 1679.

Cultivating the Seed in Our Own Hearts

The Seed of Christ is already present in our hearts, regardless of how
we live our lives. However, by recognizing, cultivating, and watering
the Seed, we grow, inwardly and outwardly. The journey of silent prayer
is the path that leads us to this awareness, which then informs all our
subsequent deliberations on faith. As we realize the true nature of
our identities, this understanding shapes our spiritual journeys. The
process is gradual. We are all works in progress. Still, a foundation of
silent prayer makes us reliable people who are on the path, who have
seen what's possible.

Modern Quaker mystics, like Thomas Kelly, tell us the direct
way to access and develop our inherent divinity (Genesis 1:27), which

is mirrored in Christ's Divinity, is to practice wordless prayer. In stillness, we can cultivate awareness of the unified and unifying Word within us. "The sower sows the word," Jesus said, and then the tiny mustard seed "puts forth large branches, so that the birds of the air can make nests in its shade" (Mark 4:14, 32).

When we touch the Seed of Christ through silent worship, everything changes. We peel back the layers of our identities, and we see at last the glorious cores. In Light, deep integration and true character become possible.[80] We discover the eternal foundation upon which we can build something extraordinary for Christ. As Jesus said, "Everyone who listens to these words of mine and acts on them will be like a wise man who built his house on rock. The rain fell, the floods came, and the winds blew and buffeted the house. But it did not collapse; it had been set solidly on rock" (Matthew 7:24–27).

Think about a marigold seed and an acorn. When you look at these seeds, there is nothing to indicate that one will grow into clusters of orange blossoms or that the other will one day be a towering tree. Each seed, however, is a tiny potent blueprint for a complex organism. If neglected, that imprint is sidelined and inconsequential; the marigold seed that remains inside the packet will never produce flowers, and the acorn that lies on a stone won't be able to sprout and grow. If watered and mulched, however, seeds expand into something beyond what we can now imagine.

It's up to us to take care of the Seed, this image of God that is dormant within us, yet yearns to awaken. The Seed is the blueprint for what we can be. We can grow from a tiny Seed of Christ into a tree that gives shelter to many. If we fail to nourish the Seed, we stunt our identities.

Jesus spoke of the vulnerabilities the Seed of Christ faces. "The seed is the word of God," he said, and then he explained:

> Some seed fell on the path and was trampled, and the birds of the sky ate it up. Some seed fell on rocky ground, and when it grew, it withered for lack of moisture. Some seed fell among thorns, and the thorns grew with it and choked it. And some seed fell on good soil, and when it grew, it produced fruit a hundredfold. . . . Those on the path are the ones who have heard, but the devil comes and takes away the word from their hearts that they may not believe and be saved. Those on rocky ground are the ones who, when they hear, receive the word with joy, but they have no root; they believe only for a time and fall away in time of trial. As for the seed that fell among thorns, they are the ones who have heard, but as they go along, they are choked by the anxieties and riches and pleasures of life, and they fail to produce mature fruit. But as for the seed that fell on rich soil, they are the ones who, when they have heard the word, embrace it with a generous and good heart, and bear fruit through perseverance. (Luke 8:5–8, 11–15)

Each day offers a new opportunity to water the Seed or neglect it. Our every choice determines the Seed's outcome. Will weeds choke it? Will hard soil prevent the Seed from growing roots? Or will the Seed find fertile soil and produce an abundant crop, just as Jesus described?

Silence is the fertile soil where the Seed grows. "And your growth in the Seed is in the silence," wrote George Fox, "in which ye may find a feeding of the bread of life . . . and there is innocence and simplicity of heart and spirit."[81]

We do not cultivate the Seed merely by talking about it or by listening to sermons about it. As Penington cautioned, "Oh my dear Friend, let not any part of your life lie in notions above the Seed, but let it all lie in the Seed Itself, in your waiting upon the Lord for its arisings in you, and in your feeling its arisings." [82] The Seed must be *experienced*, and this only takes place in silence.

As we cultivate the Seed of Christ in silence, it grows from a tiny seedling to a sturdy and reliable plant, which influences us on many levels. In the beginning, we may be reluctant to trust the Seed and its nudges. Over time, however, as we lean on it more and more, especially during adversity, we realize we can trust this hidden interior aspect of ourselves. First, the Seed carries us. Then it carries our unique mission in the world.

We can let go. We can even surrender the energy and labor used to think and breathe, for now, the Seed within us thinks and breathes for us. As Isaac Penington wrote in his journal, when we give our "own willing . . . own running . . . own desiring to know or be anything," we are then free to "sink down to the seed" that God sows in our hearts. We not only let it be in us, but we also let it grow and breathe and act, so that we "find by sweet experience that the Lord . . . will lead it to the inheritance of life which is God's portion for you."[83]

All resistance is gone. Various thought patterns and the tension they produce are released. There is no more effort spent on anything; there is just Being itself, and we discover that "just to be is holy."[84] We lean back on the secret Divinity within us, which on some level always remains incomprehensible—and yet we trust it with our lives. We even trust it with our colossal foibles, self-destructive urges, and weaknesses. We surrender everything that threatens to fragment and divide us, so that we can be true to the Seed's blueprint.

Over time, the Seed takes our brokenness and refashions each of us into a unique expression of Christ's image. This may look different from the outside at various phases of our lives. After all, as we grow older, we experience many epochs, chapters, and layers of our lives. Sometimes all the pieces feel disparate—and yet in reality, like a fractal image, each one reflects the same Reality. We see unity within unity, holons upon holons, which at each level, transcend and include the prior stages.[85]

Recognizing the Seed in Others

As George Fox and Isaac Penington discovered, belief in the Seed of Christ changes the way we think of others. It changes how we interact, for regardless of how annoying or shallow a person may be, how cruel or violent, the Seed of Christ still lies buried within them.

The Seed of Christ may lie dormant. It may have never been watered. Nonetheless, it exists before any distortions arose, before any abuses were suffered. That precious primordial Seed is tiny and seemingly insignificant, but it can move mountains. It may be so minuscule that you may think it has been permanently lost—and yet, even then, it can grow into a shelter for songbirds and squirrels. The Seed of Christ calls us to re-know each other—to see beyond the limitations of today to the potential of eternity.

"Now, to re-know another is not to condone their acts," wrote author Paul Selig, "not to let them off the hook for their behavior. But it is to re-see them." When we re-see the individuals in our lives, we see their Divinity. We still may not like their behaviors and beliefs, but we see beyond them to their inherent Divinity. The Seed of Christ can be hidden, distorted, disfigured, yet nevertheless, beneath the layers of cultural scripting and trauma, it remains luminous, glorious, "bright shining like the sun" (to use the words of John Newton in his hymn, "Amazing Grace").

Sometimes when I'm dealing with difficult people, I visualize them as children, before the dysfunction began in earnest. A friend of mine, who has a difficult and abusive relationship with her mother, keeps a childhood picture of her mother on her mantle to remind her of her mother's true identity. The Seed is pure. The child is pure. Dysfunctional people and degenerate social scripting make us neurotic, but the Seed remains.

Recognition that some portion of God's Light is in every person helps us to overcome the dissonances that seem to separate us; it leads to a sympathetic awareness of their needs and a sense of responsibility toward them. This love is for the lost and the broken; the cantankerous, ugly, and lonely; yes, and even the brutal, the murderous, and cruel. If we are to love God, we must love them as well, not for their cruelties, but for the hidden Seed that would live and grow in them. We, who are loved with a love that will not let us go, are to let that same love flow through us into the world.[86]

I believe a small percentage of people have so disfigured the image of God within them through their life choices that the Image is buried under an enormous pile of refuse. Can such people dig themselves out from under the piles of refuse? Yes, but such changes are herculean and highly unlikely. (Alas, I am both a romantic and a realist!)

Not many people, though, have dumped gargantuan piles of refuse onto the Divine Light within them—but at the same time, few people have deeply cultivated that Light. Most people are somewhere in between. In other words, the Seed has been neglected. As we learn to cultivate the Seed within our own souls, we are called to help cultivate the Seed in others.

The Transformative Power of the Seed

Jens Soering is a German citizen who became known for his involvement in a high-profile murder case in the United States in the 1980s. Soering was a student at the University of Virginia when he fell in love with Elizabeth Haysom, the daughter of a wealthy couple. In 1985, Haysom's parents were found brutally murdered in their home, and Soering and Haysom fled to Europe. They were eventually arrested in England and extradited to the United States to face trial. Soering was convicted of the murders and sentenced to two consecutive life terms in prison.

While in prison, Soering began practicing centering prayer. Today, Soering credits his practice of centering prayer with helping him cope with the challenges of prison life. "In future," he wrote, "I will continue to emphasize the importance of the inward journey, seeking peace and meaning within. My experience has been that this inward turn, ironically, leads to community and friendship, the most important factors in my own survival. . . . I have spent 30 years fighting for the light in the darkest places, and I have survived. Now I would like to help and perhaps even inspire others who are struggling to keep the light alive in their own lives."[87] Soering has written several books, in which he reflects on his spiritual journey and the role that centering prayer played in his life.

When Thomas Keating visited Soering in prison, Keating remarked that Soering was not the same man. He was a new man.[88] In my experience, people are rarely capable of deep change, so how is this possible? Soering changed because, through centering prayer, he found his true identity, a secure Center that gave him the courage and wherewithal to change. The Seed of Christ sprouted in him, and it continues to blossom and produce fruit.

Still confined in prison, Soering has found his mission. The immense energy born of silent prayer must always go somewhere, and even prison bars cannot contain it. Despite the circumstances of his life, Soering is actualizing his unique, tailor-made mission through his writing.

The Challenge of the Seed

As Soering's life—and many others'—demonstrate, once we discover the Seed of Christ within us, our outer lives change—and that change spreads outward into the world. At Rufus Jones's memorial gathering, one of his students said, "He lit my candle."[89] That is the challenge of the Seed—to not only bring Light to our own lives but to also kindle the Light in others.

To begin the journey of the Seed, we only need to enter a Quaker Meeting House and bathe in silence or schedule a centering prayer retreat and marinate in days of prolonged silence. Silence is the gateway into the Divinity within us. Then, to stay true to the Seed's challenge, we need firm resolve.

With persistence, the spiritual life reorients us, so we no longer read the Gospels "out there"; we read them mirrored "in here." We no longer pray *to Jesus* out there; we *pray Jesus* from the inner core of our beings (the omission of the "to" is intentional), mirroring his Divinity and humanity. We even begin to realize that mythology such as the hero's journey is not necessarily a story out there; its deepest meaning emerges from our own lives as we confront the dragons within us and emerge integrated and whole.

Notice I used the word *confront* and not *slay*. Our dragons, whatever form they take, may not go away. Over time, though, we learn to handle them with more skill. And we remember that in all the old stories, wherever there are dragons, there is gold. The greatest gifts we can offer the world lie at the gnarled feet of our dragons (or what Christian tradition sometimes refers to as our "demons").

As the Seed of Christ grows within us, we realize that the point of the hero's story is not to end up standing on a mountain with a crown and sword. That might satisfy our egos, the needy external shells we wear, but our inner selves learn that the real point of the old stories is to become the hero of our own lives. This means we fight for what we love, even in the face of tragedy and daunting odds. We fight for what we value, even when cruel people persecute us. We believe that buried within us is luminous gold put there by God, and that one day, against the odds, that gold will shine.

The Seed of Christ now directs our lives, and we listen to its voice, no matter what our peers and family may think. This gives us an inner authority that doesn't depend on the approval of others. The Seed helps us complete the unfinished business of "weaning" that's necessary for mature adulthood; we wean ourselves from external motivators and compulsions like shopping, gambling, sex, alcohol, or anything that *fills in the gap* we sense within us. Now, as we allow the Seed of Christ to expand into that emptiness, we rely more and more on what Augustine called the *Magister Internus*—the Master Within.[90] We become less dependent on everyone else's agendas. Then, the sense of acute homesickness begins to release, and we no longer feel that something vital is missing. (The seventeenth-century philosopher Blaise Pascal described this feeling as an emptiness within the human soul that only God can fill.[91])

The Seed of Christ mysteriously drives us toward our innate purpose—the reason God put us on earth. In time, our sense of purpose is no longer forced in any way. We utilize every chunk of time to further it, not because of external pressures and not for monetary gain. We simply pursue our passion. The Seed nudges us forward daily. In the language of scripture, Jesus must increase, and we must decrease (John 3:30); Jesus is the Vine, and we are the branches (John 15:5), our lives fed and sustained by his larger life. In the story of our lives, Jesus is now the Hero (uppercase), and we are the heroes and heroines (lowercase).

"Each one of us has the Seed of Christ within," wrote Thomas Kelly, ". . . the amazing and dangerous Seed of Christ."[92] We are drawn to the "amazing" aspect of the Seed, but we may not be as happy about the "dangerous" piece. Many of us are more comfortable living our lives on the surface. We go through the motions, yet on some level, we feel a deep skepticism, if not cynicism, about the spiritual life. Perhaps a part of us wants to give life our all, but we are not quite there yet. We are not all in. Another part of us is absent, distracted, undecided.

A deep and daily relationship with the Seed of Christ is too scary, demands too much; it's far easier to keep Christ at a safe distance. As

Robert McAfee Brown wrote, "He's not a safe or a tame God, securely lodged behind the bars of a distant Heaven; He has the most annoying manner of showing up when we least want Him; of confronting us in the strangest ways."[93] On some level, we prefer the distant and authoritarian Western image of God to Jesus' intimate Abba. After all, look where Jesus' profound interbeing with God led him—to the cross!

And so, we sometimes pray to the Christ *out there*, on the altar, instead of interacting with the Seed within our own hearts. Keeping the Divine Christ at arm's length is easier on heart and mind. The human Jesus' profound vulnerability and compassion make us uncomfortable; his Reality threatens our complacency and cowardice. Yet Jesus Christ's paradoxical essence, which holds the creative tension between Divinity and humanity, Creator and creature, absolute and relative, eternity and time, interior Christ and incarnate Son of Humanity, strikes us as true.

The Seed of Christ is a subtle and exquisite inner guide that was always there, underneath layers of cultural conditioning, scripting, and peer influence. As we finally give it free rein in our lives, this Guide inspires creativity and art. Musicians and artists often refer to the Guide as their Muse.

In time, relationship with the Seed deepens. We discover we have many layers to remove: First, we take off the winter coat and scarf. Then we remove the sweater, boots, and hat. Then we go naked before our Beloved. Finally, our greater vulnerability and abandon leads to what some mystics have called the bridal chamber, a place where we enter into union with the Beloved, as described in the Song of Songs.[94]

Like any real-life romance, there is no "happily ever after." The difficulties in our lives continue, and they sometimes challenge our interrelationship with the Seed within us. No deep, long-term love relationship is easy.

This is the fate of all Christ's disciples. They don't just float along in happy serenity; they are often in trouble. They may even face literal danger because they dare to speak out against injustice, taking a stand for suffering people. They have the audacity to cross the line, whatever that line is and regardless of who drew it, on behalf of God's beloveds.

"As a black Quaker," wrote Ayesha Clark-Halkin Imani, "I see the Inner Light as the great liberator and equalizer . . . the indestructible power in us that is able to create from nothing, able to make ways out of no way, able to change what appears to be the natural order of things. It is the power in us that can never be overcome by the darkness of fear and hatred or altered by the might or money of people."[95]

Who You Were Always Meant to Be

Seventeenth-century Quaker Robert Barclay wrote: "As the whole body of a great tree is wrapped up potentially in the seed of the tree, and so is brought forth in due season . . . even so the Kingdom of Jesus Christ . . . is in every man's and woman's heart, in that little incorruptible Seed, ready to be brought forth as it is cherished and received."[96] The tree doesn't think about what it is supposed to be; the tree's being emerges naturally.

Unlike the tree, we can choose to walk our unique path toward the true self—or we can opt for the false self. The road to our authentic self is narrow, sometimes as thin as a rope bridge across a precipice (Matthew 7:14). With each choice, we solidify our identity.

Be who you are intended to be. Let the Seed of Christ grow in you. Experience the Real Presence of God in each aspect of your life.

Come to the seed and wait to feel and receive the power
which raises the seed in the heart;
and brings the heart, soul, mind and spirit
into union with the seed. . . .
My religion, which I now daily bless my God for,
began in the Seed.

—Isaac Penington[97]

7

Real Presence

Refuse to be content with just the knowledge of God.
But insist on experiencing his presence.

—Kerri Weems[98]

Ever return quietly to him and wait in his Presence.

—Thomas Kelly[99]

When Quakers dispensed with the outward trappings of traditional Christianity, they distilled their faith down to its purest essence: Christ's Real Presence.

The term *Real Presence* was not new to Christianity, but always before, it had referred to the belief that Christ is truly present in the

Eucharist or Communion. This belief had been a central part of Christian theology for centuries. Now, in Quaker theology, the concept of Real Presence took on a different meaning.

Quakers believe the presence of Christ is not limited to the bread and wine of Communion. Instead, Friends believe every person has the potential to experience the Divine Presence when the Seed of Christ awakens within them. This can happen through silence and stillness, through intentional life-giving relationships, and through Nature. This experience is not limited to any intermediary ritual or sacrament.

A Radical Idea

During Quakerism's early days, this new understanding of the Divine Presence was radical and upsetting, for it challenged the traditional hierarchy and authority of the church. If every person has a portion of the Christ-Light within them, then intermediaries such as ministers and priests were no longer required. Quakers were egalitarian, although elders were generally the ones who steered their Meetings into life-giving pathways.

Professional clergy, however, was a centuries-old English establishment integral to the government and courts. Clergy worked alongside municipalities to promote law and order—so this Quaker principle brought outrage, especially from the clergy. How dare these quiet rebels question a foundational pillar of society!

Always before, the clergy had controlled and overseen life's great events, such as marriage, baptism, and death. The Quakers, however, understood that ceremonies such as baptism and marriage do not necessarily accompany a conviction of the heart, nor do they ensure honesty and fidelity. Just as college diplomas are simply pieces of paper that do not guarantee a lifelong love of learning, even the Bible can be simply a collection of pages read at arm's length without genuine engagement.

As a matter of conscience, Quakers thought paid clergy were unnecessary.[100] All people are made in God's image, and when we take the time to be still and listen, each of us experiences a portion of Christ's infinite Light. Throughout Margaret Fell Fox's letters, she referred to "the measure of Christ" in a person—a portion of the Christ-Light within every soul.[101] Some may shine like a candle, others like a headlight, and others like a stadium floodlight, yet it is the same Christ-Light in all. Each of us has access to the Real Presence, and each of us has the potential to express this Presence through our unique gifts. Christ calls us all—not just paid clergy—to experience his Presence and witness to its Light, in whatever portion is allotted to us.[102]

Quakers don't want professionals to pray for them; they want to pray for themselves. They don't want an eloquent pray-er to intercede on their behalf before God; their approach to God is direct, without an intermediary. Quakers don't leave their faith to "spiritual experts." Like the shepherds and nomads who wrote the Bible, they stand before God's Presence with rough hands, chiseled chins, and straight eyes.

As God became incarnate in Christ, so too you and I are parts of the Body of Christ, visible signs of grace. Christ's Real Presence within us manifests uniquely in each individual. Each person receives a vision only they in their one-of-a-kind context can embody. In Christ, Christians find their blueprint, their metanarrative.

A metanarrative is an overarching story that makes sense of our smaller, individual stories. The Greeks called this principle the Logos. Christians call it the preexistent Word (John 1:1). Just because we don't understand the universe and world history doesn't mean it's all chaos. On some level, a profound pattern is being worked out. There's a bigger story going on—the story of the Real Presence that is active at every level of our world.

This verbal description of Christ's Real Presence is one thing; experience is another. No matter how many words I use, I can never fully express the meaning of Real Presence. Some people accidentally stumble into this experience, but for most of us, it takes years of silent prayer and extended retreats.

Then, once we experience it, nothing is ever the same. A new-found resilience shields us from poison darts and tragedy. We are surprised by fresh passion, zeal, and endurance, even in the face of betrayal or apparent ruin. We discover the ways in which this holistic mysticism—the Real Presence fully integrated into our lives—changes us at both spiritual and practical levels.

A Life Shaped by Real Presence

We can see the role Real Presence played in the life of Thomas Kelly, a prominent Quaker theologian and writer in the early twentieth century. Kelly discovered, through personal experience, that the inner Presence of Christ can guide individuals toward spiritual transformation. He believed shared worship was essential for experiencing this Presence, as well as for working together for societal transformation. His understanding of Real Presence led him to a life of service and activism.

This Presence, wrote Kelly, "is no mere doctrine, belonging peculiarly to a small religious fellowship, to be accepted or rejected as mere belief. It is the living Center of Reference for all Christian souls and Christian groups—yes, and of non-Christian groups as well. . . . He is the center and source of action, . . . the locus of commitment, not a problem for debate." Above all, Kelly concluded, we must practice "the perpetual return of the soul into the inner sanctuary" in order to bring "the Light into the world with all its turmoil and its fitfulness" and recreate the Light for others to see.[103]

Kelly taught that we experience the Real Presence of Christ on ever-deepening levels of surrender.[104] This progressive letting-go leads us to an energized and reliable inner center we come to trust. We discover none other than the Real Presence of Christ, who lets go of all self-centered desires, the Christ who empties himself (Philippians 2:7).[105]

Thomas Kelly was rooted in experiences of Real Presence in the eternal now. His inner experience of Real Presence—abiding joy and equanimous peace—became his Reality. External realities, like clothing and cars, became secondary. Attempts, however valorous, to become content and happy through exterior experiences are folly, he realized, misdirected and inevitably frustrated attempts at happiness. Like so many sages before him, he took the "narrow road" (Matthew 7:14); he became inner-directed.

Thomas Kelly's interior journey of disciplined silences progressively relaxed his mind and body into that condition that is our birthright: great natural peace. Instead of getting swept away by titillating objects along the river of the senses, he experienced the river's free flow. Like the author of the Twenty-Third Psalm, he had everything he needed.

The Real Presence is all in all. Once we taste it, nothing else is needed. Nothing else satisfies at that level. Once we experience it, we are, in a foundational sense, content. At last, we are home.

Who Was Thomas Kelly?

Born in 1893 to a Quaker family, Thomas Kelly initially hoped to be a missionary. At seminary, he met Rufus Jones, who taught him about Quakerism's more mystical side. Thomas also met his wife-to-be there, Lael Macy.

When World War I broke out, Thomas signed up to work with men serving in the armed forces. Eventually, however, as he became increasingly ardent about pacifism, he was asked to leave. He returned to the United States to complete his seminary training—and get married.

Thomas never became a missionary; instead, he worked as a professor at Haverford College in Pennsylvania. He was known for his deep commitment to social justice, which included being actively involved in the civil rights movement. Thomas believed the Presence of Christ existed only not in individuals but also in society. As we work for justice and equality for all people, we also serve Real Presence.

Thomas Kelly wrote extensively on the importance of silence and listening, stating that deep, inner stillness is the gateway to Divine Presence. Throughout his book, *Testament of Devotion,* he emphasized the importance of surrendering ourselves to the Presence of Christ, allowing this Presence to transform our lives. Thomas died after a heart attack at the age of forty-eight, but he left us the rich legacy of his spiritual wisdom.

Abandoning the Senses in Silent Worship

The Real Presence of Christ is everywhere—but the purpose of silent worship is to magnify the Presence so that it reverberates in our inner being. Then the "invisible but eternal stream of reality"[106] reveals itself. We don't exert effort to do this. We simply wait expectantly (see chapter 2), until eventually we enter a primordial Reality that has been there from the beginning—the preexistent Word found in John's Gospel.

Reality has two aspects: absolute and relative. Relative consciousness is tied to the senses and is given to constant change. As a result, it has an unsatisfactory transient quality. Every experience of the senses is ephemeral. When we disengage from the senses, however, the eternal Real Presence of Christ makes itself known. Jesus said in the Gospel of Matthew, "Whenever you pray, go into your room and shut the door and pray to your Father, who is in secret" (6:6). Many Christian mystics have interpreted Jesus' words as meaning "close the door to your senses." Freed from the bombardment of sensory experience, we taste the eternal absolute dimension of Christ. No matter our personal limitations, we are never the same. We realize that Real Presence is not found in the passing temporal fancies of the senses. It is found in primordial stillness and silence: timeless, immaculate, exhilarating.

And yet all reality is based on the gratification or deprivation of the senses, is it not? Here we must take the mystics on faith, that there is a deeper Reality beyond our physical perceptions. As Quaker mystics and others attest, we discover the doorway to Reality ("Real Presence" in Quakerism and "Kingdom of Heaven" in the older Christian tradition) is the brief periods when the senses are renounced, and we focus on stillness and silence. Then, as we habitually set aside time to close the door to the senses, we glimpse the eternal. These moments of infinity satisfy us on a cellular and cosmic level far beyond the delights of the senses. Thomas Keating used to say, "Sensory pleasures simply can't compete with spiritual consolations in prayer."[107]

We need the senses to navigate daily life, and they are God-given gifts that add beauty and pleasure to our lives. But our physical senses are not equipped to perceive luminous spiritual Reality. Our inner selves, however, are hardwired to experience the absolute, which satisfies us more than anything else can. When the nervous system is completely quieted and healed (usually after many months of disciplined silent prayer), long-standing tensions in our muscles release. In this context, we can experience a blissful calm we didn't even know was possible. We enter "a peace that passes all understanding" (Philippians 4:7).

People sometimes look for excitement and satisfaction in bars, virtual realities, and skydiving adventures, but none of these ultimately satisfy. Only Real Presence that lies beyond fleeting sensory pleasures can give us what we thirst for most.

We glimpse the eternal not through the senses but through what Eastern Orthodox writers, such as Kallistos Ware, refer to as the spiritual intellect.[108] When we habitually suspend the senses in silent prayer, our innate spiritual intellect awakens and develops. This habit is utterly countercultural, especially in the West—and yet we, like the Quakers and other mystics, have access to this life-giving practice.

In silent worship, we seek to find Christ's Real Presence within— and at the same time, we experience communion with the "Body of

Christ" without. In other words, silence has interior and collective aspects. There is the preexistent Word of John's Gospel, which is timeless, and there is the incarnate Word in time. There is communion with the eternal Real Presence, and there is also communion with the Body (community) of Christ that exists in a specific time and place.

Communion with the Real Presence does not participate in that deadening word—*objectivity*. Instead, it is characterized by the transformation of the subjective self. In reality, objectivity is an illusion, for all perspectives are unavoidably shaped by their locations in time and space. In the final analysis, the subjective self is the most real starting point, our paradigm through which we filter all experience. If our inner eyes bathe in stillness, silence, and the Light of Christ, the afterglow illumines everything we see.[109] Acute isolation and fragmentation are healed, and profound belonging and participation arise.

The Ground of Our Being

As we settle into silence, after we sift through the various layers of chatter, images, symbols, and physical sensations, we reach a baseline that Kelly called the "Last Rock." Eastern Christian writers referred to a similar concept as our Original Nature, and Meister Eckhart said it was "Absolute Unity."[110]

We might think that the deeper we dig into our own being, the further we travel from God; that's one way Christianity has regarded the inner self, as a source of sin and separation from God. Quakers, however—and other holistic mystics through the ages—believe that at the deepest level of our beings lies Kelly's Last Rock, the preexistent Word of John's Gospel (John 1:1–5). Mental and emotional commotion obscure this bedrock, but someone practiced in disciplined silence spends more and more time absorbed in this Ground of Our Being.

At first, the Ground doesn't shimmer, beckon, or entice (though that may come later). Someone untrained and unaccustomed to it may simply overlook it, even during silent prayer. We are hardwired for interior immensity and intimacy. In contrast to other security symbols like bank accounts, property, and titles, the last Rock is reliable and solid through and through. It is the "Ancient of Days," known by the priests who attended the Ark of the Covenant, known and witnessed by Moses, Peter, and Mary Magdalene—and still available to us today.

The Real Presence turns us all into priests—accountant-priests, parent-priests, homemaker-priests, lawyer-priests, factory-worker-priests, computer-science-priests, and so on; no matter our profession or role in life, we bring to it the Presence of Christ. His Real Presence is available in and through all that we are and all that we do. We may start on the meditation chair or the seat in Meeting, but then, in time we bring the fully embodied Presence that we have practiced on the chair to the rest of our lives. These are not just words but an abiding state of consciousness, an experience rooted in healed nervous systems as well as renewed spirits.

The life of George Fox demonstrated this. His distilled essence, gleaned from his journal, was his gospel-rooted principles. The consequences he faced for standing up for his principles, such as prison time and bodily assault, were immaterial to him, for everything he did and said was firmly rooted in the Ground of his being—a bedrock underlayer, unshakable, not even in death—the constant Real Presence of his Lord.

The lives of people like George Fox, Thomas Kelly, and other holistic mystics show us that everything passes in the end. Everything changes—all except for the Last Rock of established Presence in wordless prayer. The Last Rock is with us always, even when we are thrown hellacious curveballs and stampeded by life. Establishment in the Last Rock gives us a foundation that can withstand life's tragedies, cruelties, heartbreaks. It can even survive an all-out tsunami that destroys the house or flattens the village. "God is our refuge and strength, a very present help in trouble," wrote the psalmist (46:1). Even when it feels like the mind might unravel during a crisis, the refuge of our Last Rock stands. The Ground of Our Being holds firm.

The Divine Intruder

Sometimes, though, especially in the early stages of our spiritual journeys, we may see the Presence of the Divine as an unwelcome intruder in our lives. As Thomas Kelly wrote, Real Presence can be "aggressive . . . an intruder, a lofty lowly conqueror on whom we had counted too little, because we had counted on ourselves."[111] We are no longer in control—and we hate that! When we allow our Higher Power to take the reins, our elaborate agendas are not only dropkicked; the entire set of rules we've been using is also replaced. We may regret that we invited this Divine Intruder into our lives.

Over the years, I've encountered people who, through a car wreck, a death in the family, or a terminal illness, finally came to know Christ's Real Presence. At first, though, they felt Christ was an imposter who ambushed them at the worst possible time; under the guise of tragedy, he snuck into their lives. In tragedy, God removes all filters and scripts designed to insulate us from the Divine. Then the raw reality hits us like thunder, and we stagger around, blinded and bowed, like Paul when he had his vision on the road to Damascus (Act 9:1–19).

Let me clarify that God never causes tragedy. We have free will, and we are vulnerable to unpredictable economic trends, viruses, natural disasters, and people. When, because of chaotic circumstances, tragedy does strike, Christ draws near. According to many people I have visited in emergency rooms, when the veil between life and death thins, Christ's Presence shines, energizes, and comforts.

Without wholesome and sustained experiences of Christ's Real Presence, we may try to fill our sense of desperate need with recreational drugs, gambling, daredevil speed, reckless sex, or other compulsive behaviors. The body and mind crave intimacy and connection with our Source, but instead of healthy, patient cultivation of this intimacy, we fall for surrogates. When a crisis strikes, we are forced to realize that all surrogates leave us empty. They cannot give us the stability we need to face tragedy and hardship.

Rufus Jones described his childhood anxieties and then wrote, "My deliverance from fear was my childlike discovery that God was with me and that I belonged to him. God . . . was as real to everybody in our family as was our house or our farm."[112] The Real Presence of God is just that—*real,* even more real, in fact, than our homes or any other possession.

Personal integration produces positive ripple effects in our environment.[113] Christ's Real Presence reveals the Bible's inner meaning for us at this moment, in these particular circumstances. As we submit to the Word, we then learn to submit to our life as it is.[114] When we stay close to the Real Presence, everything blossoms around us.

Union

Cyril of Alexandria wrote, "Although we are distinguished by our very different personalities, as were, for instance, Peter, or John, or Thomas, or Matthew, yet we are merged as it were in a single body in Christ by feeding on his unifying body."[115] In our experience of the Real Presence, we too can find the answer to our world's divisions and polarity.

Within that unified field or Real Presence, there is diversity, not division. There are distinctions, not animosity. A Christ-centered life emphasizes communion, and in a vibrant faith community, we enter relationship with both other people and the Divine. We experience the dynamic unity of Jesus' humanity and Divinity.

Thomas Kelly refers to this contemplative dynamic as *simplified multiplicity*.[116] In other words, silent prayer simplifies our inner lives, so we can then respond to the multiplicity of people in our community. Each individual whom we have the opportunity to serve in Christ is extraordinarily unique and precious. To behold and attend to a diversity of people and organisms within the context of an exquisite larger unity is the ideal of holistic mysticism.

Many ecosystems and organisms exist in the natural world, differentiated in numerous ways, yet, as biologists tell us, they are interdependent. If the worms die off, some crops fail, and many humans don't eat. If the photosynthetic plankton on the surface of our oceans die, 60 percent of our oxygen supply vanishes.[117] Interdependence is the operating system of both our biosphere and the Real Presence.

Ignorance divides, dominates, threatens, and coerces. The Light of Christ honors and celebrates distinctions, yet also transcends and includes diverse elements. As Paul put it in his first letter to the Corinthians:

There are varieties of activities, but it is the same God who activates all of them in everyone. To each is given the manifestation of the Spirit for the common good. All these are activated by one and the same Spirit, who allots to each one individually just as the Spirit chooses. For just as the body is one and has many members, and all the members of the body, though many, are one body, so it is with Christ . . . that there may be no dissension within the body, but the members may have the same care for one another. If one member suffers, all suffer together with it; if one member is honored, all rejoice together with it. Now you are the body of Christ and individually members of it. (12:6, 7, 11, 12, 25–27)

Dualistic thinking insists that things must be either-or—my identity can be as *either* an individual *or* as a member of a unified body but not both. The holistic mysticism of Paul saw past the illusion of division; he recognized a both-and reality, where unity does not cancel individuality, and individuality does not undermine unity.

A unique insight of Quakers is that gathered communities, not just individuals, can collectively access this contemplative Ground in waiting worship. And so Christ's Real Presence guides us—through scripture, through the promptings of the Spirit in prayer, and through the circumstances of our lives—drawing us together, individuals in union.

Gladly committing ourselves in body and soul,
utterly and completely, to the Light Within,
is the beginning of true life.
It is a dynamic center, a creative Life
that presses to birth within us . . .
to become the soul we clothe
in earthly form and action.
And He is within us all.

—Thomas Kelly[118]

8

Group Mysticism

We may not know these our neighbors
in any outwardly intimate sense,
but we now know them, as it were, from within,
and they know us in the same way, as souls now alive
. . . blended into the body of Christ
Such gathered meetings I take to be
cases of group mysticism.

—Thomas Kelly[119]

The holistic mysticism of the Quakers is different from any other. In the words of twentieth-century Quaker theologian Howard Brinton, most "mystics generally think of [the experience of union] only as union with God, but the Quakers . . . think of it also as union with their fellows."[120] Because the Seed of Christ is present in all people, as we gather with other spiritual seekers, we enter a state of possibility, where the Real Presence of Christ manifests itself in our togetherness. The heart of Quaker mysticism is found in the interplay between beholding sacred silences and beholding the Seed of Christ in each person as we interact in community. As Ursula Jane O'Shea wrote, the spirituality of Friends "has never been a private matter."[121]

A Sense of Unity

Thomas Kelly wrote of the sense of unity or oneness that can happen between Friends: "It occurs again and again that two or three individuals find the boundaries of their separateness partially melted down . . . wrapped in a sense of unity and of Presence."[122] You can see this same concept expressed in William Tabor's classic Pendle Hill Pamphlet, *Four Doors to Quaker Worship*, where he said that in the gathered Meeting, "the sharp boundaries of the self can become blurred and blended as we feel ourselves more and more united with fellow worshipers and with the Spirit of God" and that this experience can bring "joy, peace, praise, and an experience of timelessness."[123]

Here's another way to put this: in mysticism, the line where skin ends and air begins is a permeable continuum, rather than a rigid boundary; we are in no way separate from the air we breathe. In a similar way, in the collective silent prayer of Quaker Meetings for Worship, no tangible line is drawn between the individual and the collective. It too is a continuum, and in gathered Meetings, we are in no way separate from our sisters and brothers. We are one community. To use an analogy from quantum physics, a photon of light behaves as a particle or a wave, depending on how it is observed—and we too have the potential in communion with Real Presence to behave as individuals or as a collective.

Another way to understand union in individuality (and individuality in union) is to think of watching a movie in a theater. Each person there will interpret the movie through their own unique filters, and they will come away with their own internalized memories of the movie—and yet, at the same time, the movie itself is a common ground of experience that produces similar experiences and emotions in the viewers. Chances are, when we laugh at the end of the opening scene, those sitting beside us in the theater are laughing too, and when we cry at a particularly moving moment, we hear sniffles and sighs from our fellow viewers. In a similar way, in Quaker Meeting for Worship, gathered silence is common ground that can produce congruent states of consciousness among worshipers. The silence becomes a communal experience.

This group mysticism is a shared experience of spiritual connection and insight that can arise when individuals come together with a mutual intention to seek a deeper understanding of the Divine. In contrast to individual mysticism, which emphasizes the personal quest for spiritual insight and Divine union, group mysticism highlights the power and potential of collective spiritual experience. Thomas Kelly explained this experience during Quaker Meeting, saying that even when we are sitting with people all around us, "the Eternal Presence is over all and beneath all." Kelly goes on to say that worship "does not consist in achieving a mental state of concentrated isolation." Instead, in communal worship, "it is as if we found our separate lives were all one life, within whom we live and move and have our being."[124]

Marcelle Martin, a Quaker scholar, has written extensively about group mysticism. According to Martin, the characteristics of group mysticism include a sense of shared presence and awareness, a deepening of spiritual understanding, and a feeling of interconnectedness and unity with others.[125] When individuals come together in a group with a shared intention to seek the Divine, they can create a powerful field of energy that can facilitate a collective mystical experience.

This group experience can provide spiritual support and community that can be difficult to find in individual practice. By coming together with others in a common pursuit of the Divine, we find belonging and connection that can help to sustain and deepen our spiritual journeys. While individual mysticism is usually a solitary pursuit, group mysticism highlights the potential for spiritual insight and transformation that can arise when we share a quest for the Divine.

Twenty-first-century Quaker Thomas Jeavons breaks down Quakers' group mysticism into three features. First, he said, comes an understanding "rooted in experience" that we can enjoy an intimate relationship with God that will give our lives "meaning, purpose, and wholeness." Second, he noted that Quakers have a "fervent desire to live out, to fully embody" the Light that shines from this relationship with the Divine, and third, Quakers recognize that they need each other; they need the support of a spiritual community in order to live a life of faith and integrity.[126]

The Meaning of Quaker Community

The lived experience of community is essential to Quaker mysticism. In fact, it is implicit in the very name—the Religious Society of Friends. This community is grounded in solitude, but it is a solitude that is supported and nourished by community. As Quaker author Parker Palmer put it, we need to "hold solitude and community together as a true paradox." Parker describes a state of solitude we can experience when we are "fully present to ourselves, whether or not we are with others." At the same time, Parker said, "Community does not necessarily mean living face-to-face with others; rather, it means never losing the awareness that we are connected to each other."[127] Palmer affirmed that "community happens as that of God in you responds to that of God in me."[128]

Author Martin Buber speaks of three progressive stages of relationship: the "I–it" relationship, which is exploitive; the "I–you" relationship, a relationship of equals; and finally, the "I–Thou" relationship, when we see "that of God" in the other person.[129] This to me is the essence of the transformation that takes place in Quaker sacred silences. Over time, we begin to see the Real Presence in our sisters and brothers gathered with us in stillness. We move from I–it and I–you relationships to I–Thou relationships. As we make this shift, we can also, as Parker Palmer noted, move from the loneliness of perceived separation, even when we're surrounded by a crowd—to solitude, where we maintain our sense of connection with the community, even when we are geographically alone.

"Although Quakerism emphasizes the direct relationship that exists between each person and God," wrote Marcelle Martin, "we have always found spiritual companionship helpful, often crucial, in accessing that direct relationship."[130]

Who Is Marcelle Martin?

A prominent Quaker scholar, author, and teacher, Marcelle Martin has spent her life exploring the intersection of spirituality, community, and social justice. She is widely recognized as a Quaker elder and teacher.

Raised Catholic, Marcelle was still searching for something more in her spiritual life. She studied the practices of many spiritual traditions, seeking to discover the "Great Mystery" she sensed in and around her. Then she had a mystical experience. Looking up at a starry sky, she said in her blog, she "experienced a divine Light, a cosmic wholeness that infuses all things, what an early Quaker might have called 'the hidden unity in the Eternal Being.'" Marcelle knew in that moment that this Light can heal all the brokenness in our world. The experience inspired her to dedicate her life to helping humanity "open fully to that divine Light that flows within all things and within each of us."[131]

Today, Marcelle shares her insights and experiences with others, leading workshops and retreats on Quaker spirituality and the practice of group mysticism. Her life and writings continue to point the way toward a practical and holistic mysticism. "It is my whole-hearted desire to help individuals and communities seek Truth and find the Way of love, wisdom, and peace," she wrote on her website. "May we see a restored earth, enjoy the Peaceable Kingdom, and together grow into our inheritance as children of God."[132]

Movement in the Stillness

The stillness of communal mysticism is not static. With practice, as you sit in Meeting, you notice an odd phenomenon: at particular points in a silent Meeting for Worship, the collective silence increases in depth and breadth; at other times, it dissipates. Rufus Jones referred to this as "spiritual waves" or "silent hushes."[133] The silence surges like the ocean, which crests and falls. These waves are often tangible when we enter collective silence.

Sometimes, after I've experienced one of these collective waves of silence, I hear Friends refer to it as a *gathered Meeting.* This sense of being gathered into union, all our differences suspended, is what makes Quaker mysticism unique.

This doesn't just happen all by itself. As in a marriage, union requires individual commitment. When Friends meet for worship, the group depends on each individual's wholehearted presence. As modern-day Quaker Calvin Keene remarked, when those present at Quaker Meetings are not committed to this responsibility, "spirit will be largely absent, distractions will be sensed, and spoken messages, if there are any, will tend to be shallow and superficial. It is in this regard that it is true that no form of religious expression makes so great a demand upon the worshiper as does the Friends Meeting for worship."[134]

Discernment

Holistic mysticism can be a useful tool for decision-making. Quakers use group discernment processes to clarify personal life choices; they also use them to test directions for the community as a whole and to seek unity. Discernment—the act of searching for truth—requires remaining open to the Light within as well as the Light of the gathered Meeting.

Friends have faith that those who sincerely question and seek will find life-giving ways forward. As Jesus said, "Ask, and it will be given to you; search, and you will find; knock, and the door will be opened for you. For everyone who asks receives, and everyone who searches finds, and for everyone who knocks, the door will be opened" (Matthew 7:7–8). In saying this, Jesus was not promising that our every selfish, ego-oriented desire will be satisfied. Instead, he meant that as we honestly search for solutions to our life's dilemmas, we will find answers.

There's an old Quaker saying: *A way will open.* Lao-Tzu, the Chinese philosopher who wrote often about the Way (what he called the *Tao*), said, "Do you have the patience to wait till the mud settles and the water is clear? Can you remain unmoving till the right action arises of itself?"[135] This is what happens in Quaker group mysticism: together we let the mud settle, so that we can see with greater clarity. We wait together for the way to open.

In our world of rugged individualism, however, we may prefer to do our own analysis and come to our own conclusions regarding decisions we face. We may not feel the need to talk things through or to draw out other people's thoughts and perspectives. In this case, our thought process may become heavy-handed and narrow. We don't take into consideration each other's insights. Instead, we keep our own council, and we do not invite the council of others. In our beleaguered twenty-first century, this truncated and reductionist approach abounds.

When our approach to decisions is narrow, our personal relationships are constricted. People keep us at a distance because we haven't taken the time to value and explore their opinions. But, as the author of Proverbs attested, "Fools think their own way is right, but the wise listen to advice" (12:15).

Two or three heads are always better than one is a profoundly Quaker statement. Yes, when faced with a decision, it often helps to spend time alone pondering the pros and cons; writing a risk-benefit analysis down on paper can help with discernment. But (as the ancient world knew, though we have sometimes forgotten) a good discernment process includes conversations. This doesn't mean we give away our inner authority. When we are open to different perspectives, however, we make better-informed big-brain decisions.

While Quaker Meetings for Worship are fundamentally about inclusion, inclusion doesn't mean absolute equality. We can invite everyone to participate in a discussion about a decision we face, but we are free to discern which voices carry the most weight. It wouldn't make sense if every voice were given the same weight regardless of experience, age, spiritual maturity, mental acuity, education. That would lack discernment. In a Quaker Meeting for discernment, all have equal voices, but not all voices carry equal weight.

As Howard Brinton pointed out, the Quaker process of discernment is different from other group decision-making processes. "At its best the Quaker method does not result in a compromise," he wrote. "A compromise is not likely to satisfy anyone completely. The objective of the Quaker method is to discover Truth which will satisfy everyone more fully than did any position previously held."[136] No one claims that this is easy! All groups of human beings will have differing perspectives and ideas—but when these are experienced within the Real Presence of Divinity, these differences can become strengths. As any strong leader knows, a diverse advisory cabinet that rivals and challenges their thought processes is far better than a bunch of boot-licking cronies who parrot their ideas.

If we relegate mysticism to individuals, we isolate, sideline, and trivialize it. Meeting for Worship changes everything, even the details of our interpersonal relationships. If my reference point is my egalitarian Quaker Meeting, then I try to draw out my friends' ideas. I ask clarifying questions. I naturally advocate open-ended conversation. I open myself up to others and their diverse views. I open myself up to be influenced.

We need a community of contemplative mentors. That's a gift that Quaker tradition collectively passes down through generations.

Standing on the Shoulders of Giants

The English word "tradition" comes from the Latin *traditio*, which means to transmit, hand over, or give for safekeeping. Tradition is not meant to be an inflexible set of rules or a rigid box that prevents us from seeking out creative change and expanded awareness of the Divine. Instead, it's a way to stand on the shoulders of those who came before us, so that we can see further than our own limited perspectives—and in doing so, discover new options for today's dilemmas.

People often see mystics as tangential to Christian tradition. For me, however, mysticism is the core of the tradition. People like George

Fox, Caroline Stephen, Rufus Jones, and Thomas Kelly are my spiritual mentors[137]; I turn to their writings when I seek wisdom from beyond my own limitations. Although these individuals are no longer alive in the flesh, they continue to be a part of my experience of Quaker group mysticism. Their spiritual insights live on. The Real Presence of Christ is still visible in them, and when I stand on their shoulders, I see the panorama of holistic mysticism.

The standing-on-the-shoulders-of-giants figure of speech is often credited to Isaac Newton, who wrote in a letter to a colleague regarding his scientific insights, "If I have seen a little further it is by standing on the shoulders of Giants."[138] In other words, Newtonian physics would never have come to be without the centuries of mathematical and scientific thought that preceded Newton.

This is the creative interaction that comes about as we interact with the mystic community that transcends time and space. Furthermore, in group mysticism, when we "stand on the shoulders of giants," we are not only standing on human shoulders, for in each human life, shines the Seed of Christ, the Light that enlightens us all.

In silence, in union, we climb onto the "shoulders of love." Then, in the fullness of time, we emerge with new insights, fresh passion, and creative zeal for building the Divine Reality in our lives today. There is no better revitalization of religion than the emergence of living masters.

You and I are each called to carry the Light of Christ, making it visible in our world again. In doing so, we bless ourselves and others. Together, we discover the "original blessing" that is our birthright.

*Community happens as that of God in you
responds to that of God in me.
. . . The silence of the Quaker meeting for worship
can be an experience of unity. . . .
Words can divide us,
but the silence can bring us together.*

—Parker J. Palmer[139]

9

Original Blessing

[Quakers] met the pessimism of depravity
with a rival optimism about human potentiality.

–Rufus Jones[140]

S ome of us were born into religious communities that insisted that
every human being had been "born in sin," deserving of eternal
damnation. When the first human beings sinned, we were all contam-
inated with their original sin.

This belief can lead us to relate to the Divine with fear and anxiety.
On the one hand, we may try as hard as we can to jump through the
church's hoops in order to escape hell's fire. Eventually, however, we may
become discouraged; if we were born damned, maybe we should just
give up and accept it. Belief in the grace of God is the only escape hatch.

Quakers, however, believe that grace is not triggered by human sin; instead, Divine grace is expressed in the inherent goodness of all human beings. "Original blessing" stands in contradiction to the traditional Christian doctrine of "original sin." George Fox believed all people had the potential to experience a direct, unmediated relationship with God, and that this relationship could lead to a deep sense of peace, joy, and love. He saw this relationship as evidence of the inherent original goodness of human beings, and rejected the notion of original sin. Fox knew original goodness could be distorted and twisted by detrimental influences; still, the soul's origin is fundamentally good.

In the twentieth century, Rufus Jones further developed the concept of original blessing by emphasizing the importance of cultivating the inner light within oneself; he believed that by nurturing this inner light, individuals could tap into their inherent goodness and bring about positive change in the larger world. Thomas Kelly also emphasized the need for individuals to surrender their egos to the Divine in order to fully realize their inherent goodness. He saw this surrender as a path to spiritual transformation and the fulfillment of human potential.

Quakers disengaged from the church's doctrine of original sin. They replaced this gloomy, entrenched belief with the Light-filled doctrine of original blessing.

Unpacking the Concept of Original Sin

The third chapter of Genesis, which describes the "Fall" of Adam and Eve, is generally offered as the biblical foundation for original sin.

However, the story in Genesis never uses the word *sin*, and no mention is made of eternal punishment.

There are, however, consequences for Adam and Eve, just as there are for each of us whenever we over-indulge our selfish cravings rather than patiently cultivate the Seed of Christ within us. Adam and Eve lose their intimate relationship with God—and when that happens, humanity's relationship with animals and the relationship between genders are disrupted (see Genesis 8:14–24). The Fall, as it's described in Genesis, does not lead to total depravity but to broken relationships.

In the parables Jesus told of the lost coin, the lost sheep, and the prodigal son, we see that when separation exists between our hearts and God's, that separation is painful. The Divine, as shown in the metaphors of housewife, shepherd, and father, eagerly works to heal and find what has been lost. Jesus never mentions punishment, only the restoration of relationship.

Similarly, in the Book of Acts, the Apostles never talk about damnation or hell. Like Jesus, they spoke only of Divine love and restored connections between human beings. So when did the church start believing in original sin instead of original blessing?

It happened in the fourth century after Christ, when Augustine of Hippo made it a permanent part of Western theology. "We have all become one lump of clay," he wrote, "that is, a lump of sin. . . . We as sinners deserve nothing other than eternal damnation."[141] According to Augustine, it was a "moral and legal liability" that was passed on genetically from Adam to the entire human race; all descendants of Adam were condemned to hell from birth for a sin committed before they were even born. For the Western church, this teaching became official dogma at the Council of Orange in 529. Human beings were by nature congenital sinners.[142]

Augustine's influence is a primary distinction between Eastern and Western Christianity. In the West, the influence of Augustine's writing is second only to the Bible; his ideas became the bloodstream of the Western church. In the East, on the other hand, Augustine has little influence. So, although Augustine overshadows all Western theology, Eastern theology is not enamored with him. Quakerism often has more in common with Eastern Christianity than it does with most of the Western church.

Original blessing reminds us that since the beginning of Creation, God has called us good; we are beloved of the Divine before we are anything else. We do not need to suppress or eradicate our humanity in order to follow Real Presence. Instead, we need to be more like Jesus, more fully human, while embodying the image of God.

Jesus came to bring us good news. If his message had been "You are all going to hell," that would have been bad news, but original blessing is the heart of the gospel. Blessing brings healing. It allows us to experience what is sometimes referred to as humanity's *pre-fallen state*. The pre-fallen state, original blessing, and original purity are synonymous.

Before the "Fall"

Eastern mystics wrote about a "pre-fallen state." Hundreds of years later, George Fox wrote that he came into "the state of Adam before he fell." Fox had never read the writings of the Eastern Fathers, and yet through habitual deep silences, he came to their same conclusion of original blessing, not original sin, as the primordial state of purity before the Fall. Across generations, Fox and other Christian mystics knew that in rapt silence, we may stumble upon the radiant Source who calls us into being before any defilement or Fall.

Mystics who speak of this pre-fallen state repeatedly refer to joy as its primary characteristic—not a marketer's joy after a sale or a pleasure-seeker's joy after a skydive, but rather a deep and steady joy that surpasses all our fancies. It is like a sailboat floating on a still sea: undistracted, spacious, liberated. The sailboat is in perfect alignment, water below and sky above. There is symmetry, effortless inherent order, peace.

Blessing and Healing

Emphasizing original blessing has therapeutic effects, a deep healing that inoculates us against tragedy. When there is a crisis, the human psyche often shuts down and quits taking risks; it finds a hole to crawl into and then assumes the fetal position. The profound affirmation of original blessing is the antidote that integrates body, heart, mind, and soul on a neurological level. That intense affirmation and synthesis then give us the strength to survive life's hurricanes. Our steadiness is rooted in the very essence of Reality.

To understand that primordial Reality a little better, picture yourself at a movie theater, where the moving picture on the big screen seizes your attention. If you were to follow the light projected on the screen, however, you'd come to a hole in a wall at the back of the theater with a small projector room behind it. Then, if you were able to enter the mechanical encasing of the projector, you would come to a brilliant bulb giving copious light. Without this light, there would be no projection. There would be no movie.

Like the Light of original blessing, the source of the movie—the brilliant bulb—is not apparent. It takes determination to find it. But upon it, everything else depends. The bulb itself is not involved in the drama on the screen, yet it is the source of light for every dialogue and action sequence. The bulb's detachment and brilliance are pure, like a wild river at its mountain source before pollution and debris accumulate downstream. The bulb is the original Light, from the beginning, primordial. It gives light to all (Genesis 1:3). It is none other than the preexisting Word, which inspired the poetry of John 1:1–5.[143] Because of the bulb, the movie and the whole spectacle have their being.

Experiences of our original nature in Christ give us the power to dust ourselves off, get up again, and risk everything again. No matter how many times life knocks us down, we continue, again and again, to get up. The affirmation of our original primordial nature inoculates us from those schoolyard bullies, the demons of despair and lethargy. Each time, we lose our balance and stumble, we hear a sturdy whisper from the labyrinthine depths of our being: "Get up, get up."

Hannah Whitall Smith, a nineteenth-century cradle Quaker, must have heard that stubborn whisper, for heartbreak after heartbreak, she got back to her feet and continued to claim the blessing of her God. In her book *The Christian's Secret of a Happy Life*, she described people who seem to think that God wants to make us miserable, when instead, "the will of love is always blessing of its loved one."[144] Smith also described people who feel they are unworthy of claiming their identities as God's blessed ones. "Their false humility prevents them from seeing it," she wrote.[145] Hannah found she could rest in the blessing, no matter how challenging the circumstances. Despite financial fears, a broken marriage, and the deaths of five of her children, Smith trusted what she called "the mother-heart of God." Like a baby on her mother's breast, she said, she relaxed into the loving blessing of God.[146] "Your part," she said, "is simply to rest."[147]

Who Was Hannah Whitall Smith?

Born in 1832 into a strict Quaker home, Hannah Whitall Smith grew up to be an important public preacher, women's rights reformer, and a bestselling author. At the age of nineteen, she married her husband Robert, who was also a Quaker.

After Hannah and Robert encountered John Wesley's teachings, they became deeply involved with the Holiness Movement, but Hannah continued to see Quakerism as her spiritual home. In fact, she wrote in a letter to a friend, her bestselling *The Christian's Secret of a Happy Life* was simply "old Quaker doctrine" laid out in a new way. In her autobiography, she devoted an entire chapter to explaining the Quaker faith. Although many evangelical Christians now claim Hannah as their own (while, ironically, many others condemn her for her radical ideas), Hannah said her popular books and speeches had actually brought the Quaker faith to the masses.[148]

> Although Hannah often wrote about comfort and joy, her life was full of loneliness, doubt, and sorrow. In the years before her death in 1911, she was confined to a wheelchair. Despite all that, her belief in God's blessing never waned, and today she continues to inspire and encourage twenty-first-century seekers.

Our Original Nature

Unfortunately, as a baby develops and matures into adulthood, she confronts numerous negative influences that stifle and truncate her potential. Although she may find it harder to "simply rest," her origin in God remains pure. It shares in "Uncreated Light."[149]

Darkness scatters before the spacious uncreated Light of Christ. So too, our pretenses and duplicity scurry away. Prayer empowers us to touch the original blessing that predates and overpowers all subsequent influences. In doing so, we connect more deeply with the Divine—and we may discover anew the life-giving properties of scripture.

The gospel is not a story of us being separated by sin from God. . . .
It's a story of invitation and participation. . . .
Sin is not at the heart of our nature;
blessing is.

—Danielle Shroyer[150]

10

Scripture and the Spirit

The words of the Bible are good words,
but they are not superior to the Eternal Word,
from which they came.
The best way to use the Scriptures is to employ them
as a means by which we are led into the same spirit
which impelled them who first gave them forth.

—Elton Trueblood[151]

The Bible plays a unique role in Quaker beliefs, both past and present. Quakers consider the Bible to be a valuable source of inspiration and guidance, but they do not see it as the only or ultimate source of religious truth. Instead, Quakers believe the Inner Light—the direct and personal experience of God's presence and guidance within each person—is the ultimate authority. So, Quakers value the

Bible and draw inspiration from it, but they do not view it as the only authoritative source of religious truth. The rely instead on the Spirit of Truth that Jesus described in the Gospel of John (16:12).

Quaker author Calvin Keene wrote, "Used as starting points for meditation, these Scriptures have the power to awaken and deepen insight and faith."[152] For Quakers, scripture is not an infallible or absolute authority—but it is a precious resource that connects us to our spiritual heritage. It is a starting point.

Howard Brinton described scripture as part of the living network that connects us. The Quaker sense of connection extends through both time and space, including those who lived thousands of years ago in Bible times. They are "bone of our bone, flesh of our flesh," wrote Brinton, "and we can no more separate ourselves from them than a plant can separate itself from its roots."[153]

"The Spirit which produced the Bible," Brinton also wrote, "still works in hearts, revealing new truth and new aspects of old truth, so the biblical canon is never closed." The Quaker experience of holistic mysticism, he explained, "can only be upheld by an attitude which accepts the spirit of the New Testament as a whole, rather than stressing the literal meaning of certain isolated texts."[154] For Howard Brinton, the Inner Light must always come first—and then it illumines everything we see, including the Bible. But the Bible can never be the source of the Light. Instead, we participate in "an eternal gospel not exclusively related to particular historical events."[155] The Bible gives testament to the Inner Light Brinton championed (for example, the Transfiguration [Mark 9:2–30] and Paul's conversion [Acts 9:1–19]), but the Bible is not itself the Light.

Each generation has its unique challenges and these lead to unique relationships with scripture, based on the context of the times.

Therefore, the Spirit moves and adapts to the needs of each generation, keeping faith vital. The way the Spirit moves today mirrors past revelation in scripture. At the same time, the Spirit has a limitless capacity to enter scripture through the fine print of our present context. Quakers' direct experience of the Divine is "informed by the Word."

Who Was Howard Brinton?

Howard Brinton was born in 1884 into a family that had been Quakers for at least eight generations. He is sometimes credited with creating a vital modern version of Quakerism that is true to its historic roots while at the same time meeting the needs of today's world. Throughout his writing, he stressed the connection between roots (including Christianity's biblical roots) and direct, personal spiritual experience.

During World War I, Howard worked with conscientious objectors who were imprisoned because of their beliefs. This experience inspired him to join the American Friends Service Committee, which allowed Quakers and other pacifists to serve during wartime in nonviolent ways. After witnessing firsthand the horrific consequences of war, Howard became a pacifist speaker and writer.

Howard met and married Anna Shipley Cox, also a Quaker and a historian, who worked closely with him on many of his projects. They became co-directors of the Quaker center at Pendle Hill. Howard continued to write and speak, spreading Quaker ideas around the world. He died in 1973.

Light Is Light

"Informed by the Word" is a phrase Caroline Stephen used to describe the relationship between her individual Inner Light and the Bible. "Some, no doubt," Stephen acknowledged, "have gone too far in the direction of transferring the idea of infallibility from the Bible to themselves. But, on the whole, I believe . . . that the 'Word of God' is Christ, not the Bible."[156] Stephen recommended neither putting the Bible "under a bushel" nor slavish obedience to it, but a healthy, middle-of-the-road approach.

Stephen went on to explain, "There can, indeed, be no rivalry between inward and outward light." Light is light, regardless of whether it comes from a candle or the sun. You are not required to shine using the exact same methodology I use (although my light may serve as a "lamp" that helps you see the way, just as your light may shine in such a way that I too am illuminated). Although scripture serves as a standard we all can share, it does not replace our inner light but rather guides and undergirds it. At the same time, Stephen affirmed, Quakers have "always had the courage to trust . . . the Spirit which gave forth the Scriptures for their interpretation, and for the leading of each one 'into all truth.'"[157]

When George Fox helped found Quakerism, he did not deny the value of scripture; the Quakers, like the rest of Christianity, treasures the scriptures, but, said Fox, "they wanted the power and spirit that they had that gave them forth."[158] Classical Protestantism had replaced the infallible authority of the church with the infallible authority of the Bible; now, the radical reformation of the Quakers replaced the infallible authority of the Bible with "the power and life of God . . . which gave forth the Scriptures, which was before the Scriptures."[159] In other words, Quakers realized the inward Spirit that inspired the scriptures is primary, and the outward manifestations of Real Presence are the glorious byproducts.

Our guidance from the Spirit has biblical roots. If we want to know how God will manifest in the future, we remember how God manifested in the past. That is our best indicator of how God manifests tomorrow. For people of faith, future revelation reflects past revelation. A common thread links past and future. Our nudges from the Spirit reflect the experience of past mystics and prophets. And at the same time, our nudges have a unique angle, given our aptitudes and circumstances; our revelations are tailor-made.

Scripture and the personal insight that comes from our Inner Light should not be in conflict. Instead, they work together. Each helps us understand the other more deeply. "Nothing is revealed truth to me, as doctrine," wrote Hannah Barnard at the beginning of the nineteenth century, "until it is sealed as such in my mind, through the illumination of the word of God, the divine light, and intelligence."[160]

The Spirit That Permeates Scripture

"The Scriptures were given forth by the spirit of God," wrote George Fox, "and all people must first come to the spirit of God in themselves."[161] Here, Fox made another distinction between inner and outer. The Bible is not magic. Lying on a dusty shelf, it has no power to heal and transform. The letters of the Bible, its binding, and its pages are empty externals that only come alive when animated by the internal Spirit. Our interaction and relationship with the words of the Bible are what make it come alive. Even more profound, in my opinion, is the singular unifying Word that permeates the many scrolls that formed what we know today as the Bible.[162]

We are not able to tap into the wellspring of life alluded to in scripture unless we experience some portion of the raw, unadulterated Spirit that gave forth scripture. In the apostle Paul's second letter to the church at Corinth, he spoke of the "new covenant," which is "not of letter but of spirit, for the letter kills, but the Spirit gives life" (3:6). The letters of the law are one thing, and a dynamic faith and relationship with those letters is another. The love of scripture takes us beyond the scripture to the Spirit that gave them forth.

Fox's distinction between the scriptures and the "Spirit that gave them forth" corresponds to this same separation between life-giving Spirit and deadening legalism. The Spirit of the law gives life. Absolutism about the letter of the law smothers life. When the Bible is seen as a solid fixture, it can sometimes be used to club people. It becomes a weapon rather than a vehicle of Divine Light.

"I was to direct people to the Spirit that gave forth the Scriptures," George Fox wrote in his journal.[163] Relationship with the Source is always primary. Scripture is a magnificent byproduct. Fox declared that the state of mind that produced the scriptures is available to us. We can access that primary Source, fertile with prophetic seeds. Holy writ didn't end with the Bible. It spoke through Fox's quill, and it continues to speak through today's spiritual and social prophets.

In the Bible, we see the path of holistic mysticism lived out in individuals' lives. David's long silences while herding flocks inspired the Psalms. Quiet wilderness sojourns inspired Moses and Abraham. Jesus retreated into the wilderness for prayer and renewal, undergirding his speaking ministry with his direct relationship with his Father.

John alone of the Isle of Patmos had a world-shaking vision. Intimacy with the quickening unifying pulse of the universe gave forth the scriptures. The people who wrote the Bible were steeped in stillness and silence. This long kinship made their minds fertile and receptive to the Seed of Christ.[164]

Scripture opens us to revelation—but at the same time, scripture can be a crutch that shelters us from personal connection and interaction with our Source. The words of scripture point to God in Christ, but they are no substitute for a relationship with the living Word. Someone who fixates on the Bible and sidelines personal experience is like someone who fixates on the trail map but fails to hike the trail. The map is not the territory. The words are not the Word. The letter of the law is not the Spirit. Jesus-made words (as recorded in the Gospels) are not the same as Jesus-made-flesh. Sermons *about* Jesus, preached from the pulpit, are not the Real Presence of Christ within.

"We are all thieves, we are all thieves," wrote Quaker Margaret Fell in 1694, "we have taken the Scriptures in words and know nothing of them in ourselves."[165] For Quakers, experience is always primary; personal experience trumps secondary witnesses. If we don't first experience the Spirit within, how can we perceive it with any depth in scripture?

We understand the Bible better when we approach it with humility. Rather than approaching scripture with an agenda, we allow ourselves to be molded by it. We don't bend our understanding of scripture to match our preconceived notions and political positions. The living Christ is the priority rather than self-serving ideology.

Cult leaders, doomsday fanatics, and flat-Earth crusaders can find isolated Bible verses to adapt to their schema. Meanwhile, holistic mystics tend to approach scripture as a whole. The Book of Ruth, where a foreign woman becomes one of the ancestresses of Jesus, counterbalances much of the Hebrew scriptures' emphasis on kinship ties. The Book of Job counterbalances the consistent sentiment of the Psalms and other biblical books, that God rewards the righteous. Job is both righteous and cursed; Ruth is both orphan and beloved. The wrathful God of the Hebrew scriptures is countered by the loving and merciful Christ of the Gospels. Grace by faith alone outlined in the Book of Romans balances insistence on good deeds in the Book of James.[166] We can't pick and choose according to our agendas. Paradox and balance are the elixirs of faith. The point is to stay receptive to scripture as it zigzags, and not to reduce it to our agendas.

George Fox understood that what is more important than the Bible's *words* (plural) is the Word (singular). The Source (the Word) of the words is more important than the words themselves.[167] That same eternal Word liberates and energizes prophets ancient and postmodern. The Bible has multifaceted and diverse branches, but one deep taproot, a singularity, the "preexistent Word" of John's Gospel: "In the beginning was the Word, and the Word was with God, and the Word was God" (John 1:1). This taproot predates scripture.

When we let go of our egos' agendas and manipulation, and instead, ask the Bible to form us, amazing things happen. As George Fox reiterated, the most genuine way to approach the Bible is personal relationship. The Bible needs to become intimate, with our scribbles in the margins and a coffee stain on the cover.

The Living Witness

Scholar Bernard McGinn wrote, "The Bible has been both the origin and the norm for Christian mystics down through the ages. The very term mystical (Greek: *mystikos*; Latin: *mysticus*) entered Christianity primarily as a way to describe the inner sense of the Bible."[168] The Bible holds an inner meaning for us unique to our context. I read a verse and say to myself, *What does the Bible say to me in this moment?*

The same Bible verse may say something entirely different to you from what it does to me, based on our individual contexts. In other words, scripture is not monolithic. When we approach it prayerfully, it is personal. It morphs depending on our lens, filters, and context. We must walk the unique topography of our lives and read scripture in our own way. In doing so, we become "new testaments in the flesh" for our times. From a lived faith comes a living testament. The Bible is a springboard for personal transformation—but unless we internalize it and experience its Spirit for ourselves, it is a dusty, lifeless book.

I like it when people talk about their "life verse." I see a life verse as a scripture they want to live into fully—a trail they want to hike repeatedly. They want to birth that verse in their own lives. They want to *become* that verse. One of my favorite life verses, revered by a Quaker I know, is this: "We know that we have passed from death to life because we love one another" (1 John 3:14).

Wrestling with Scripture

My mother introduced me to scripture. From my youth, she taught me the Lord's Prayer and Psalm 23. When she taught me these words of life, she invited me into the inner sanctum, the prayer room where her core being, her essence, was nourished. Her lessons sowed seeds that loitered in my heart and mind for years, then germinated later.

My mother's example and our relationship taught me far more effectively than if she had tried to pressure me or enforce her beliefs through parental authority. "The autonomy of the soul"—our spiritual freedom to decide for ourselves—"should be protected and safeguarded," wrote Rufus Jones. Quakers "had seen enough, and more than enough, of outside compulsion in religious matters."[169]

Like Brinton, we may come from a long line of religious people—or like George Fox and Caroline Stephen, we may have struggled to discover a faith that meets our needs. Either way, ultimately, Quakerism teaches us we must question and probe the tradition handed down to us. We need to exercise individual conscience and reason. We must wrestle with tradition like Jacob wrestled the angel (Genesis 32:22–31). Only then will our faith be authentic, something hard-won and precious that's our very own.

When I take ownership of my faith, scripture is no longer the church's Bible. It is now *my* Bible that I underline, dog-ear, and internalize. My favorite verses compel me and form me. In the long run, it is not the faith of the church that matters most to me; rather, what counts is my hard-won faith after thousands of hours of worshiping, soul-searching, and prayer. What matters most is not what Matthew, Mark, Luke, and John said a couple thousand years ago, but what you and I can say now.

My Bible, faith, and witness are dynamic living phenomena. They require no secondary sources or reference points. I don't mouth the words or formulas of others, no matter how noble. My faith's origin is within, and therefore, is real, authentic. It is no hand-me-down, cookie-cutter faith. My faith is unique to me as every snowflake is original and unique unto itself.

When we wrestle with our faith, it gives birth to original tailor-made missions. We connect with the profound and mysterious Holy Spirit that not only permeates and animates scripture but also all Reality.

> *No creature can read the Scriptures to profit thereby,*
> *but who come to the light and Spirit*
> *that gave them forth.*
>
> —George Fox[170]

11

Mystery and
the Nature of God

God cannot be fitted into performed notions
bounded by expressions in words.
Faith must allow for elements of radical unknowability
and mystery about God.

—Jonathan Hewett[171]

As a boy growing up in Virginia, I would lie in the tall grass with my mom and look up at the stars. She pointed out to me the shapes of the Big Dipper, Orion's Belt, and other constellations, but all the while, her unspoken message was this: *The wonder of this night sky, the silent mystery that carries our prayers and our breath are what matter. When we remember the Great Mystery and address it, we address what is most real. When we forget, we become small.*

My artist mother revered the Great Artist who carved the Grand Canyon, set planets in motion, and wound Sequoia roots together. I loved her reminders that awe and wonderment prevail. She taught me by example when it came to practical religion. The minister might get it wrong, or the acolyte might stumble in the aisle and fall to a knee—but my mother's faith would remain unshaken. Something of immense beauty animated her faith, something deeper than external religious trappings.

This luminous Mystery lies behind the shadows and smoke screens, the Ultimate Good that gave us our first breath and receives us at the end. The world's bullies can't change this. Their insular froth can't alter the largess of the One, who transcends all (Luke 9:28–36), yet welcomes all (Luke 4:18). The rigidity of our society's thinking can never contain the vast Mystery that is Divinity. The God who is "life, light, beauty, everywhere," as Whittier wrote, is woven throughout all life.

Quakers' emphasis on individual spiritual experience has led us to develop a unique perspective on the nature of God that differs in some respects from other Christian traditions; the emphasis on the ineffable and unknowable nature of the Divine has some similarities with Eastern Orthodox Hesychast tradition. Most Quakers believe in Jesus, both as a historical person in Galilee whose life, death, and resurrection are the revelation of God, and as a Presence here and now who guides and sustains. We acknowledge that the Spirit of Christ—what some have called the *Cosmic Christ*—is bigger than the human life of Jesus and also greater than our human ability to comprehend. We cannot put Divinity in a box. For most Quakers, the Divine Mystery is defined by Jesus but not confined to Jesus.

The Mystery of God

Twentieth-century Japanese Quaker Yukio Irie wrote, "It was not the life and death of Jesus alone that was mysterious. Strictly speaking, every bit of any life and death is mysterious!"[172] "Spirit is so universal and eternal," wrote Yukio, ". . . and I believe that it is living more or less in all human beings in the world."[173] What we think of as *self-reliance,* he said, is, in its truest sense, God-reliance, for God lies at the center of each person's mystery.[174]

Who Is Yukio Irie?

Yukio, who was born in Japan in 1908, studied philosophy and religion at Tokyo University and then became interested in the work of Western philosophers such as Heidegger and Nietzsche. At the same time, he felt a deep connection to traditional Japanese religious and philosophical traditions, including Zen Buddhism and Shintoism. Then, in 1950, Yukio met Quakers Thomas and Eliza Foulke.

For the first time, wrote Yukio, he felt he had encountered "real religion," the "Truth and Life" he had always sensed since childhood. When he told Eliza Foulke he wanted to join the Quakers, she immediately said, "Enter our Society of Friends? Quakerism has entered you through His direct Guidance. That's all!" This wasn't a conversion experience, said Yukio, so much as a discovery of something he had always known. "What a sublime moment it was!" he wrote.[175]

Throughout his life, Yukio sought to integrate his spiritual understanding into a unified worldview. He emphasized the interconnectedness of all things and the importance of embracing the mystery of the Divine. The concept of Divine Mystery, an ineffable and unknowable force present in all things, is essential, he believed, for understanding the nature of Reality and the human experience.

Faith as a Journey, Not a Destination

By this point in the book, you have probably noticed that the Quaker faith cannot be reduced to a tidy package of words, an "elevator summary" you can rattle off. This faith is an experience of discovery, but it is a matter of individual discernment, rather than something we can pick up ready-made, passed down from a parent or priest. Faith is something we wrestle with and discover for ourselves—and once we discover it, we realize there is always more. We are on a journey of unending discovery.

This journey leads us into the vast, unknowable Mystery of God. The more we explore, the more we realize still lies ahead, still unknown. Divinity is always *more.*

Outside the Box

People are often threatened by "more." Many of us prefer a reductionist, entirely materialistic worldview. A mechanistic world reduced to numbers and chemicals may give us some illusion of security and control.

The point of Christianity in general and Christian mysticism in particular, however, is to behold the Great Mystery—the infinite

More. This More is wholly unpredictable, and so it frightens us, even petrifies us at times. It can also quicken our pulse and senses, filling our hearts with wonder and joy as we perceive an enchanted and mysterious Reality.

Our language for the Divine is always approximate. It can never corner, pigeonhole, or completely define the Great Mystery. We sift through all the chatter and niceties and find them wanting. All is secondary to that immaculate Light at the center. Like the Quakers, we can call it the Seed of Christ or the Real Presence of Christ. Like Meister Eckhart, we can call it the Absolute Unity. The jaw-dropping Mystery remains as surprising today as it was thousands of years ago. And in the presence of the Mystery, there are no answers. God is not a question to be answered. God is a Mystery to behold.

We cannot solve this Mystery. There is nothing to name or define. Striving and effort do not draw us further into it. All we can do is surrender to it. The great Mystery is within our own 4.5-billion-year-old genomes. When our hearts and minds are still and quiet, we are receptive to its luminous, primordial Presence. We knock on the door of contemplation. We don't yet have the ability and interior resources to open the door—but when we are ready, the door will open from the inside, probably when we least expect it. This goes along with the saying, "What you search for cannot be found by seeking [that is, our own abilities], but only seekers find it."

When someone says to me, "I don't believe in God," I often respond, "Tell me about the God you don't believe in." I usually get a list of reductionist, anthropocentric caricatures—an Old Man with a white beard, for example, a selfish and angry celestial Dictator, or a magic Wish-Granter in the sky. Then I say, "I don't believe in that God either.

That God is not big enough. It doesn't inspire the appropriate awe, like when we gaze up at the infinite night sky." This invites a conversation about the Great Mystery, the God beyond all boxes.

Some people use the term "G-d" for Ultimate Reality, indicating that we need a new term for the Divine because the old ones carry too much baggage, politics, and quackery. I can respect the colossal challenge of clumsy attempts to name what is ultimately beyond names and images. When God told Moses, "You shall not make for yourself an idol, whether in the form of anything that is in heaven above, or that is on the earth beneath, or that is in the water under the earth" (Exodus 20:4), this is what God meant: that when we try to restrict our understanding of God to any one image, one gender, one thing, we end up with an empty box—an idol—that's far too small to contain the Infinite.

When referring to the Divine, the ancient Hebrew scriptures use the consonants YHWH.[176] The Hebrew language lacked vowels, which allowed for a wider range of meanings to be contained by the same word. In the case of YHWH, the meaning has to do with *being*. Bible scholars suggest the following options: "One-Who-Is," "One-Who-Is-Becoming," "I AM," "Self-Existent One," "Real One," and "Life-Giver." Some Hebrew experts believe the original word was a "God-cry," an instinctive exhalation of hope and need, the very sound of our breath as we gasp in fear or delight. Still others say the four letters are a verb meaning "becoming," "being," "happening." And finally, some Bible scholars believe the name expresses a relationship, the covenant commitment between Divinity and humanity.[177]

For the ancient Hebrews, the name of God, whatever its precise meanings, was too holy to be uttered, so they replaced it with the word *Lord*. A better approach, I believe, might have been simply a silent pause when we read YHWH, an acknowledgment that we can never comprehend or fully define Divinity. Through the cultivation of deep stillness and silence, we come closest to true Reality.

"The sense of God is the ultimate reality of our life," wrote Quaker Rex Ambler. He went on to explain that *God* is that which "answers our own inner longing for reality, our deep personal need for meaning and security and identity, which nothing else—nothing in the world around us—seems to be able to answer."[178]

Spiritual seekers often emphasize *light,* but it is only the false dualism of good-or-evil, black-or-white, that perceives light as good and darkness as bad. "Darkness is no less desirable than light," wrote Quaker Elizabeth Watson. "It is rather, a rich source of creativity. . . . We say that God is the Inner Light, but I want to affirm also the Inner Darkness, and I do not mean desolation or evil, but a quiet waiting and creativity."[179] I once heard someone at a centering retreat with me refer to "luminous darkness"[180]—and I was reminded of Psalm 139:12: "Even the darkness is not dark to you; the night is bright as the day."

We are called into an intimate communion with this Great Mystery. Regardless of our perceptions, even when all we sense is darkness, "God is never far away. God's Spirit is always so close—closer than breath. But unless we stop and listen, we might not notice. We practice listening. We listen with our whole selves—with our bodies, our minds, our hearts, our imaginations, our souls."[181]

Mystic Listening

Stillness is not just the absence of noise. It is a waiting attitude that's free from expectations. Zen Buddhists call this the Beginner's Mind, a state of mind without assumptions, without agendas. As Irwin Abrams put it, "In a word, the essence of Quaker spirituality is right listening."[182]

This means we're open to hearing the Divine Voice come to us in unfamiliar ways. We listen patiently, in a posture of "empty cup," with humility and an open mind. We acknowledge that our own understanding of Divinity will never be complete; we accept we may be mistaken. We also accept that each person has their own experience to which they must seek to be true.

We are like the blind people trying to describe an elephant; no matter how much we seek God, we can only know God in glimpses and partial impressions. Sometimes, God may need to smash all our ideas about Divinity, so we may go further on the long journey into the Mystery, a journey that leads us deeper into ourselves.

Every moment is a mystery.
This air is God's, the light is God's. . . .
I am living with all the universe,
and all the universe is living with me, in God.

—Yukio Irie[183]

PART III

Tools for the Inner Work

12

Mindfulness and Inward Focus

*It is foolish to think that we will enter heaven
without entering into ourselves.*

—Teresa of Avila[184]

*The Light nurtures a Seed in us but to grow,
that seed must be repeatedly exposed to the Light.*

—Robert Griswold[185]

E lder Thaddeus of the Eastern church stated that "our thoughts determine our whole life." He went on to say: "If our thoughts are destructive, we will have no peace. If they are quiet, meek, and simple, our life will be the same, and we will have peace within us. It will radiate from us and influence all beings around us."[186]

We often conceive of thoughts as insubstantial. But thoughts are as substantial as silverware we place in a drawer. Each piece has a distinct outline and weight. In the same way, once a thought is accepted and allowed to loiter in the mind—as a spoon lingers in a drawer—that thought subtly manifests itself in our lives. If we lazily allow indiscriminate thoughts to propagate our minds, we may think, "Oh they're just thoughts." But make no mistake; those thoughts influence us subconsciously. Like the half-forgotten spoon in the drawer, these thoughts are what we pick up when we interact with the world—and then they shape our interactions in ways we may not even notice.

That is why we carefully watch the gate of our minds, so that our inward focus is healthy and life-giving. Greek church fathers referred to silent prayer as *nepsis,* which means "wakefulness" or "watchfulness." We vigilantly watch for any thoughts that might disturb our inner stillness. We are hypervigilant. We are hyperaware. Our aim is undistracted prayer. We do not let our thoughts run away with us, sinking deeper and deeper into a swampland of despair or anger or monkey mind, nor do we open our thoughts to violent movies and other forms of potentially damaging entertainment. Instead, we learn to cull destructive and self-absorbed streams of thought. We turn off the television or walk out of the theater, rather than expose ourselves to destructive ideas that might take root in our minds.

When our minds go off on tangential flurries of speculation during prayer, we gently bring our minds back to their center. This is a difficult exercise in the beginning, and our success may be spotty. But after years of silent prayer, the practice will become almost automatic—muscle memory, in other words. At first, we seek peace in prayer, but in time, our minds simply abide in peace, stillness, and deep calm.

Just as negative thoughts can lead to a nonproductive life, positive thoughts can produce a life of creativity and constructive action. Journaling and writing are powerful tools that can aid and support an inward focus, because they probe our thought processes for the Light that shines through, below, and around our thoughts; they train us to be more aware of our thoughts and where they lead. One tiny butterfly of an idea can change the course of our lives (like, for example, the thought, "She is amazing. I want to marry her!").

Entering Heaven by Entering Ourselves

Richard Rohr recounted an experience he had on retreat at a monastery. One morning a monk walked by him and said, "God really is within you." This is the secret of contemplatives everywhere. We do not find the deepest layers of experience when we indulge our senses in externals. The most profound and satisfying layers of experience are *within*—where God is.

Extended retreats can dramatically enhance our awareness of the Light of Christ within. After a few consecutive days of silent prayer, perhaps four hours a day, the luminous ground of our being usually becomes unmistakable, reverberating throughout the day. Of course, such extended retreats are not "practical," considering our busy schedules. And yet they surprise us with what's possible. After such deep dives into silence, most people, including me, will exclaim, "I had no idea this deeper big-brain reality was even possible!"

Gil Scott-Heron has a famous blues album titled *The Revolution Will Not Be Televised*,[187] in which he made clear that transformation is not a spectator sport. The revolution of the heart and mind is an inside job. It does not come from outside, where it can be observed or filmed! The journey of transformation does not begin in the mall, movie theater, or concert hall. The quest begins from an invisible interior nudge, so small that at first, we may barely notice it.

This quickening within us opens a door we never realized was there. When the hinges squeak open, at first, we look around in bewilderment. Everything looks different from what it did before—and yet at the same time, nothing has changed. Sometimes, when we enter the heaven within us, a dramatic outward change does take place, but other times, "Everything changes, nothing changes." As a Zen Buddhist saying reminds us, "Before enlightenment: chop wood, carry water. After enlightenment: chop wood, carry water." The house, the clothes, the family, the daily responsibilities, all remain the same—but our subjective identities are transformed; our perceptions are different.

"In the silence," wrote Elfrida Vipont Foulds, "I feel the presence of the Divine, like a still pool in the midst of my being. It is in this sacred space that I come to know myself and God more intimately."[188] Maturity had brought this understanding, but at first, Foulds had resisted turning inward as a spiritual practice. She wrote:

> When I read that I was supposed to make "a place for inward retirement and waiting upon God" in my daily life, as the Queries in those days expressed it, I thought:

"Oh, those stuffy old Friends, they don't understand! Do they think I'm going to be able to sit for an hour, or half an hour, or a quarter of an hour, or for any time at all, in my very busy life, just to have some kind of feeling of 'inward retirement'?" I felt irritated and misunderstood, and I tried to put the whole thing out of my mind.

Now, she no longer considered this time "a formality or an obligation; it was a place which was there all the time and always available."[189]

Who Was Elfrida Vipont Foulds?

Born in 1902 in Manchester, England, into a Quaker family, Elfrida became known for her contributions to children's literature, poetry, and religious writings. In 1930, she married Percy Foulds, a science research technologist, and their married life provided Elfrida with a supportive foundation from which to begin a writing career. She was a prolific writer, in many genres, including history, music, and spirituality. She wrote nearly two dozen novels, stories, and anthologies for children and young adults, including *The Lark on the Wing*, which won the Carnegie Medal in 1951.

Elfrida understood that the external world could be overwhelming and deceptive, but by turning inward, she discovered a reliable source of truth. "The truest answers are not found in the clamor of voices around us," she wrote, "but in the silent depths of our own hearts, where the Divine speaks, softly, gently."[190]

The Practice of Inner Mindfulness

Although Quakers value and practice group mysticism, they also recognize that the communal experience must be undergirded by daily private moments of mindfulness. As Christopher Holdsworth wrote, "I am convinced that the vitality and practical effectiveness of our Society, as of any church, is directly related to the degree to which each of us manages to find time to explore our inner space during the week."[191] From our inner journeys, we bring wealth to share with the community.

Holdsworth referred to this practice of going within as a way to redirect our attention and refocus our thoughts. Without this intentionality, our awareness becomes scattered. Moments of mindfulness allow us to course correct; they wake us up and redirect us.

In the seventeenth century, a French monk named Brother Lawrence referred to daily mindfulness as "practicing the presence of God." "God is within you," he wrote. "Don't look for the Divine Presence anywhere else. . . . When you realize the treasure you can find in yourself, you no longer need to search anxiously for it outside yourself. The treasure chest is always open."[192]

Brother Lawrence's words point to something mysterious beyond the constant chatter of our minds. I like to visualize each thought as a boat on a river; in moments of mindfulness, I let go of all the boats and focus on the river itself and its current. In that water are profound subtleties, unnoticed by minds that dwell on the surface. When all distractions are set aside, we can observe the still and silent source of our thoughts. We can become self-aware of nudges and flickers of insight that are at the root of our thought processes, which we might otherwise overlook.

"Whenever you enter the spiritual realm," wrote Brother Lawrence, "take a close look at yourself. Examine your thoughts and feelings, seeking out the very bottom level of who you are."[193] This self-examination reveals that everything we allow into our senses and thoughts influences us—people we befriend, books we read, food we eat, movies we watch. Over time, it all subtly shapes us. A practice of daily inner mindfulness sensitizes us to these influences. It may spur us to cultivate some influences and reject others.

As we become more adept at this practice, we find we can enter into stillness even when we are surrounded by people. Even in a busy office cubicle, for example, we can intentionally minimize distractions by wearing earplugs, avoiding frivolous chatter, and taking a walk during a break or lunch hour. We can bring intention and care to each phone call, making each encounter a conscious opportunity to serve, each moment a connection to the Divine.

Mindfulness and the "Now"

"In the immediate experience of the Presence," wrote Thomas Kelly, "the Now is no mere nodal point between the past and the future. It is the seat and region of the Divine Presence itself."[194] In spiritual terms, "now" is everything. Yesterday is gone. Tomorrow is not yet here. All we have is now. Now is precious. Now is most often neglected, especially among Westerners.

It takes concerted effort to recapture the now. We must stop driving after an agenda and pushing toward goals. To recapture the now, we clear our minds of their aspirations. We clear the calendar and inbox. (Or if that is not possible, we neglect the calendar and inbox!)

This doesn't mean we abandon our children to unsupervised video games or phone time, nor do we hover over them like a helicopter (hence the modern term "helicopter mom"). We find a happy medium between absence and presence. We attend calendar appointments when necessary and neglect them when possible. In other words, we nix both abdication of responsibility and hypervigilance. We cultivate balance.

Now is our ultimate priority. Everything else can wait. Now requires that we neglect all pressing demands and attend to what is most important, this precious moment in its infinite possibilities and potential. Then, as the quality of our presence in the now increases, every other aspect of our life improves. This is the best possible use of our time! We have this moment, no other. And if we cannot embody full presence now, nothing will prepare us to be present in the future.

Of course, the now cannot be captured. Heraclitus wrote, "No person ever steps into the same river twice, for it's not the same river and they're not the same person."[195] Heraclitus understood both the beauty and foreboding of the present moment. The beauty is its ever-morphing creative dynamism. The foreboding is its ever-morphing impermanence. When we embrace the dynamism and shrug off the impermanence, we find the present moment, resplendent, supreme.

Now is where the energy is. Now is the pivotal point between the past and the future. Now is the moment to change dysfunctional patterns in our family system. And, as Thomas Kelly reminds us, now is the only place we experience Divine Presence.

Past and future tenses fall miserably short of Real Presence. We can read about how the Divine became known generations ago. We can speculate about how the Divine will reveal itself to future generations. But these are not firsthand experiences. They are once or twice removed from the original experience. Original experience in the here and now is the precious taproot of authentic religion. If we neglect the taproot, the tree withers.

In some forms of meditation, we focus on the now by fixing our attention on the breath where it enters and exits the nostrils. We can bring a similar attention to our ordinary daily activities. As we wash dishes, we focus on each dish. If we attend to children, our single-point focus is on these small people, constantly scanning their expressions and body movements for clues about their needs. Are they sleepy or hungry or frustrated? (Then we encourage better self-monitoring and self-awareness on their part so they can use their words to identify their needs instead of relying on mom or dad's vigilant awareness. This is the beginning of the road to adult maturity, self-reliance, and self-care.) No matter what occupies us during the day, as we bring our full attention to it, it becomes a vehicle for inner mindfulness.

Building a Habit of Inner Mindfulness

Eventually, this practice will become habitual, our automatic fallback state of mind, but at first, we may find that reminders are helpful. Quaker Josephine Duveneck wrote, "But to establish the presence of God so that it becomes as natural as breathing—that requires a rigorous apprenticeship." Duveneck undertook her apprenticeship by using "some trivial and seemingly ridiculous ways of keeping myself reminded. For instance, I fastened a large safety pin to the front of my dress and I carried a button in my pocket that I felt every time I reached in to find a pencil or a handkerchief."[196] Another possible reminder in today's world might be setting a timer on our phones.

On an external level, there may be much activity. But our actions are not dissipated, mindless, or distracted. Our minds are single-pointed. When we master this serenity, we can maintain it even in crisis, when our job, family, or future is at stake. This kind of subterranean serenity amid personal tsunamis brings foundational security. We know that even if everything falls away, even if our bodies waste away before our eyes, there is Something deeper. There is Something even more Real than the catastrophe at hand. We are part of an infinite whole, not reduced to separate parts. Each of us organisms is a cell in this larger body—vast and multilayered, interdependent on all other organisms. We are not alone.

And so, we submit to the present moment and to our lives as they are in this moment. We repel anxiety-ridden daydreams and regrets. We say, "This is the way it is. So be it. This day, hour, minute, moment has something to teach me, and I no longer squirm or whimper. I no longer look away." Not only that, but we also unequivocally accept everything that has happened in our lives. We accept it all, which frees us to be completely present in this extraordinary moment.

When the world began, chaotic waters swirled in the deep. Then came the Word, which gave form, utility, and poise to the chaos (Genesis 1:2–3). So too, when the waters rage around us: the everspacious and life-giving Word creates openness and possibility where there was gridlock before. The Word creates peace where there was chaos. It creates acceptance and release where there was nagging self-recrimination. It creates healing and a fresh start where there was stagnant decay.

Setting aside daily time for interior stillness provides an infrastructure that supports our spiritual journeys, like an unseen root system that silently and unsuspectingly hydrates, feeds, and nourishes us. And these quiet times are also fertile ground for prayer.

Enter into yourself
and break down all that hinders
the flow of God's grace. . . .
I say it again: enter into yourself.

—Brother Lawrence[197]

13

Silent Prayer

Do we pray, or does God pray through us?
I know not. All I can say is, prayer is taking place,
and we are graciously permitted to be within the orbit.
We emerge from such experiences of infused prayer
shaken and deepened and humbled
before the Majesty on High.

—Thomas Kelly[198]

Prayer, according to a Quaker definition, is "spending intentional time in the presence of the Divine,"[199] and this can take many forms. We may come to God with "groanings too deep for words" (Romans 8:26)—or we may pour out all the day's events into God's listening ear, sorting through our emotions and ideas, the way we would with an intimate friend. We may seek God's spiritual and practical help—or we may simply offer up our gratitude and praise. We pray in bed when we can't sleep, in the car as we drive to work, and while we do household chores. We pray in the silence of centering prayer—and we pray as we weed our gardens. We pray when something beautiful stirs our emotions, when we hold our children and our hearts swell, when we are moved with compassion for refugees and others in our world who are confronting oppression and tragedy.

Contemplative prayer embraces all life. This is what the apostle Paul meant when he wrote, "Pray without ceasing" (1 Thessalonians 5:17).

Based on their prayer lives, Quaker mystics speak of God-drenched experiences of Real Presence. A quickening Light laid Thomas Kelly's conscience bare and put everything into perspective, and then, instead of fixating on distractions and trivialities, Kelly focused on the life of prayer. In a quite different way, harrowing experiences in English prisons ushered in George Fox's profound consolations of Christ's Real Presence.[200] People who knew George Fox best, like William Penn, said Fox "excelled at prayer" above all.[201] "The most awe-filled, living, reverent frame I ever felt or beheld . . . was his in prayer. And truly it was a testimony that he knew and lived nearer to the Lord than other [people]."[202]

From the perspective of Christianity's Desert Tradition, prayer is the most vital aspect of faith. Without prayer and experiences of the infinite, Christianity loses its guts. It loses its primary reason for being, which is to experience the Real Presence of Christ and the primordial freedom we find in him.

The sixteenth-century mystic Teresa of Avila understood, however, that not all people are ready for silent prayer. It's a developmental process, with stages along the way. For nearly twenty years, Teresa herself found this form of prayer challenging. Her advice to the members of her convent was to simply focus on Jesus and "desire no other path even if you are at the summit of contemplation." At whatever level of silent prayer, if we use Jesus as our entry point, said Teresa, we do not need to strive and push ourselves. We simply look at Jesus. "We are always in the presence of God," she wrote, but "the manner is different with those who practice [silent] prayer," for they are in a reciprocal relationship where they see the Divine seeing them. To enter the Divine Reality, said Teresa, "all that is needed is the will to love."[203]

Centering Prayer

Thomas Keating was a monk drenched in experiences of Real Presence. He left an indelible imprint on the world's contemplative landscape through his profound teachings on centering prayer. Keating understood that we always have access to prayer, no matter where we are or what we are doing. "We rarely think of the air we breathe," he wrote, "yet it is in us and around all the time. In a similar fashion, the presence of God penetrates us, is all around us, is always embracing us."[204] All we need to do is tap into it. "The chief thing that separates us from God," wrote Keating, "is the thought that we are separated from God."[205]

This understanding that the Divine Presence is always available was central to Keating's spiritual growth. He often quoted Teresa of Avila, who said, "All difficulties in prayer can be traced to one praying as if God were absent." According to Keating, this "is the conviction that we bring with us from early childhood and apply to everyday life and to our lives in general. It gets stronger as we grow up. . . ." The spiritual journey, he said, "is a process of dismantling the monumental illusion that God is distant or absent."[206]

I first encountered Thomas Keating in person at an interfaith service at St. Michael's Parish in Olympia, Washington, in 2007. I was amazed by how controversial his interfaith dialogue had become; when I arrived at the service, picketers in the parking lot touted signs that read "Keating is not a real Catholic," "Real Catholicism draws the line at Buddhism," and so on. Despite the controversy, Keating's openness and willingness to learn from other traditions contributed to the ongoing dialogue between Christianity and Buddhism, fostering mutual understanding and appreciation.

In the 1970s, Keating, along with fellow monks William Meninger and Basil Pennington, developed centering prayer. They contemporized the ancient English monastic roots of centering prayer, found in the fourteenth-century classic, *The Cloud of Unknowing*. They clarified and shared this practice, making it accessible outside of monastic settings. Centering prayer gained recognition as a form of Christian meditation that transcends denominational boundaries, a catalyst for spiritual awakening and inner transformation.

As a result of Thomas Keating and others in the centering prayer movement, tens of thousands of people were drawn back to contemplative Christianity. Keating was nothing less than the foremost apostle of centering prayer in our time. And make no mistake, he never advocated retreat from the world to do centering prayer. His work went far beyond that, reaching out into the world.

Like George Fox, Thomas Keating excelled in prayer. For both, prayer was the taproot from which their life missions emerged.

Who Was Thomas Keating?

Born in 1923, in New York City, Thomas was raised in a devout Irish Catholic family, steeped in the traditions of the Catholic faith. He entered St. Joseph's Abbey in Spencer, Massachusetts, as a Trappist monk in 1944 and was ordained a priest in 1949. During his time in the monastery, he immersed himself in the ancient Christian contemplative practices of Lectio Divina (sacred reading) and the Liturgy of the Hours (praying the Psalms). These practices became the crucible of his spiritual growth. Then, while serving as the abbot of St. Joseph's Abbey in the 1960s, Thomas encountered the writings of the Desert Fathers and Mothers, particularly their teachings on silence and interior prayer. This encounter sparked his desire to explore a fresh contemplative approach.

As Thomas Keating deepened his understanding of Christian contemplative traditions, he embarked on a profound journey of exploring other spiritual paths as well. His encounters with Buddhist teachings, particularly those related to meditation and mindfulness, brought a fresh perspective to his understanding of prayer. Thomas recognized that both traditions emphasize stillness, silence, and the direct experience of Ultimate Reality. This realization opened doors for him to explore dialogues between Christian contemplation and Buddhist mindfulness.

Thomas Keating also helped create a mission organization—Contemplative Outreach, which brings centering prayer to groups and churches around the globe. Today, the Contemplative Outreach newsletter has more than a quarter million subscribers worldwide.

Root Consciousness

When the chatter of the mind settles and quiets, we become aware of a deeper layer of mind. In silence, we bypass the habitual dialogues inside our heads and go somewhere altogether different from the predictable fishbowls of the senses. When the sensate chatter subsides, we intuit a deep primal stillness, uncharted and luminous. It greets us at the entrances of ancient stone monasteries and old-growth forests. We can pick up its primordial trail in our reptilian brains' lizard DNA; this old brain is visual, not auditory, attuned to silence.[207] This root consciousness, here long before us, reveals the mysteries of our Origin; it generates an existential peace.

Silence is a powerful antidote to the pervasive noise around us, and as we enter it in both daily and weekly prayer, it begins to shape and steer us. Our minds soften, become more receptive to the Word that transforms us. As the Word came into the world on Christmas ("silent night, holy night, all is calm, all is bright"), we too invite the Word to enter us anew during pregnant silences. Then, as our unruly thoughts become settled, our minds become fertile for the Seed of Christ.

The Seed cannot germinate in noise, chatter, and crowds. As Quaker mystics tell us, to awaken the Seed requires habitual disciplined silences. This is perhaps the deepest form of prayer, to simply "Be still and know that I am God" (Psalm 46:10). This place of centered, silent prayer is the incubator that brings forth something new into the world.

As we marinate in deep stillness for years, it washes all our actions. At that point, whatever we do is a form of prayer. At the same time, we are awake and engaged, absorbed in each detail of the job, not given to distractions and daydreams. We are fully present and little escapes our notice. As Thomas Kelly wrote, "On one level we may be thinking, discussing, seeing, calculating, meeting all the demands of external affairs. But deep within, behind the scenes, at a profounder level, we may also be in prayer and absorption, song and worship, and a gentle receptiveness to divine breathings."[208]

As I said at the beginning of this chapter, prayer can come in many shapes and forms, all valuable, all aspects of a healthy growing relationship with the Divine. The small, daily times of prayer shape us as gradually as dripping water shapes stone; weekly Meeting for communal prayer forms another ongoing crucible for transformation. Sometimes, though, we may need times when we withdraw completely from the demands of our ordinary lives, so that we can focus on the Seed of Christ.

Silent Retreats: Greenhouses of Prayer

For centuries, monasteries did not emphasize silent prayer. They did not need to because they lived it. The natural rhythm of monastic life immersed them in silence. They simply absorbed silence and simplicity as part of their regular monastic routine. In our busy, modern world, however, we will probably need to seek out an extended experience of silent prayer. Silent retreats are ideal for this.[209]

"Powerful hours of unbroken silence frequently carry a genuine progression of spiritual change and experience," wrote Thomas Kelly.[210] Nothing compares to extended silences of forty-five minutes or more repeated over many days. Awash in stillness, the cumulative effect of this discipline resets our inner balance. It counterbalances the frenetic activity of our ordinary lives, generating transformation from the inside out. We swim in the deep end of silent prayer. By the end of such retreats, we find ourselves drenched in light and wonder. (Incidentally, when on retreat, I would recommend at least two thirty-minute silent prayer sessions before breakfast, two thirty-minute sessions before lunch, and the same before dinner.)

Absolute Consciousness

"The deep level of prayer and divine attendance," wrote Thomas Kelly, "is the most important thing in the world." He contrasts this with what he calls the "secular mind"—an "abbreviated, fragmentary mind, building only upon a part of [a person's] nature and neglecting a part—the most glorious part—of [a person's] nature, powers, and resources."[211]

Kelly often wrote about these two aspects of human consciousness, which I call absolute and relative.[212] Kelly differentiated between the qualities of these two states. He discerned the state of the absolute/eternal/Divine/nondual/unified mind as superior to the state of the relative/temporal/human/dualistic/chaotic mind.

The relative sphere is familiar to us all. Experiences of the absolute, on the other hand, are rare. Because of their rarity, we desperately seek them. We draw instinctively toward them for meaning, purpose, and fulfillment. We encounter Divinity there.

Although prayer can thrive in group settings, as it does in Quaker Meeting, we must also take care to claim its intimate, personal quality as our own. The spiritual journey is both communal and deeply individual. Absolute consciousness cannot be experienced vicariously.

I have learned much about prayer from reading books by people like Thomas Kelly, Thomas Keating, and Cynthia Bourgeault, but ultimately, I must participate in prayer for myself. It is dangerous, I've learned, to try to fast-track the spiritual journey via transmission from a holy "expert"[213]—far better to embark on the long road of daily centering prayer and other means of tapping into Christ's Real Presence for myself.

This daily practice brings Divine Union into my life on a cellular level—but without the external trappings of a particular religious denomination or doctrine. Thomas Keating taught that centering prayer should be free of excessive overlays of sectarian teaching and denominationalism,[214] and as a result, today the centering prayer community spans many denominations and nations.

Prayer and the Exterior Life

Our capacity to take risks and endure the consequences is directly related to our prayer life. Quakers teach that a rooted and embodied prayer life gives us the courage to exercise a social conscience, no matter the perils.

When Anthony of Egypt, one of the Desert Fathers, emerged from years of silent prayer in his cave, he was markedly different. He had awakened in the same sense that Jesus resurrected; in other words, there was total transformation. After years of silent prayer, Anthony was aglow, awash in the Spirit. He had returned to a purified state before any fall or defilement. He was drenched in God, a condition the Orthodox call Christification.[215] Although it was not necessarily his intent, there are accounts of spontaneous healing in Anthony's presence. His biography whispers what is possible: that when we enter Divine Union,[216] we heal the nervous system and become whole—and then, like Anthony, our presence may help heal wounded people, as well as our wounded Earth.

Notice what comes first: first we are healed, and then we heal others; first we are transformed from within, and then we transform our relationships and world. When Thomas Kelly reflected on the lives of John Woolman and George Fox, he praised their outward deeds to a "suffering" humanity—but Kelly stressed that these external actions were only possible because of Woolman's and Fox's "practice of orienting their entire being in inward adoration," so that Christ became their "living Center of Reference."[217]

Despite the daunting obstacles, prayer shapes us into instruments of beauty. Instead of being "conformed to this age," we are "transformed by the renewing of the mind," so we can see "what is the will of God—what is good and acceptable and perfect" (Romans 12:2). We are drawn into ever-deepening trust, no matter the circumstances. We understand that even in death and dying, we are not alone. We are intertwined with God.

But this doesn't happen automatically. It requires persistence and self-discipline.

Prayer is a process of inner transformation
a conversation initiated by God and leading,
if we consent, to divine union.
One's way of seeing reality changes in the process . . .
with increasing sensitivity to the divine presence
in, through, and beyond everything that exists.

—Thomas Keating[218]

14

Persistence and Steadiness

As long as we are persistent
in our pursuit of our deepest destiny,
we will continue to grow.
We cannot choose the day or time
when we will fully bloom.
It happens in its own time.

—Denis Waitley[219]

The aim of all spiritual practice, including prayer, according to Thomas Kelly, is to increase "steadiness in the deeper sense of his Presence."[220] Some people, who have done spiritual practice for years, experience a permanent backdrop of joy that lights up their features. Their steadiness comes from their ongoing, nearly continual awareness of the Real Presence.

Kelly described this as "an amazing stayed-ness . . . a well-nigh unbroken life of humble quiet adoration in His Presence, in the depths of our being. Day and night, winter and summer, sunshine and shadow . . . children in Paradise before the Fall, walking with [God] in the garden in the heat as well as the cool of the day. Here is not ecstasy but serenity, unshakableness, firmness of life-orientation." This sense of firm commitment, Kelly stresses, is not only for those the church regards as "saints" but rather "they are housewives and hand work-ers, plumbers and teachers, learned and unlettered, black and white, poor and perchance even rich."[221]

To know Primordial Light through consistent experience makes us steady. It rarely leads to outward recognition and glory. In fact, because this energy often threatens the status quo, society may try to squash it. Interior spiritual consolations are sometimes accompanied by persecution and deprivations. Once there is resolve about our mission in the world, however—that we were created to be in relationship with Divinity and with each other— from then on, the word that guides us is *persist*.

Resolve and Persistence

Ordinary water can carve out enormous canyons like the Grand Canyon. How? Persistence. Day after day, week after week, water wears down the rock. Like the lineage of apostles, the water persists for thousands of years.

When tragedy struck, as it has more than once in my life, the word *persist* became my mantra. That word has helped me brush off my tattered soul, get out of bed, put one foot in front of the other, and begin again.

We keep going on. That's what we do.

The mystics of the Eastern church often celebrate the virtue of patient endurance,[222] which the Bible refers to as "perseverance"[223] and Rufus Jones often called "patient suffering." According to many mystics, this is one of the keys to the ongoing spiritual life. Patient endurance resists the impulse to despair; it also resists the compulsion to become reactive or rash. Patient acceptance of pressures, suffering, and Herculean endurance tests produces something beautiful. Extraordinary pressures over time form both diamonds and saints. Be prepared—it might take forty years (Numbers 14:33)!

"Growth in the life of the spirit is slow and uneven," wrote Quaker Rachel R. Cadbury. But, Cadbury affirmed, "patience, persistence, and prayer have solved insoluble problems, and narrow strained lives have burgeoned into great beauty."[224]

Patient endurance and self-discipline mean we submit to the present moment as it is, not as we would like it to be. This is easy to say but difficult to practice. It means, moment by moment, we resist the regrets and reminiscences about yesterday, as well as the daydreams about tomorrow. Again and again, we bring ourselves back to the present moment as it is. If there is suffering, pain, or regret in the present moment, we accept it. We no longer avoid it or numb it through addictions or fetishes.

We persist.

George Fox is a good example of someone who did not judge reality by the exterior circumstances of his life. He looked past the hardships and kept his focus on the Divine Presence—even though the hardships in his life were frequent and severe. "I was so weak with lying about three years in cruel and hard imprisonments," he wrote in his journal, "my joints and my body were so stiff and benumbed that I could hardly get on my horse.[225] Between 1647 and 1664, he was imprisoned eight times, for a total of at least six years.[226] Prison time breaks people, especially in Fox's day, with its filthy, cold, rat-infested jails. But Fox's resolve did not falter.

Once, a winter storm tore open the prison roof where Fox was confined, exposing him to frigid winter elements. For months after this, Fox curled up in a ball and shivered all night. He had no blanket, and exposure swelled his joints. Others in that part of the prison froze to death. Fox barely survived.[227]

He wrote from prison to his followers, who were facing persecution of their own: "Sing and rejoice, ye Children of the Day and of the Light. . . . And never heed the tempests nor the storms, floods nor rains, for the Seed Christ is over all and doth reign. And so, be of good faith and valiant for the Truth."[228]

Twentieth-century Quaker activist Bayard Rustin followed in Fox's footsteps, inspired by Fox's example of courage and perseverance. As Rustin wrote in his book *Time on Two Crosses*, "God does not require us to achieve any of the good tasks that humanity must pursue. What God requires of us is that we not stop trying."

Who Was Bayard Rustin?

Born in 1912, Bayard Rustin grew up in a Quaker home. Later in life, he said his Quaker background was the foundation and framework for his social activism. He was a committed pacifist who was imprisoned during World II due to his conscientious objection to military service. In the 1960s, he became a prominent figure in the civil rights movement, an advisor to Martin Luther King Jr., and a strong advocate for nonviolent protest.

As a Black man, Bayard faced prejudice and discrimination; as a gay man, he endured opposition even within the civil rights movement. Despite attacks against his work from the FBI and the Senate, Bayard persisted. His perseverance pushed the civil rights movement forward, bringing about new legislation that protected the rights of all people.

After his death in 1987, he posthumously received the Presidential Medal of Freedom for his contributions to the advancement of civil rights and social justice. Despite facing hatred and opposition, Bayard's dedication to nonviolence and social justice continues to inspire activists and advocates worldwide. Throughout his life, he always said his Quaker beliefs were the source of his strength and inspiration.

Acquainted with Suffering

Persistent and steadfast resolve in the face of the cross is what Quakers revere about Jesus (Luke 22:42), and their founder George Fox's unwavering conviction was his honor and mantle, the reason his followers honored him. George gained zeal from his imprisonment and ordeals—an energy not of the body but of the spirit. After his years of imprisonment, he visited far-flung Quaker communities, even into the frontier wilds of North America, where his charisma and ardor drew thousands of people.

Another Quaker activist, John Woolman, wrote that we should be "acquainted with the hardships and difficulties of our fellow creatures."[229] The Prophet Isaiah described God's Servant as "a man of sorrows, and acquainted with grief" (52:3). Acquaintance with sorrow and suffering is not on most people's bucket list. We prefer to skip that part, opting instead for hedge-fund portfolios, creature comforts, hypertense jaw muscles, and impressive titles. We want nothing to do with soup lines, prisons, poverty-stricken countries, and crosses.

Jesus stumbled and bled beneath the heavy wooden beams of the cross. We are called to follow him, in his life and in his death, but people instinctively flee from the crucifixion, the most odious and rejected part of Christianity. Fox and other Quaker activists, however, bore their crosses and suffered with forgotten jailbirds. Meanwhile, sensual pleasures and piles of money attract most of us, until we realize that concealed within the ill-begotten stash is folly and disaster. On the other hand, hidden within the drawn-out heart-wrenching ordeal is a blessing.

The early-church father Tertullian (155–220) wrote, "The blood of the martyrs is the seed of the Church."[230] When people died for their Christian principles rather than recanted, people thought, "There must be something to these beliefs if they matter so much." As Tertullian and others understood, this impression made people pay attention, and ultimately, it converted thousands of people—and eventually spread Christianity around the world.

Soul-Force

Fox had the same persistent fortitude as the early Christians. A much later activist, Mahatma Gandhi, also had a firm resolve that was not cowed or broken by threats and beatings. I admire this strength, especially when coupled with the iron will not to retaliate with violence. Gandhi called the high ground of nonviolent resistance *Soul-Force* (*Satyagraha* in Hindi).[231] In the case of both Fox and Gandhi, their steady inward conviction accomplished extraordinary results far beyond stump speech and pulpit. In Gandhi's case, it achieved nonviolent Indian independence, and in Fox's case, it converted fifty thousand followers to Quakerism by 1661.[232]

A persistent prayer life is the necessary bedrock for Soul-Force. It is what changes our habitual attachment to pleasure and our aversion to pain. This is not to say that we become masochists, taking pleasure in pain, nor do we seek it out for its own sake; the aversion to emotional and physical pain is a healthy, protective, and God-given aspect of human nature. We begin, however, to realize the hidden snares of enticements, especially addictive substances and sexually reckless people. We see past the lure of shallow ego-pleasures and discover deeper spiritual delights. We discover that the luxuries of a high standard of living can feed anxiety, addiction, and mood disorders—the opposite of what we might think. We begin to understand the meaning and sources of true joy, which stem from personal authenticity, holistic healing, and genuine bonds of relationship.

We also see that the painful chapters of our lives have therapeutic value; they empower character growth and establish humility. The experience of downward mobility and sharing the suffering of our fellow humans and Earth's devastated life can, paradoxically, revitalize us.

This was the experience of Henri Nouwen when he joined a community of people with developmental challenges (called L'Arche Daybreak) in Toronto, Canada.[233] There, as Nouwen cared for a marginalized, undervalued, and vulnerable person named Adam, he found his soul growing beyond what he had experienced as a popular professor and author. His move to L'Arche mirrors Jesus's ministry in the Gospels.

Isaac Penington wrote from a jail cell to a fellow Quaker, Thomas Ellwood, who was also at the time imprisoned: "May your . . . spirit be kept fresh in the midst of your sufferings. May you find everything pared off that hinders the bubblings of the everlasting springs, the breaking forth of the Pure Power."[234] As we remain steady through hardship and suffering, we discover the meaning of Gandhi's Soul-Force. The things that previously obscured our vision are "pared" away, and our eyes and hearts are opened.

A Self-Disciplined Faith

To hear the call to a unique ministry and to hold fast to that call—despite all obstacles—is faith tempered by self-discipline. Although the spiritual journey has its moments of exquisite joy and loveliness, those do not fuel a lifelong journey.

The authentic path does not always lead to good times. Going in a new direction, against the norms and vested interests of our day, can bring hard times. "Great moments we shall have," promised Quaker Elizabeth Gray Vining, but then she cautioned: "they will be comparatively rare. There will be more stretches of dimness and dusk when we plod along in faith and determination."[235]

The legacy of both biblical and Quaker witnesses is that we can hold on. We can endure the suffering and emerge. We do not merely survive. We reflect the light of Christ—we reflect his wounded and disarming humility. We reflect his unassuming glory, which comes from marinating in his Light.

Despite the hardship of outer circumstances, finding our call and actualizing it is good news, the best news. Amid the endless throng of naysayers, our calling fills us and provides our reason for being (Psalm 23:5). Our existential angst subsides, and our true self emerges radiant. As we persist in lengthy meditation sessions, we release tension stored deep in our muscle tissue, another step toward the deep healing of our nervous system. The cumulative release of tension makes us able to be present and unworried in our relationships with our loved ones.

Resolve and willingness to persist may be the ultimate testimony to the Divine Presence. The Seed of Christ germinates and flourishes within our lives, despite hellacious obstacles, leading us into ever-deepening self-surrender.

Follow steadfastly after all
that is pure and lovely and of good report.
Be prayerful. Be watchful. Be humble.
Let no failure discourage you.
When temptation comes, make it an opportunity
to gain new strength by standing fast,
that you may enter into that life of gladness and victory
to which all are called.

—Ohio Yearly Meeting Book of Discipline, 1992

15

Deepening
Self-Surrender

*There is no way to find yourself
until you discover how utterly to lose yourself.*

—Rufus Jones[236]

"**U**nless a grain of wheat falls into the earth and dies, it remains alone; but if it dies, it bears much fruit" (Matthew 12:24). These words of Jesus speak to a paradoxical spiritual phenomenon: the more we surrender what we consider to be ourselves, the more fruitful we become. The outer shell of the ego cracks open, allowing the true Seed within us to emerge. Adversity, tragedy, and the humility that follows are often part of this process.

Dying and Fruitfulness

Thomas Kelly's life reveals the connection between dying and fruitfulness. Kelly is remembered as a modern model of Quakerism's holistic mysticism—but he did not easily achieve this level of spiritual perception. As a young man, he told Rufus Jones, "I am just going to make my life a miracle!"[237]—but the years that followed were full of questioning and disappointment.

These painful years, during which Kelly's life seemed to lack direction, served a spiritual purpose. Like the grain of wheat Jesus described, Kelly's life cracked open. After years of self-doubt and stumbling, he surrendered his ego-self—and in his forties, he was healed and restored. According to one of his colleagues, Douglas Steere, "A fissure in him seemed to close, cliffs caved in and filled up a chasm, and what was divided grew together within him."[238]

Kelly's spiritual advice in *Testament of Devotion* was honest and unselfconscious. It came from the depths of his spirit, from the Seed of Christ within him. If he had clung to his ambition and striving, he would never have been able to write this spiritual classic. His book grew out of the soil of self-abandonment.

The Ups and Downs of Thomas Kelly's Life

Thomas graduated college with a degree in chemistry, but this did not seem like quite the right fit for his life's vocation. He went back to earn a second bachelor's degree and then taught at a prep school, but this still did not feel like his life's calling. Next, he felt led to missionary work in Japan, and so he entered a theological seminary. Once there, he no longer felt called to Japan and decided to pursue ministry in the United States.

By this time, Thomas had a wife and family to support, which further complicated his life. Nevertheless, he continued to bounce back and forth between teaching and studying, convinced multiple academic degrees would fill the gaps he felt within himself. All the while, he suffered from kidney stones and "woozy spells" that left him physically exhausted and mentally depleted. He was very nearly drained dry, spiritually, emotionally, and physically, but still, he soldiered on. Then, when the time came for the oral defense of his doctoral dissertation, he had one of his "spells" in the middle of his presentation. He did so badly the university told him he could not try again.

Thomas was nearly drowning in despair and depression—but when he deepened his prayer life, everything changed. In the years that followed, he wrote *Testament of Devotion*, a monument of contemporary Quaker spirituality and mysticism.

Letting Go

This description of Thomas Kelly's life would probably not be attractive to an ambitious capitalist. The Desert Elder who left occupation, title, and village for desert hut would have understood, though. So would the artist who let go of the law-school treadmill for the one-room studio, open canvases, and a bucket of brushes. Many people in this post-Covid world can also relate to Kelly's biography.

People I know have floundered in the years since the pandemic, and many are still floundering. Restaurant workers and film industry workers, in particular (which describes two of my friends), have experienced major upheaval that uprooted their families and led to financial adversity and chaos. And yet, as English artist and mystic William Blake wrote in the early nineteenth century, "crooked roads . . . are the road of Genius."[239] People like Thomas Kelly, like those of us whose lives have been constantly uprooted, constantly shifting direction like a tumbleweed, are not actually wandering aimlessly in the wilderness, as it may seem at first glance. Somehow, when we surrender all the details of our lives, they all come together in ways we could never have predicted. All the schemes, all the "strive and drive" machinations of the ego, could never have created such genius.

As we let go of everything we thought mattered, we also discover what truly matters. We stop searching for external achievement—and we rest in our true vocations in the Real Presence of Christ.

For most of us, this will not come easily or quickly. Like Kelly, we may experience years of searching and doubt before we can finally surrender to the abundant riches God had in store for us all along. But we don't have to wait until failure and disappointment drive us to our knees. Instead, we can choose to practice letting go, day in, day out, week in, week out. We do this in centering prayer and in the centered-down silence of Meeting.

During silent prayer, in the process of settling (see chapter 2), we let go of all thoughts that pass through our stream of consciousness. We allow them to come—and then we let them go. We acknowledge each thought, but we do not cling to it; we realize our thoughts are temporary, just passing through. In Fox's words, we become "still and cool in your own mind . . . from your own thoughts,"[240] a perspective that mirrors the teaching of many contemporary schools of meditation.

Sooner or later, we will all get thrown a sidewinding curve-ball—a tragic death in the family, a terminal disease, a natural disaster, or a bankruptcy. Whatever it might be, if we are established in silence and stillness, we will have the resilience to weather the storm. During a crisis, the need to let go and change direction happens in rapid-fire succession, so if the reflex is honed, our chances of survival are higher—and through the practice of silent prayer, we will have already developed the automatic reflex to let go; it's become a reflex in our muscle memory. Just as we learned to habitually let go of thoughts that enter the mind, now we learn to habitually let go of expectations in life. Instead of resisting and making a situation worse, we let go and let Christ.

As we learn to drop the reins, we release our grip on agendas and schemes. We may laugh, we may cry—but whatever our emotional reactions, we don't resist them. We simply allow the present moment to unfold as it is, not as we would like it to be. Our time on our meditation cushions or centering-prayer chairs has groomed us, and we are ready for whatever comes. Whether our crises are of the trivial, privileged sort—or more serious, such as doing jail time despite our innocence, living through natural catastrophes, or enduring a life-shaking tragedy—we are anchored in silence. We have created a habit of self-surrender. In time, because of habitual letting-go, we come to rest in a fruitful power. We discover a Resource that not only carries all our thoughts but also all the details of our lives. But this only happens when we release our white-knuckle grip on our lives.

Don't expect to completely change overnight, though. Instead, you will know you are making progress in prayer when the individuals who once drove you all the way up the wall now only drive you half-way up the wall. Those around us don't change; they are still doing the same old frustrating things and making the same ignorant statements. But we have changed. Instead of wringing our napkins and grinding our teeth when they speak (as we used to do), now we simply give the napkin a couple of tugs and roll our eyes—and this is a triumph, real nitty-gritty progress on the spiritual path. It may not make the news or gain us fame on social media, but our teenage child may stay around after dinner and talk to us, the neighbor won't duck and hide when they see us, our spouses may be more willing to compromise—and other wonders may occur.

Emptying Ourselves

Christ's spirit is perhaps best encapsulated in the scripture "He emptied himself" (Philippians 2:7). This also sums up my understanding of the journey of holistic mysticism.

As we saw in Thomas Kelly's life, most of us will reach a tipping point, a watershed moment, when the cumulating junk in our life, our tormentors, or our failures are too much for us to handle. We crack in one form or another—and then, we become empty of all posturing and hubris. We realize our interior resources are not enough to get us out of our quandary.

The first stages of this process are seldom pretty. Recently, on a walk, I saw a man with physical challenges become so frustrated that he slammed his crutches into a guard rail. Then he shouted and hurled the crutches over the bridge. In doing so, he made his situation even more vulnerable and desperate, since without his crutches, he had lost his means of ambulation. I pray that in that state of desperate vulnerability, he found the internal resources to get through and to begin again. This is the specialty of contemplative Christianity: to build such resources; to instill abiding resilience and self-love.

But we don't have to be like that man; we don't have to keep going until we blow a gasket and throw our crutches over a bridge. Instead, we can choose to let it all go *now*, before we reach the crisis point. Consciously, deliberately, we can empty ourselves and lay down at Christ's cross each aspect of ourselves and our lives. This is genuine self-surrender, self-abandonment. We drop to our knees, wave the white flag, submit.

Isaac Penington described this attitude as waiting to "feel the light of life" that draws us away from what is destructive in our lives. We do not try to control this process or direct it from our desire to be in control; instead, we let the Light choose where it wants to focus, and, "though it be little and very inconsiderable in [our] own eyes," we don't argue or try to tell our own stories about what's been revealed. We simply wait for the first inkling of light and "there begin to follow."[241]

As we empty ourselves of our self-serving agendas, we are freed to be faithful to the incrementally revealed Divine purpose in our lives. We move from self-centered to Christ-centered.

Surrendering to Christ

Becoming Christ-centered is not an abstract, theological concept. It's practical. It's something we live out daily in our ordinary lives. But before we can surrender our selfishness to Christ, we need to recognize Christ.

Christ comes disguised in an ingenious costume that stumps us every time. He comes hidden in the details of our lives. He comes to us disguised as our life. Just as we resist Christ, so too we resist our lives.

We resist adversity. We fight back against the most challenging aspects of our lives—the marriage that plummets, the friend who commits suicide, or the parent who constantly criticizes. Still, as Christian mystics attest, adversity often bestows soul treasures. You might ask, "What kind of damn soul treasures?" I answer, "The spiritual kind, such as humility and inner light." Then you might ask, "What the hell good is that?" To which I respond, "What at first seems a blessing often turns out to be a curse—and what looks like a curse often proves to be a blessing. So when Christ reveals himself in the form of deprivation or our tailor-made cross, we wait to see what else he has in store for us. What can we learn from this experience? What hidden treasures does it contain? How can we use it to draw closer to Christ and to our True Selves?"

Some people may think this strategy is childish wish-fulfillment. But a mysterious, contemplative sphere of existence is at play here. I've heard Thomas Keating refer to it as "a fourth dimension." This mysterious realm is as plentiful and as accessible as air. We simply need to tap into it. And in Christian tradition, adversity is often the very thing that wakes us up enough to perceive the contemplative dimensions of reality.

Submission and surrender to our unique cross bring eventual serenity. When we go through our gauntlet, family and friends may assume we have lost our way, based on our external appearance or utterances. All the while, however, the glowing embers within grace us with imperceptible stability, determination, and release. In "losing" by the world's standards we may find our true selves (Matthew 16:25). In letting go, we may release what is false about ourselves. In this letting-go, we find our refuge in Christ's Real Presence.

"Behold I stand at the door and knock," said Jesus in the Book of Revelation (3:20). Through adversity and crisis, Jesus "knocks" on the doors of our hearts. In these difficult events, we can find Christ—"a testimonial to the secret presence and working within us," in Thomas Kelly's words.[242]

Kelly loved the Gospel narrative of Christ knocking at the door. Although artists have portrayed Christ as outside the doors of our hearts, knocking to be let in, in reality, the voices of our higher Selves—the Christ *within*—knocks from the inside, asking to be released. Kelly knew from experience that we usually only hear these faint knocks at our interior doors after a calamity has forced us to set aside our usual distractions. Often, we don't hear until we have no other alternatives. When we have exhausted our resources and there is seemingly nothing left to hold on to, those are the moments we hear Christ's gentle tapping.

Empowerment in Prayer

As we've already mentioned, George Fox spent years in a prison with horrible conditions. As a result, all his joints swelled and ached. During Fox's fiercest prison torments and tempests of mind, he felt God draw near to him, comfort him, and put him at ease. When Fox wrote, "You will receive [Divine] strength and power . . . to allay all tempests," he spoke from experience. Like the biblical prophets, Fox touched the deepest chords of his soul and thereby the deepest chords of humanity. This ultimate common ground gave him wisdom and strength to navigate all the tempests in his soul and in his community, even his struggle to stay alive in a frigid prison.

The "power" that Fox referred to is "from whence life comes." In other words, its source is the Creator, not the creatures; the Tree, not the offshoots; the Vine, not the branches (John 15:5). Although counterintuitive, numerous other Christ-followers have reported similar experiences during suffering. We are hardwired to connect with this primal Singularity, which satisfies and grounds us more than anything else.

When we surrender to this awareness, something ancient and magnificent awakens deep within our cells and organs. This Something was fully formed in Christ (Colossians 2:9), and each of us, in our unique ways, can participate in and reflect some fraction of that original glory. Day by day, we participate in Christ in down-to-earth, unassuming ways, sacred in their ordinariness. Other times, because of deep interior resources developed in prayer, we survive what most are unable to survive.

On the spiritual journey, eventually, we surrender our autonomous choices—and in doing so, the agonizing choices become much fewer. Instead, our decisions are choiceless choices because they are predetermined according to our conscience and mission. The dissonance and resistance are gone. The need to stand out is gone. We simply yield to the current of Divine activity. We experience a free flow in which we no longer pray but are *prayed through*.

New Life

People are okay with the concept of surrender as long as they remain in control of their calendar. As soon as the still small voice within (1 Kings 19:12) bumps pet projects off the agenda and adds despised ones, however, we realize we are no longer in control. If we can accept this, this is the point when we enter a new life. We evolve into servant-leaders who follow the example of Jesus. We are willing to wash grimy feet (John 13:1–17), dress wounds, mop floors—whatever is needed.

But the transformation from self-servant to Christ-servant is a long journey, often reluctant and begrudged. No matter how much progress we make on the spiritual journey, we still resist Christ and his cross. The cross is the last rung of a depleted ego. In its vehement will to survive, the ego clenches tight, unwilling to let go. The cross extracts the ego's final death grip, finger by finger. Then comes resurrection.

Baptism symbolizes this process: the descent into the water is symbolic of burial dirt; the emergence from the water is the resurrection from the grave. Ritual baptism cannot accomplish the real work, however. This can only be accomplished by dying to everything self-centered and false within us, so our Christ-centered life can emerge. We move from a fixation on self and self-service to community service. We move from self-absorption to a passion for active love.

This process is painful—but centering prayer and centered-down prayer help us carry the crosses life brings. Silent prayer gives us something to fall back on. If we develop spacious equanimity in prayer, we create a safety net that catches us, when everything we have known (from the ego's perspective) is lost. In Thomas Kelly's words: "We pray and yet it is not we who pray, but a Greater who prays in us.... In holy hush we bow in Eternity.... [God] works and prays and seeks [the Divine path] through us, in exquisite, energizing life. Here the autonomy of the inner life becomes complete and we are joyfully prayed through."[243]

Silent prayer gives us an advantage; not a financial advantage or increased sex appeal or added intelligence, but the ability to accept the moment in its entirety as it presents itself, without distortion or filters. It even permits us to accept the most taboo word of all, death. Only when we hit this psychological "rock bottom" are we capable of seeing Christ, the holistic Reality, from cradle to tomb—and beyond, into the resurrection that leads to an active and empowered life.

Sacrifice, surrender, negation, are inherently involved
in any great onwardmarching life.
. . . But sacrifice, surrender, negation,
are never for their own sake;
they are never ends in themselves.
They are involved in life itself.

–Rufus Jones[244]

PART IV

Outer Expressions
of Inner Work

16

Taking a Stand

The paradox of true mysticism
is that individual experience leads to social passion. . . .
Love of God and love of neighbor
are not two commandments, but one.

—Thomas Kelly[245]

In these lines, Thomas Kelly offers us a succinct synopsis of the integral relationship between contemplation and action. Contemplation and action, he implies, intertwine like lovers in a bridal chamber. They may seem like two different things, but they move as one. Talk to a social prophet, and we usually uncover a mystical experience that gave birth to activism. First, come the fiery interior insights, and *then*, years of tireless passion for the cause.

Kelly's first sentence—"The paradox of true mysticism is that individual experience leads to social passion"—is the rallying cry of contemporary contemplative activists. The cry is heard and realized in Quaker Meetings, in the Center for Action and Contemplation (which Richard Rohr founded), and in countless other organizations that work to express their intimate connection with the Divine by bringing positive change to the world in which they operate.

I love Kelly's paradoxical statement that "love of God and love of neighbor are not two commandments, but one." When an activist is steeped in contemplative arts, she acts with empathy and tact. She also has a built-in mechanism to decompress from stress. Then activism becomes most effective. This effectiveness does not happen through some artificial tactic or sales gimmick but because of increased quality, depth of spirit, and self-care. Without this interior contemplative quality, activism is prone to cynicism and burnout.

Activism and Intimacy with Our Source

Quakers are the most contemplative wing of the Protestant Reformation, and at the same time, they also intensely engage in social activism. They know the key to the Social Gospel: to connect with one's Source through prayer and then engage in social and environmental missions. Prayer revitalizes; it is the refuge from the storm. A genuine connection with our Source, even a small fraction of complete union with Christ, energizes and electrifies.

Individual experience and social conscience simultaneously arise. The first is about interior wholeness. The second is about restoring what is broken in society back to wholeness. They are sides of the same coin.

To draw near to Christ's Real Presence, we move away from the world, words, and noise (Luke 5:16). Then, from this calm place of refuge, we move into the fray of the world and its problems. We take refuge in solitude to rekindle our individual light, then venture out into the world to pass on the light.

Have you ever passed candlelight from one to another at a Christmas Eve vigil? This passing of light is done one-on-one, one person at a time, one candle at a time. I don't know about you, but the people who have most energized and inspired me did so based on one-on-one communication.

Inward Devotion and Outward Faithfulness

"The Lord taught me to be faithful in all things," wrote George Fox, "and to act faithfully two ways . . . inwardly to God and outwardly to [people]."[246] These are the introverted and extroverted aspects of the Golden Rule, which is to love God and to love our neighbors (Mark 12:30–31). Likewise, Rufus Jones wrote about the "double-edged sword" of Quakerism: one edge is inward life, and the other is action in the world. Many people see these two as opposed. Yet, Quaker mystics are unanimous: these two are in creative tension, not gridlock. And the most vital life integrates contemplation with activism. We are empowered to courageously soldier through the hail storms of dysfunction.[247]

Luke's Gospel says, "The reign of God is within you" (17:21 YLT). So, according to Luke, the Divine Realm is an inward experience of Christ's Real Presence. This realm is present now within us, but at the same time, it is also yet to come; we see all too clearly the injustice in our communities, towns, and cities that needs redress before the rule of law and human rights can prevail.

According to mystic-author Cynthia Bourgeault, the internal "Kingdom of Heaven [is] a state of consciousness."[248] The external coming of God's realm emerges when that state of consciousness becomes established in families, communities, and nations. In Paul's letter to the Romans, he wrote that the Divine Realm relies on "righteousness, peace, and joy in the Holy Spirit" (14:17). The implication here is that the "kingdom within" is expressed in "righteousness," while "the kingdom without" emerges in the form of justice (Amos 5:12). These two arms of a single embrace form a creative tension between the love of solitude and contemplation—and respect and advocacy for the rights of others (human and nonhuman). In other words, solitude and contemplation produce self-knowledge, integration, and humble righteousness (not self-righteousness). When we are righteous, we lead by example and by compassion, and people respond to our leadership. Justice, which begins at home, becomes possible.

Many Quakers embody the dynamic of contemplation and activism. Inward-focused contemplation compliments outward-focused missions to prisons, polluted rivers, and plastic-bloated seas. Contemplation and action are never isolated from one another. When the two intertwine and complement each other, Quakerism takes on robust vigor.

We walk the tightrope between contemplation and action. Too much activism without a prayer life results in burnout, all too familiar in the helping professions. On the other hand, too much silent prayer can be dangerous in another way. We can start to lose our focus on the rest of our lives, becoming so "heavenly minded that we are no earthly good."

As seasoned Friends[249] know, balance is the key. We balance silent worship with activism. This mutually beneficial combination deepens and compliments, so we don't just become contemplative but contemplative with a social conscience. And we don't just become short-lived activists; we become long-term advocates in solidarity with oppressed people. We know how to find the Center, where we revitalize both our spirits and our nervous systems. Then, our long-lived activism gives birth to lasting change. We are called to shine our light, not hide it (Matthew 5:15).

Touching That of God Within and in All

"Let your lives and conversation preach," wrote George Fox, "that with a measure of the spirit of God you may reach to that of God in all."[250] As we learn to be in touch with what the Quakers call "that of God" within us, we can touch that same Presence in all people.[251] In other words, according to Fox, we connect with the Ground of Our Being that is at the same time, shared by everyone.[252] Rooted in that fertile Ground, intimate connection with others comes naturally.

Recognizing "that of God in all" gives us compassion for people despite their possibly unattractive exteriors. The Japanese poet Issa wrote, "Under the cherry blossom's shade there is no such thing as a stranger."[253] In other words, at the level of Divine Beauty, no human experience is foreign to us anymore. No matter the person or situation, we share some interior reference point.

Once we realize that whatever is going on with the other is mirrored within our own hearts, we can no longer demonize others. To give just one possible example, we may be tempted to judge a person living on the streets—until we remember the time in our twenties when we might not have been able to pay the rent if Uncle Robert hadn't intervened with the needed cash. We recognize that given the right circumstances, we might be living the same lifestyles we once condemned. We come to see God in all experiences and in all people—and in doing so, we are inspired to reach out our hands to help.

Jesus never saw in partials; he saw in wholes, and this perception healed people. The way we see will also determine if we are healers. A vision based on a holistic consciousness fosters integrated families, communities, and businesses. It gives us both the strength and the desire to take a stand wherever we see brokenness and need.

Quaker witnesses assert that each person has a mission; each of us is put on earth for a reason. When we find the reason, everything else comes into clear focus. Everything in our lives integrates like discordant metal shavings that organize themselves around a magnet. When we align with our mission, our actions are no longer self-originated. They arise without effort from our core purpose.

This is not to say the road is easy. Far from it! Yet, with every step, synergy from a newfound center guides us. As Caroline Stephen wrote, "To yield one's self unreservedly to divine guidance; resolutely, and at whatever cost, to refuse to participate in that which one's own

conscience has been taught to condemn; this is the ancient and ines-
timable Quaker ideal."[254]

Activism Sustained by Faith

When Rufus Jones wrote about the "double-edged sword" of
Quakerism, he meant that one edge is the inward life, and the other
is action in the world. Jane Addams is a prime example of a lifelong
balance between the inner and active aspects of the spiritual path.

As a young woman, Addams read Leo Tolstoy's *My Religion*,
in which Tolstoy described his work with Russian peasants. When
it came to the exterior expression of his faith, Tolstoy rejected both
condescending benevolence and harsh expectations of compliance.
He wrote that when we apply scripture to our own hearts at the same
time that we respond directly to injustice, complacency is impossible.

Personal and societal wholeness, Tolstoy wrote, interact in
an essential relationship where one cannot exist without the other.
The inner work nourishes and deepens the outer work, infusing it
with compassion. Activism without interior work is half-hearted and
ineffective, and at the same time, "a righteous life cannot be lived in
a society that is not righteous," and so spirituality "cannot flourish
without action."[255]

Though Addams seldom spoke publicly of her spiritual beliefs,
her writings reveal the importance scripture played in her life. As she
mapped out her work in the world, she relied almost exclusively on the
life of Jesus. Again, as I've said before, Quakers teach that Jesus is the
singularity, the Word, while the Gospels are plural written accounts
of his life.

From Jesus, Addams learned that taking a stand for justice requires the recognition that we are equals with those we seek to help. Less concerned with doctrine and interpretation, Addams focused instead on how the "very existence of Jesus and the power of his teachings ought to direct her own life."[256] She realized: "Things that make us alike are finer and stronger than the things that make us different."[257] She also wrote, "The essence of immorality is the tendency to make an exception of myself."[258] In other words, the mark of someone who is on the spiritual journey in earnest is humility and concern for the poor. Pride and self-preoccupation, on the other hand, indicate false prophets.

Addams insisted that societal factors caused poverty, not laziness or a lack of responsibility. Her work differed from the philanthropy of her day, because she endorsed what she called "a cooperative ideal of mutual assistance."[259] Those we consider the "poor," Addams realized, may be rich in ways where we are deficient. In the living organism of Christ's Body, all are needed—and all need one another.

Meanwhile, only a few miles from where Addams devoted her life to the poor, the rich elite were enjoying the extravagances of the Gilded Age. Addams challenged these complacent and prosperous people to look beyond the glitter and exhilaration of new inventions, fashions, and opportunities—and see the sweatshops and slums, the factory workers and children living in despicable conditions. As John Woolman and other Quaker social prophets through the centuries all saw, solidarity with those who suffer is the ticket to deeper communion, both internal (getting in touch with our common humanity) and external (as we seek societal justice). The compartmentalized "divide and conquer" mindset cannot experience deep communion.

"I need religion in a practical sense," Addams wrote, "that if I could fix myself with my relations to God and the universe, and so be in perfect harmony with nature and duty, I could use my faculties and energy so much better and could do almost anything."[260]

Who Was Jane Addams?

Jane Addams (1860–1935) grew up in a Quaker home. As a teenager, she attended a female seminary, which, according to one of her biographers, helped foster "a mystical-intuitive turn of mind" combined with "down-to-earth" practicality.[261]

As a young woman, Jane wanted to become a doctor to the poor. When illness and family crises forced her to surrender her dream, the promises of Psalm 23 strengthened her. She wrote, "If I could claim one promise in the Bible I would care for no other—'He restores my soul.'"

On a trip to England, Jane encountered new ways to serve the poor. Inspired by what she saw, she established Hull-House in Chicago. There, she offered social services to women and children, including job training, legal aid, childcare, and health care.

When World War I began, Jane spoke out for pacifism. As a result, she faced harsh criticism. That didn't stop her from working tirelessly to bring peace, even though newspapers called her a traitor and a fool.[262] Physically ill for much of the war, as well as being isolated and shunned, Jane never gave up her work on behalf of the poor. Because of the many ways in which she consistently lived out the gospel, in 1931 she was the first American woman to receive the Nobel Peace Prize.

The Cost of Taking a Stand

As we read about Jane Addams' life from the safe perspective of the twenty-first century, we may not realize the full price she paid for her consistent and holistic spiritual activism. High principles encounter opposition, which may turn violent. The path can be lonely and painful.

Quakers, starting with Fox, have been ready and willing to sacrifice themselves in the service of their calling. To be "a great sufferer," as Fox puts it in his journals, our ideals must be expressed in external resolution. In other words, according to early Quakers, we do not fully live until we find a principle for which we will die. Holistic mystics courageously accept persecution if it comes. Like Jane Addams, they walk with Christ, carrying their crosses.

The cross takes many forms: persecution, brokenness, poverty, illness, misunderstanding, ignorance, addiction, scapegoating, and abuse. Each person's cross is unique. At the same time, we are not alone; we encourage and support one another. What's more, when we experience the cross, we draw closer to Christ's Real Presence. The cross is the holy experience of solidarity with sufferers, while we simultaneously encounter the Divine Presence. There, we empty ourselves so we can be filled.

Christ understands our tailor-made crosses, even though everyone else may misinterpret and misunderstand them. Sometimes, when people publicly criticize a failure of character, it may actually be a part of a cloaked smear campaign, persecution in disguise. To feel as though no one understands is painful—yet Christ understands, not just in general but in detail.

Meanwhile, the enemies of our self-concepts can serve a positive role in our lives: they compel us to dropkick the lie of total self-reliance. All of us who experience adversity know we do not get through it independently. We lean on visiting angels of both the human and prophetic variety. Empowered beyond our own abilities, we see the Seed of Christ even in those who intend us harm.

Catalysts for Transformation

When we touch the deep healing well of fulfillment, unshakable security, and "the peace that passes understanding" (Philippians 4:7), we naturally radiate our inner joy and peace outward. Like the prodigal son in the story Jesus told (Luke 15:11–32), we have made colossal mistakes—and yet God embraces our souls, heals them, and gives them royal robes. Now, spiritual homecoming defines us and our relationships. We pass on the forgiveness and largess we received. We become catalysts for positive change.

While many people spread their dis-ease, we are called to spread our wholeness. The quality of our being sends ripple effects throughout our families, extended families, and community. Toxic emotions, such as malice and jealousy, poison the waters of a community, but positive emotions like tolerance and joy enliven the community's life.

Sometimes, in my experience as a Quaker, Friends bless us and encourage us by simply living in union with God, no matter what. When everyone thought my friend Terry would go down in flames, his cancer went into remission, he saved his marriage, and his business rose from the brink of bankruptcy. Terry's powerful faith instilled potent interior resources, including resilience, which then served as an example and inspiration for his community.

We don't know how our lives may trigger reactions that spread farther than we ever dreamed. Simply by remaining faithful to our calling, we may be helping others have the backbone to survive rather than crumple, to keep fighting for justice rather than surrendering. Simply taking a stand, firmly, lovingly, and persistently, has the power to set off a chain reaction of positive change.

Avoiding Burnout

Taking a stand for justice, in whatever way we're called, doesn't always produce the change we'd hoped for, nor does it follow the timeline we may have anticipated. As a result, activism can be exhausting work. When we are praised for our efforts, we feel encouraged, but we are as likely to find ourselves the butt of social media trolls who criticize our stance. Long before social media, Elizabeth Fry, a great Quaker prison reformer, understood this dynamic. "There are times of encouragement and building up," she wrote, "and of discouragement and treading down."[263]

The front lines of poverty, prejudice, and polluted oceans require a warrior-like resolve coupled with deep interior resources of prayer. When we develop these resources, we are more effective servants who are empowered to tackle challenging ministries. Without these resources, burnout is around the corner.

Burnout is particularly likely whenever our egos are involved. Instead, of focusing on service as an act of self-giving love, we may find ourselves acting in order to garner others' praise and approval. So long as our egos are stroked, we feel good about our work—but when our work is rejected or criticized, we quickly become discouraged.

Quaker reformer Elizabeth Fry offers a helpful answer to this problem: "I have always considered the work not mine," she wrote, "and have desired that self may have no reputation in it; if trials of this kind come, they may be for our good." What we perceive as "trials," Fry went on to say, may be the very things the circumstances require (when we look with God's eyes rather than our own).[264] When genuine kindness and concern guides everything we do, what society calls success or failure is no longer important. Fueled by Divine love, rather than our own resources, we are inoculated from the ABCs of dysfunction: Act out, Burn out, Check out.

Humility

Because we carry the Seed of Christ within us, we have enormous potential for transformation; we embody the transformative power of the Christian community. At the same time, we cannot preen or take the credit when we see signs of transformation in the lives of those around us. Instead, we get our egos out of the way, so that the Real Presence of God has space and freedom to move. No matter what gifts and skills we may have, we ultimately can't take credit for them, since the Divine planted those talents and aptitudes within us in the first place.

According to the traditions of the Desert Mothers and Fathers, humility is the primary virtue and the principal way to discern the Divine Presence. Wayward souls transgress boundaries, the first and foremost boundary being the truth. They lie and, by doing so, lack humility. They puff themselves up with exaggeration and untruths.

Meanwhile, true pilgrims know they are jars of clay (2 Corinthians 4:7); in other words, they are containers carrying the Seed of Christ, aware that no matter how wonderful the contents, containers are breakable and flawed. As we realize we are dependent on Christ's grace, we are respectful of all creatures.

In every situation, there are two options, the humble response or the less than humble one. There is the high, proud retort on the one hand and the low, unassuming reply on the other. A sibling may say something to get a rise out of us; we can take the bait, or we can maintain silence. A parent may say something belittling to us at a family gathering; we can return snub for snub, or we can maintain silence. Silence is inherently humble.

Contrary to popular opinion, silence qualifies as a response—an eloquent response. Silence allows us to resist arrogant comebacks in the heat of the moment. Speech on the other, hand, draws attention to ourselves and assumes others want to listen.

When faced with a set of challenging circumstances, we can choose to wait for God—or we can rush in. The first posture is humble, the second rash and arrogant. Acting prematurely, sinking our teeth into unripe fruit, benefits no one. But humility is not the same as timidity. At some point, when the fruit is ripe, we act. A more skillful reply may be forthcoming when we can talk with a person in private, and so, instead of a public ambush, we wait for an opportune private moment. We speak the truth in love. We embody an exquisite balance. We are tough and nice, courageous and courteous, strong and loving.

When we are called to positions of influence, genuine humility allows us to hold power in the form of servant leadership.[265] Humility protects us from others' projections, sabotage, and reprisals. It allows us to set aside our ego-needs and rely instead on the Spirit working through circumstances, always in process. Instead of relying on our knee-jerk first response to circumstances, we realize events that seem profitable may hold the seeds of ultimate misfortune, while circumstances that seem like utter disasters often bestow great blessings. The inconclusive nature of so-called tragedies and so-called blessings teach us to withhold judgment. They teach us to wait for a way to open. They teach us to fight for justice with humility.

The Fight for Justice

The Bible uses military language at times to describe the outer expression of our spiritual lives. "Put on the whole armor of God, so that you may be able to stand," wrote Paul to the Ephesians. He goes on to say: "For our struggle is not against enemies of blood and flesh, but against the rulers, against the authorities, against the cosmic powers of this present darkness, against the spiritual forces of evil in the heavenly places. Therefore . . . put on whatever will make you ready to proclaim the gospel of peace" (6:11–12, 15). Although the Bible uses the metaphor of a warrior, note that this is a "gospel of peace." Quaker activism, the expression of interior relationship with the Divine, has always followed nonviolent paths.

True godliness does not turn us out of the world,
but enables us to live better in it
and excites our endeavors to mend it.

—William Penn[266]

17

Quaker Nonviolence

The spirit of Christ, which leads us into all Truth,
will never move us to fight and war . . . with outward weapons,
neither for the kingdom of Christ,
nor for the kingdoms of this world. . . .
[To do so] is contrary to the spirit of Christ,
his doctrine, and the practice of the Apostles.

—George Fox[267]

Notice that George Fox in the quote above referred to "outward weapons." Fox and his followers understood that while we may "fight" to make the world a better place for all people and creatures, our struggle is not carried out with human-made weapons of violence. The early Quakers stood for prison reform, women's suffrage, and the abolition of slavery—but they didn't fight for these causes with outward weapons.

Of course, as we take a stand in the world, we often engage in an interior fight with our own demons and despair, especially during times of persecution and adversity. It is this internal battle that allows us to speak out, take the hits, and accept the consequences, without defensiveness or retaliation.

"Love your neighbor as yourself" is the familiar Golden Rule that Jesus taught—and without nonviolence, loving our neighbor is impossible. This understanding is also rooted in the Ten Commandments: "You shall not murder" (Exodus 20:13). Ultimately, what separates the path of selfishness from the path of love is the willingness to murder on the one hand and the rejection of murder on the other. Quakers know that as soon as we take up arms for a cause, even a good cause, the spilled blood stains our hands and undermines our cause. Violence always leaves scars, not only on the victim but on the perpetrator as well.[268]

Listening as an Alternative to Violence

"An enemy," said Quaker activist Gene Knudsen Hoffman, is one whose story we have not heard." "We peace people have always listened to the oppressed and disenfranchised," she wrote. "That's very important. One of the new steps I think we should take is to listen to those we consider 'the enemy' with the same openness, non-judgment, and compassion we bring to those with whom our sympathies lie." Hoffman went on to say: "Everyone has a partial truth, and we must listen, discern, acknowledge this partial truth in everyone—particularly those with whom we disagree."

"Compassionate Listening," she said, "is adaptable to any conflict. The listening requires a particular attitude. It is non-judgmental, non-adversarial, and seeks the truth of the person questioned. . . . Listeners do not defend themselves, but accept what others say as their perceptions. By listening they validate the others' right to those perceptions."[269]

Our deepest challenges and wounds are tender, and so we protect them as best we can, hiding them out of sight. The average listener will never get there. Only vigilance to details, keen intuition, and precise clarifying questions (after rapport and trust are built) can heal. The compassionate listener couples these skills with infinite patience to discover the wounds nobody knows about. Once gently exposed to the light, the wound can begin to heal.

By listening with the "spiritual ear," said Hoffman, we stop "deciding in advance who is right and who is wrong, and then seeking to rectify it." We become open to the Seed of Christ working in all people. We build a world of kindness and peace, one person at a time. This is the pacifist software missing from most policies of international diplomacy. What we need most are good listeners, who can perceive and intuit the opposition's underlying needs. What makes highly perceptive intuitive listeners so valuable is that they dig beneath the layers, to what is the root source of a problem. This perception can make the difference between an ally and an enemy.

Who Was Gene Knudsen Hoffman?

Gene Knudsen Hoffman (1919–2010) was a peace activist, teacher, and author. When she became a Quaker in her early thirties, she remembers "dancing down the street, feeling exultant that I had joined so great a company of seekers, people of God." She felt, she said, that she "would perform miracles."[270]

The miracles Gene would perform were quiet, yet radical. As she studied post-traumatic stress disorder in Holocaust victims and Vietnam veterans, she realized that a large cause of violence is unhealed wounds. "To reconcile," she wrote, "we must realize that both sides to any violence are wounded." She described a life-changing experience she had when she saw a sign outside a Quaker Meeting: "Meeting for Worship for the torturers and the tortured." She suddenly understood she had been focusing on listening to the "tortured," but until then, it had never occurred to her that she needed to also hear the torturer's story.

Gene went on to work for reconciliation between Palestinians and Israelis, and in other conflicts throughout the Middle East and around the world, including in Libya and Russia. As she did so, she realized "there really are divine possibilities in every situation." She developed a tool for reconciliation she called *Compassionate Listening*, which still today provides nations, organizations, and individuals with a nonviolent path forward.[271]

Quiet Rebels

Gene Hoffman's nonviolent yet active stance is rooted deeply in Quakerism's beliefs. Like Hoffman, George Fox and his followers worked for peace in their society in practical ways, holding firm to their convictions even while they refused to let their principles escalate into violence. Quakers didn't fight fire with fire.

The British authorities of the seventeenth century were accustomed to rule-breakers who engaged in violent resistance, which, in the eyes of the government, made the rebels' guilt obvious. Magistrates were ill-prepared for nonviolent, quiet rebels, however, whose principles came before all else, including their possessions, freedom, and good name.

"They took our ploughs and plough-gear," wrote Fox in his journal,

> our cows and horses, our corn and cattle, and kettles and planters from us, and whipped us, and set us in the stocks, and cast us in prison . . . because we could not conform to their religions, manners, customs, and fashions. . . . Sometimes they would come with a troop of horse and company of foot, and they would break their swords and muskets, carbines and pikes, with beating Friends and wounding abundance, so that the blood stood like puddles in the streets. And Friends were made to stand, by the Lord's power.[272]

Quakers' principle-driven nonviolence produced ripple effects worldwide. It created a roadmap that was later followed by civil disobedience movements in India, Korea, the United States, and elsewhere. Gandhi, India's civil rights leader, befriended Quakers and involved them in his nation's reconciliation work.[273] Quiet rebels like these transform nations. They take a stand. They don't back down. Yet, they don't resort to violence either, except perhaps in rare circumstances, such as self-defense.

The Nonviolence of Jesus

George Fox believed in "the power which saves lives, and destroys none."[274] His nonviolence was not, however, the radically new approach it seemed to the authorities of his day. Actually, he was merely advocating a return to the teachings of Jesus in the Gospels, as interpreted by the early church before subsequent distortions. Opposition to military service and violence was nothing new; it was the witness of the church's first three centuries.[275] George Fox and the Quakers reclaimed it for their time.

In Jesus' Sermon on the Mount (Matthew 5–7), he revealed the shining facets of the Divine Realm. Peace, Jesus said, characterizes God's people, and God calls them to be peacemakers in the world around them. The apostle Paul wrote that Christ's followers are to do whatever possible to live peaceably with all people (Romans 12:18), and many other scriptures support this central facet of following Jesus (for example, Hebrews 12:14, 2 Corinthians 13:11, Galatians 5:22, James 3:17).

When faced with conflict, we may think we have only two options: passivity and cowardice on one hand, or aggression and violent resistance on the other. The nonviolent stance of George Fox, Gandhi, Martin Luther King Jr., Bayard Rustin, Gene Knudsen Hoffman, and Jesus reminds us that we always have a third option: what Walter Wink calls the *Third Way* of "militant nonviolence."[276] We don't settle for the extremes; instead, we hold the tension between them and seek creative alternatives. We never blackball one side and embrace the other. We avoid dualistic reductionist thinking, and instead, we realize people on the opposing side of an issue may also be listening to the higher angels of human nature. At the same time, individuals on "our side" may actually be listening to the selfish demons of human nature.

"Be Far from Oppression"

One of John Woolman's favorite Bible verses was Isaiah 54:14, which in the King James Version reads: "In righteousness shalt thou be established: thou shalt be far from oppression." Today, most Bible scholars interpret this as a promise rather than an exhortation (in other words, God will protect us from oppression), but Woolman did not receive these words passively; instead, he sought to *live* them, choosing to be part of the Divine plan to build a world free from oppression and injustice.

Woolman's life goal was to embody justice in every aspect of his life. This is never easy, because on close examination, our possessions contain what Woolman called "the seeds of war." In earlier centuries, slavery was interwoven into American society, which meant that even those who refused to directly participate in enslaving other human beings still benefited from the economy that was built on slavery. In today's world, our clothing may be made in a sweatshop in Bangladesh; the jewelry we wear often comes from exploited regions of Africa dominated by ruthless thugs; and the meat we eat is raised and slaughtered in inhumane ways.[277] Whenever we drive a gasoline-powered car, we bloat carbon emissions, contributing to our planet's environmental crisis. The ordinary objects made of plastic that we use every day are filling up the oceans, threatening the extinction of sea life.[278]

Nonviolence and the Earth

As we experience the exquisite stillness and rapt silence of both centering prayer and centered-down prayer, our vision becomes clearer, and we see the Seed of Christ not only in other people but also in ecosystems. With this clarity of perception, we naturally want to protect the precious Seed in all life. Even the smallest act that protects one strand of life's web helps preserve the entire ecosystem.

Elitist and reductionist thinkers don't understand that every strand in the web of life matters. They don't realize that if one strand dissolves, it weakens the whole. As an eco-contemplative, however, my starting point is the holistic symbiosis of the natural world reflected in the contemplative mind. In other words, my spirituality does not exist in some ethereal otherworld; instead, it is grounded in Creation, for I too am woven into the web of life on Earth, and it is within this web that I experience my relationship with Divinity.

Meanwhile, scientists say we are amid the sixth mass extinction in Earth's history. From elephants to albatross to coral reefs, species are dying off at alarming rates.[279] This reality requires a colossal shift in consciousness, where responsibility to the planet takes priority over short-term profit. In a world in the throes of climate change, holistic mysticism is often expressed in environmental activism. Without devotion to silence and stillness on the one hand and to devastated ecosystems on the other, Earth doesn't stand much of a chance. Our majestic Earth has given us everything; in return, we owe her not only our outrage but our solidarity and firm devotion in the struggle to protect her.[280]

George Fox said that as we begin to see the wisdom of God in Creation, we learn to recognize what he called the "natures and virtues" of the different creatures in the Creation. We begin to have a greater sense of how we fit into that picture. We start to realize that human beings have placed a burden on Creation. As Fox, said, we humans are "devouring the creation." We are "strangers to the covenant of life with God," using the natural world to satisfy our own selfish desires.[281] We need to ask ourselves: *How much is enough? What can we do without, in order to nurture and protect Creation?*

A commitment to nonviolence in relation to the environment may mean we get a loan for solar panels, invest in an electric car or an eco-friendly refrigerator, or take other practical steps to reduce our carbon footprints. Elise Boulding said that one of the best ways to work for ecojustice is to teach our children about "respectful and reverential relationships with the planet" in order to "create human beings who are oriented that way from their earliest memories."[282] The children in our lives can learn from our example to value the Earth and her life more than convenience or bank accounts.

Eco-friendly living can provoke serious pushback. As in Fox's day, people are invested in the status quo. They don't want change. When we lobby for government regulations that reduce plastics and restrict omissions in factories and vehicles, we may be accused of extremism. Some may even call us "eco-fascists" or accuse us of being members of "the environmental Taliban."[283] Encouraged, however, by the voices of those who practiced holistic mysticism—people like George Fox, Gene Knudsen Hillman, Elise Boulding, and many others—we can take a firm stand, refusing to participate in the oppressions of our time, including the colossal injustice of climate change.

Practicing nonviolence at every level of our lives is a radical challenge. We may feel as though it's simply impractical to think we can achieve this goal, and so we choose to turn our thoughts away from the "seeds of war" planted in our everyday lives. We tell ourselves that God must understand that we're doing the best we can.

Jesus, however, challenges us to expand the meaning of the Sixth Commandment ("You shall not murder") as we apply it to our lives. He spoke against the verbal violence that can kill others' self-confidence and self-worth (Matthew 5:21–22), and he stressed that in each action we take, no matter how small or seemingly inconsequential, we must take care that we are contributing to a world of personal accountability and justice.

Turn the Searchlight Inward

As Gene Knudsen Hoffman recognized, our hidden wounds are the root cause of the violence in our world. We may be reluctant, however, to recognize the wounds within our own hearts and minds. We'd rather address other people's issues than our own.

Psychologist Carl Jung believed that each person casts a "shadow," which contains all the unrecognized, secret things about ourselves we'd prefer not to face.[284] We all have aspects of our person-alities and histories that we hide, suppress, and deny. Jung said that when we refuse to acknowledge our shadow-side, we often "project" it outward, onto others.[285] In other words, if we're secretly uncom-fortable with our sexuality, we may be quick to see and criticize aspects of other people's sexual expression. Or if we have a hidden habit of lying, we may not trust that others are telling the truth. If we don't confront the contradictions and demons in our lives, we tend to demonize others. We might find a marginalized group or person upon which to unleash our wrath. What is not reconciled internally we project onto others.

Long before Jung, Jesus offered similar psychological counsel. "Why," he asked, "do you see the speck in your neighbor's eye, but you don't notice the board in your own eye? Or how can you say to your neighbor, 'Let me take that bit of sawdust out of your eye,' while you have a log in your own eye?" (Matthew 7:3–4). This passage of scripture is not literally true, yet it is so true that it hurts. There are parts of our journey that we don't want anyone to know about, but an authentic spiritual journey looks inward to detect the boards and logs hidden in the shadows. The human psyche tends to fault-find and blame others. Yet, as a friend of mine used to say, "When you point your index finger at someone, three fingers are pointing back at you."

When people came to Gandhi with a laundry list of complaints about a so-called "enemy" or a "subhuman element of the population," he would say, "Turn the searchlight inward."[286] In other words, instead of preparing for war with another person or community, we need to come to terms with the seeds of war in our own hearts. As we deal with the abuse or abandonment in our history through counseling, silent prayer, journaling, or talking to a trusted friend, we are less likely to scapegoat and demonize others.[287]

We must be the change we want to see in the world. And this begins with addressing and working on those truths we hide, suppress, and deny about ourselves. When that trauma is not addressed, it festers and comes out sideways, spreading dysfunction and dis-ease. Once we address it, release the emotions around it, and bring it to the light of day, a weight lifts—and we no longer feel the need to project our self-hatred, shame, or guilt onto others.

Everyone carries some trauma. Those who abuse have most often been abused themselves. We stop the cycle of violence and dysfunction when instead of arrogantly pointing an accusatory finger, we humbly turn the searchlight inward.

A Way of Life

This, wrote Rufus Jones, "is a way of life that . . . prefers to suffer injustice than in the slightest degree to do it. It wins and triumphs by sacrifice and self-giving. It . . . proposes to prepare the way for a new world by creation of a new spirit—which is essentially the spirit of the Cross."[288] This new spirit—the spirit of the Cross, the spirit of self-sacrificing love—finds its expression in a life of consistent integrity and balance.

Force may subdue, but love gains.

—William Penn[289]

18

Integrity and Simplicity

The call for honesty lies at the heart of Quakerism. . . .
[T]his kind of integrity calls for a correspondence
between what one professes
and how that translates into action in real life.

—Wilmer Cooper[290]

We often think of *integrity* as truthfulness—but if you look at the etymology of this word, it actually means "wholeness." For Quakers, this wholeness is rooted in the light of Truth that reaches into every corner of our lives. In addition to honest speech, it requires consistency of action. It is holistic, integrating every aspect of our inner and outer circumstances. (Hence the title of this book: *Holistic Mysticism*.)

"Do all aspects of your life bear the same witness?" is a modern Quaker query[291] that harkens back to the Friends' earliest years. Quakers have always sought to unify their speech, their private way of acting, and their public stance. Integrity requires speaking and acting in alignment with the Divine. It means living life in accord with the Real Presence of Christ, rather than being dominated by our desires, anxieties, and possessions.

Quaker Elizabeth Grill Watson believed that "growing into wholeness" was both her life's goal and the message she was called to carry into the world. This concept of wholeness embraced the inner journey and the outer life, as well as race, sexuality, and other issues in the modern world. "What do I mean by growing into wholeness?" she wrote, and then answered, "It is working to be all we were meant to be. (Most of us only live partial lives.)" She went on to say: "It is seeking integrity, . . . not wearing a mask, . . . acknowledging strengths and gifts without false modesty, and accepting our weaknesses and limitations as part of us."

"Wholeness" was Watson's goal, "fusing our scattered selves into a single self." To do this, we "no longer rush about, pulled in different directions." We say our "yes" and "no" with confidence, "out of the centeredness of our lives." Ultimately, said Watson, our goal is always to "reach out to those we love, truly desiring their wholeness, as we desire our own. So may we bless all whom we meet simply by being at peace with ourselves. So may we work more effectively for peace and justice, and speak truth to power courageously."[292] The best way I know to become the kind of person Watson described is to develop calmness and composure in prayer.

Who Was Elizabeth Grill Watson?

As a child, Elizabeth Watson (1914–2006) listened for God's voice calling to her. She was certain God had a specific task in store for her.

Shortly after she and her husband married, they became Quakers. Elizabeth went on to become a theologian and activist. Like other holistic mystics, her spiritual experiences drove her social justice work. "As Friends," Elizabeth said, "we are called . . . to help empower the poor, the Blacks, the Native and Hispanic Americans, women, gays, and anyone else who may be victims of disaster, injustice, indignity, discrimination, or any other form of oppression."[293] Some of Elizabeth's work focused on environmental justice as well. Environmental destruction, she said, was a greater threat to the planet than nuclear war.

Elizabeth's commitment to holistic mysticism survived even the tragedy of her daughter's death in a car accident. Her grief journey propelled her into a deeper understanding of integrity. The book she wrote about this journey, she said, was a part of her "lifelong call to the ministry."[294] Grief did not interfere with the work to which God called her, nor did it shatter her inner wholeness.

Plain Speech

From their beginning, Quakers emphasized the power of "plain truth."[295] I for one always trust a plain talker more than I do a fast talker. When we let our "yes" be yes and our "no" be no, as scripture advocates (Matthew 5:37), we cut through the ploys of con artists and blowhards. This is the opposite of duplicity. If we say "yes" we mean yes, period. And likewise with "no."

On the other hand, many eloquent words draw attention to ourselves; they spout from inflated egos that assume others want to hear what we have to say.[296] They may also obscure the truth. George Fox made his words "few and savory, seasoned with grace."[297]

The goal of holistic mystics is to differentiate between necessary and unnecessary speech. When we omit superfluous or decorative words, our speech is direct, weighty, and trustworthy. Quakers have always carefully weighed sentences and phrases and then whittled them to their minimalist essence. Still today, terse speech defines seasoned Quakers. Simple speech implies integrity. It wins people's trust.

Related to plain speech is terse writing. Good writers pare down their sentences and paragraphs until they say exactly what's intended. Four-word phrases change to two- or three-word phrases. Everything becomes succinct without waste. An economy of words inspires. It cuts through the detours and evasions and gets to the heart of the matter. Sparse, well-chosen words bring clarity of thought—and subsequently, clarity of action.

Plain Dress

In the same way that Quakers value plain speech, they also seek plain dress. They realize that the clothes we choose to put on our bodies speak of our inner and outer integrity. Often, if we stand in everyday dress with ordinary people, we are trusted. If, on the other hand, our jewelry and designer clothes turn heads, pretense and artifice creep in. Solidarity with ordinary people, said George Fox, means "homespun and solid" plain dress.[298]

In the twenty-first century, "plain dress" might also include the cars we drive and the houses we live in. Fashionable finery, luxury cars, and showcase homes are all ways we jockey for a higher position than others. These status symbols flaunt our superiority and stroke our egos. Once life becomes extravagant, however, we are left with less time for our priorities. Anxious to protect our interests, we are more susceptible to violence. The ultimate purpose of simple living is to make space to focus on our priorities. For people of faith, these priorities are the love of God and service to our neighbors (Matthew 22:36–40). The journey of mystic holism includes solidarity with the poor. It is not about runaway ambition, cutthroat corporate ladders, and status symbols.

"What does the Lord require of you?" asks the Book of Micah. "To act justly and to love mercy and to walk humbly with your God" (6:8). Quaker "plain dress" indicates an intentional choice to identify with our common humanity rather than with elitism; we walk humbly on the Earth with an ordinary shirt and blue jeans. Opulence and finery can spawn jealousy and divisiveness. While pretentious speech and clothing widen the chasm between us, down-to-earth clothing puts others at ease.

Simplicity has many forms that dispense with ambiguity and confusion. "I pass from simplicity in the inner life and worship," wrote Rufus Jones, "to the 'simple life.'" He connected the simple life to the way we do business, the way we dress, how we entertain ourselves, and how we participate in our culture.[299] Interior simplicity seeks expression in exterior life.

The Clutter-Free Life

As I said at the beginning of this chapter, integrity implies wholeness. We cannot divide our lives into pieces. The outer life reflects the inner life.

This means we seek to de-clutter not only our homes but our minds as well. Rather than starting with the exterior life and trying to work inward, we allow simplicity to transform our lives from the inside out. The mind free of clutter becomes transparent, devoid of artifice and posturing, no longer dependent on novelty and excitement. It is fertile and receptive to the Seed of Christ. Less becomes more. We seek to embody simplicity and integrity. Our lives are no longer shaped by pretense; they become sincere, whole, plain, and truthful.

In the modern world, plainness and an uncluttered life require a whittled-down and carefully crafted calendar. We clear away all unnecessary calendar engagements and entanglements so we can make room for what is essential: the love of God and service to our neighbors (Mark 12:30–31).

If you're seeking integrity and plainness in the modern world, I also recommend taking breaks from electronics. To periodically ween ourselves from our electronics, we can observe "electronics sabbaths." A family I know puts all their electronic gadgets into a lockbox in the kitchen at prescribed times. Another individual has an away message on their email that reads, "Today I am taking a 'screen sabbath.' If you have an emergency and need to contact me, please call me on the phone, leave a message, and I will return your call. Otherwise, I will get back to you tomorrow." We do not need to let social media, texting, email, and phone calls dictate our lives. Instead, we can set boundaries that will guard our inner wholeness and integrity (and our relationships, as we finish a family dinner uninterrupted or focus on a conversation while having coffee with a friend).

Simplicity of Purpose

"The essential condition of vigor," wrote Caroline Stephen, "is the severe pruning away of redundance."[300] Master craftspeople accomplish tasks with the least wasted time, energy, and resistance. No matter our profession, efficiency is high art.

Quakers often refer to an "undivided self." This is a life where every nook and cranny—from marriage to prayer, from food choices to business decisions—is influenced by the principle of integrity and simplicity.[301] Clean and tidy is not just about good housekeeping. It is about peace of mind. Simplicity of purpose and a calendar that reflects that purpose is a triumph. Clear priorities and a schedule to match contribute to a life of simplicity and integrity. As Rufus Jones wrote, the simple life "begins inside, with the quality of the soul. It is first and foremost the quality of sincerity, which is the opposite of duplicity or sham."[302]

Non-Dual Integration

Elizabeth Watson saw a problem in many forms of Christianity: "It insists on dividing things into opposites that are really halves of each other: body and soul, God and [humanity], life and death, this world and the next, self and other. . . . It has seen things in terms of straight lines that divide rather than in terms of circles that encompass."[303]

This either-or reality is not limited to Christianity; it extends throughout our entire culture. The nature of Western society's consciousness tends to be dualistic, given to duplicity and artifice. The nature of holistic mysticism, on the other hand, is nondual, integrated, and unifying. It participates in the absolute Ground of Our Being.

Profound simplicity of being and purpose results from glimpsing, or better yet soaking, in the pure essence of simplicity. This state is not static but energetic. In contemplation, we participate in Divine Simplicity, partaking of this holistic Presence, a nondual singularity that existed before any separation or division. This is the Divine Unity, where we maintain our individuality even as we experience Divine union.

Encountering this uncompounded pure Essence leads to a simplified life that includes business transactions and relationships. In this context, the Seed of Christ can awaken and grow. A quiet ecstasy and zeal come from a deep, almost cellular knowing that now we are home. Now we can rest, for there is nothing we desire that we do not already possess. Here, in this state of wholeness, we are transformed—and out of our own transformation, we become catalysts of change in the world.

If our inward leading is to be "doers of the truth,"
then integrity needs to be at the center of our being,
at the center of our consciousness,
and at the center of our outward witness.

—Wilmer Cooper[304]

PART V

Inner Fruit of Silence

19

Courageous Love

*The unlocking of cosmic power and love
can be accomplished if you will become
utterly, completely obedient
to the Light within you.*

—Cecil Hinshaw[305]

O ur society has many definitions of love. The highest form of love, which Quakers exemplify, is not the sentimental tear-stricken variety. It is a willingness to suffer and go the distance.

Love is the anchor for Quakers' nonviolent witness, as well as their dedication to an uncluttered life. Because of love, we refuse to do harm. Because of love, we clear our calendars, our homes, and our minds, to make room for what is essential: the love of God and our fellow creatures. From this perspective, love is both the starting point and the end goal. Love inspires us to spend time in silence and service—and love is also the fruit of our commitment.

Love is a two-fold dynamic. In the Ten Commandments, the first five commandments are about right relationship with God, and the second five are about right relationship with neighbors. So, we attend to sacred silences to hear the Divine—and we also listen to the voices of people in pain. Each movement complements the other. Vertical listening enhances horizontal empathy, and horizontal compassion enhances vertical communion.

Jesus summed up all the laws given in the Hebrew scriptures with this two-part commandment: "You shall love the Lord your God with all your heart, and with all your soul, and with all your mind, and with all your strength" and "You shall love your neighbor as yourself" (Mark 12:30–31). The message of Christ comes down to love!

For Quakers, *love* translates into "inward" devotion to God and "outward" faithfulness to people. These are the introverted and extroverted aspects of Jesus' double commandment. We experience communion with Christ through individual silent prayer (love of God). We also experience communion with Christ through collective silent prayer (love of God and neighbor). We experience the first through individual disciplined silences. We experience the second through collective silences. The heart of Quaker mysticism is found in the interplay between beholding sacred silences and beholding the Seed of Christ in each person as we interact in community.

Holy silence contains the Seed of Christ, and human souls contain the Seed of Christ. Silent prayer reveals the Divine Seed of Christ in us. And compassion toward our fellow human beings reveals the

Seed of Christ in them. It could easily be said that the two movements of Quakerism follow Christ's commandment in Mark 12: silence and service. When these two are established, they produce wisdom and compassion.

Love That Conquers Fear

Silence helps us to let go of our selfishness, freeing us to love more fully—but fear is another possible impediment to active love. As holistic mystics, though, we can overcome fear. We realize "there is no fear in love, but perfect love casts out fear; for fear has to do with punishment, and whoever fears has not reached perfection in love" (1 John 4:18).

Elizabeth Fry is a good example of someone who led a life of active service, despite being beset with fears. As a child, she frequently crept into her parents' bedroom at night, to make sure they were still breathing. Her mother's death when Fry was twelve only confirmed her fears. For several years, she rode a teeter-totter between her fear and her faith. "Why need I dread so much?" she wrote in her journal. "Have I not often known naturally and spiritually way made where I could see no way, and hard things made easy? Oh, that I could trust more . . . more fully committing my body, soul, and spirit, to my faithful Creator."[306]

Then, when she was eighteen years old, Fry heard William Savery, an American Quaker, preach about the love that is expressed in service to others. This was a turning point in Elizabeth Fry's life. She realized that "when covered with divine Love" she was completely secure—and as a result, she no longer had to be afraid. "Indeed,"

Elizabeth wrote, "what cannot we do? For [God's love] so fills the heart with love to all, that we become ready and willing to make a sacrifice for the good of any."[307]

Elizabeth Fry's life changed radically. She began to look for ways she could be of service in her community. She collected clothes for the poor, visited sick people in her neighborhood, and started a school in her house to teach children to read. When she heard that women were being mistreated in Newgate Prison, she immediately made up her mind to go see for herself.

What she saw horrified her. More than three hundred women and children were crowded into a small space. Although some of the women had been found guilty of a crime, most of them were still waiting to be tried. Some women had their children with them; some children were there because of crimes they had committed, such as vagrancy or pickpocketing. Women and children slept on the floor without beds or blankets, and the women had to do their own cooking as best they could in the small spaces they were allotted. Prisoners had to pay for everything, including food, water, and fuel for heat. There were no toilets, just a bucket in the corner.

Fry went home and returned immediately with warm clothing and bedding for the women and children. And she didn't stop there. She taught imprisoned women and children how to read and write. She brought the women materials so they could sew and knit, which allowed them to earn money to purchase food, fuel, and drinking water. She brought warm clothes and medicine. For the next twenty-five years, she visited every convict ship leaving for Australia and made sure that prisoners were not chained to the decks during the voyage; she also gave prisoners packages of useful things for their long journeys.

Although the name Elizabeth Fry is often connected with prison reform, her acts of love were not limited to prisons. She set up places around England where homeless people could get food and a place to sleep, and she worked to reform the poor conditions in workhouses, insane asylums, and hospitals. In 1840, she opened a training school for nurses, which inspired Florence Nightingale (who later took a team of Elizabeth's nurses to help care for wounded soldiers in the Crimean War). Fry worked to create more opportunities for working women and better housing for the poor. She was also responsible for the establishment of soup kitchens.

Elizabeth Fry and her brother together fought to abolish capital punishment. At the time, more than two hundred crimes were punishable by hanging in England, including such relatively minor offenses as cutting down a tree, damaging a turnpike, or pickpocketing what would be approximately equivalent to forty dollars. Elizabeth wrote books on the topic, and in 1823, she and her brother persuaded Parliament to pass a series of reforms in the criminal justice system.

Despite all she accomplished during her lifetime, Elizabeth was sometimes discouraged. She was often criticized, especially by her siblings, for not sticking to the traditional roles of mother and wife. Still, she reminded herself, "Love conquereth all." Love was the power that energized all her work, all her relationships. "I look not to myself, but to that within me," she wrote, referring to the love of Christ, "that has . . . enabled me to do what I believe of myself I could not have done."

The love she extended to everyone—from homeless and imprisoned women to royalty and politicians, including Queen Victoria and the King of Prussia (who once paid her a visit at her home)—brought about real change. She started a wave of prison reform that spread throughout Europe and the United States. In the words of a biographer, her passionate desire to lead a life of useful and active love "disturbed the placid, vapid existence of women in Victorian England and changed forever the confines of respectable femininity. The name of Elizabeth Fry broadened the appeal of the Quaker faith."[308]

Elizabeth's writings indicated that she never totally overcame her fearful nature—but she did not allow it to hold her back. "Let me take courage, and try from the bottom of my heart to do that which I believe truth dictates."[309] Elizabeth's continual prayer, she wrote, was based on the active embodiment of love described in 1 Corinthians 13:

> If I speak in the tongues of mortals and of angels, but do not have love, I am a noisy gong or a clanging cymbal. And if I have prophetic powers, and understand all mysteries and all knowledge, and if I have all faith, so as to remove mountains, but do not have love, I am nothing. If I give away all my possessions . . . so that I may boast, but do not have love, I gain nothing.
>
> Love is patient; love is kind; love is not envious or boastful or arrogant or rude. It does not insist on its own way; it is not irritable or resentful; it does not rejoice in wrongdoing, but rejoices in the truth. It bears all things, believes all things, hopes all things, endures all things. (verses 1–7)

Who Was Elizabeth Fry?

Elizabeth Gurney Fry was born in Norwich, England, in 1780 to a well-to-do Quaker family. Unlike other Quakers, the Gurneys did not "dress plain," and during her growing-up years, Elizabeth was fond of fancy clothes and scarlet laces. But although her parents had departed from Quaker ways in some aspects of their lives, Elizabeth's mother was devoted to both service and silence. Elizabeth loved to accompany her mother on her visits to homes where there was sickness or poverty. Her mother also insisted that Elizabeth and her siblings spend two hours a day in silent worship.

Elizabeth married Joseph Fry, also a Quaker. They had many children (some sources say fourteen, others eleven), but despite the demands of her busy family life, Elizabeth continued to seek out opportunities to serve the community beyond her own home. She worked for prison reform, lobbying Parliament to create laws to protect prisoners from abusive conditions, and she visited prisons all over England and also in other countries, including France. She asked that prison life be the means for reformation rather than degradation, and that everyone in prison might be equipped to begin a new life.

Elizabeth was also a well-known Quaker preacher during her lifetime. With her tireless words and actions, she constantly put love into practice. When she died at the age of sixty-five, her funeral was attended by more than a thousand people—and her legacy of love continues even today.

Divine Love

All our loving relationships are, in the deepest sense, relationships with Christ. When we interact with others, we also have the opportunity to experience his Real Presence. This is the same Presence that carries us in times of brokenness, injustice, and doubt.[310] "When my troubles and torments were great," wrote George Fox, "then was his love exceedingly great."[311]

By extending love to others, we extend love to Christ. This love is neither abstract nor reserved for spiritual giants but rather practical and simple. It consists of doing ordinary things for others, with our own selfish desires set aside. Elizabeth Fry describes this attitude: "We ought to make it an object . . . to oblige those we are with, and rather to make the pleasure of others our object, than our own. I am clear it is a great virtue to be able constantly to yield in little things; it begets the same spirit in others and renders life happy."[312] In these "little things," we become carriers of God's love—and in the kindness of others, we receive Divine love in return.

Divine love is inclusive, reaching out to draw everyone. When I read the Gospels, without the commentaries and doctrinal filters, my greatest takeaway is that Jesus reached out to everyone on the margins of society. Contrary to the prolific purity codes of the time, Jesus lavished Divine love on all people. (The same can be said of Quaker Meetings for Worship. All are welcome.)

Nothing substitutes for Christ's mysterious Presence, our absolute Ground, whose regenerative power of love unifies us on many dizzying levels. The mind of Christ, emptied of all preoccupations, restores and awakens us. Christ's Real Presence gives us the unshakable conviction that we are beloved. Knowing we are loved, we are freed. We enter into the joy of Christ.

To turn all the treasures we possess
into the channel of Universal Love
becomes the business of our lives.

—John Woolman[313]

20

Abiding Joy

This is the first fruit of the Spirit—
a joy unspeakable and full of glory.

—Thomas Kelly[314]

"**I** have said these things to you," Jesus told his followers shortly before his death, "so that my joy may be in you, and that your joy may be complete" (John 15:11). Joy is our legacy. And it is the natural fruit of spending time in silence with God.

Jesus was talking about the deepest kind of joy, which is not based on either the gratification or the deprivation of the senses. To find it, we shut the door to the senses and venture into uncharted territory. We become adventurers, where our topographical maps are dust and our sense perceptions useless. And when we return from the frontiers of religion, our words seem futile. The light at the Source is all in all, beyond all dualistic binary utterances.

This joy is constant and reliable, like the sun. It is our ultimate Refuge, a steady and secure place where we can rest our weary hearts. In contrast, all outward forms, such as altars and cathedrals, although they seek to reflect this Refuge, are empty shells. Joy comes from the Real Presence of Christ, which is always available to us, regardless of our circumstances. We can find this Real Presence in the sanctuary— and we can also find it in a cornfield or forest.

The joy of Christ is glorious, unified, unbroken, independent of externals, free. It lies at the center of the holistic mystic's life. It is the mainstay of saints in blue jeans. It makes ordinary people extraordinary, and it is unfazed by danger, oppression, or even death.

The ongoing journey of holistic mysticism is a cheerful voyage of call-and-response with the Divine, a continual conversation between our true selves and God. Holistic mysticism also always includes our neighbors (our friends and loved ones, our work colleagues, the person at the cash register in the grocery store). We spread our joy.

Joy and the "Measure of Christ"

Recently, my wife and I spent several weeks pouring over the collected letters of Margaret Fell. I found in Fell's writing a voice of bold insight and pure reason. In one of her moving pastoral letters, she wrote that we can triumph over "principalities and powers" when our joy is measured by Christ, who taught us to love our enemies, never to judge, and only to "reprove with equity" where required.[315]

The author of the Book of Hebrews wrote, "Let us approach [God] with a true heart in full assurance of faith" (10:22), and this assurance is a mainstay throughout Fell's letters. Her letters were treasured, read, and reread by fellow Quakers experiencing adversity of various kinds, including bereavement and prison sentences. Full of joy in Christ, her letters went out to friends and family, reminding them of their true nature and portion in Christ. Other letters were filled with biblical passages to bolster the spirits of those who were imprisoned. This is where Fell's zeal and light shone the brightest.

Each of us possesses a "measure of Christ," Fell wrote—and the size of that portion depends on our actions and words. In a letter written to imprisoned Quakers, Fell implored them to manifest and obey the "Measure of God" in each of them, for through this portion of Christ they will find their "Peace and Joy."[316]

During her lifetime, Margaret Fell was a beacon of light and joy to people in dire circumstances. She was a stable and reliable source of resilient and graceful words to Quakers suffering in the most grotesque circumstances. Nearly four centuries later, as I read through her letters, I too was spiritually encouraged. And I have learned that as we experience "Measures of Christ" in all areas of our lives, we find profound joy.

Who Was Margaret Fell Fox?

Born in 1614, Margaret Askew's early life did not indicate she would one day become the founding mother of the Quaker movement. Margaret's family were landed gentry, and when her father died, Margaret came into a sizeable inheritance. At the age of eighteen, she married a Puritan lawyer, Thomas Fell; they had seven daughters and a son. Margaret spent these years as a busy wife and mother, tending to the needs of her large family at Swarthmoor Hall.[317]

A chance encounter with George Fox in the summer of 1652 set Margaret's life on a new course. Impressed by his preaching, she created a carefully orchestrated "correspondence network of family, friends, and influential people through which she spread George's ideas; her letter-writing helped to organize Quaker principles into a recognized faith."[318] Her letters display a quick wit, an activist heart, and a profound theological mind. She had a clear understanding of law, both English law and Divine law, and she didn't hesitate to lambast anyone who maligned the tenets of her faith.

Eleven years after her first husband died in 1658, Margaret married George Fox. Together they were a force of nature that changed the landscape of England and later the world. George died in 1691, Margaret in 1702. Many historians believe Margaret profoundly influenced the Quakers' egalitarian nature. She is known today as the Mother of Quakerism.

Eternal Happiness

When we see the word "joy," we may think of good physical intimacy with the person we love or the magnificent vacation we took on Maui. But the joy Margaret Fell experienced—the joy Jesus sought to share in a portion of himself within us—has a far more profound meaning. This joy is not of the fleeting variety.

Our society is acquisitive by nature, and from an early age, we absorbed this tendency. During the silence of prayer, as we practice detachment from our physical senses' Tilt-a-Whirl, we create a new neural pattern, one that allows us to learn equanimity in all areas of our life. As we reinforce this mental "muscle memory" again and again, at some point we will become content with ourselves as we are. There is nothing more we will require.

I dedicated this book to Herb and Ellie Foster, who founded the Santa Cruz Friends, where I first attended a Quaker Meeting. This couple radiated a remarkable and contagious joy, unconsciously, simply by being themselves. Their joy came from decades of marinating in the sacred silences of Friends Meetings. It also came from the joy of their gentleness and tenderness toward each other. The Fosters convinced me that deep abiding love, joy, and peace are possible in a relationship; "happily-ever-after" is not a fairy tale. Of course, it's never that simple, but when we are motivated to work on ourselves out of love for our partners, we have yet another opportunity to practice letting go. Then, being steeped in spiritual community for years and years, joy becomes ever-present in our lives, as it was in the Fosters'.

The Bible says Divine joy is the source of our strength (Nehemiah 8:10). It's what gives us the courage to face this world's danger and oppression. It empowers us, making us shine. "For the kingdom of God is not food and drink," wrote Paul in his letter to the Romans, "but . . . joy in the Holy Spirit" (14:17). Rooted in Divine joy, we have the stability we need to not only face whatever life hands us but to also take a stand for God's justice.

*For the real difference between happiness and joy
is that one is grounded in this world, the other in eternity.
. . . Joy is the ultimate liberation of the human spirit.*

—Elise Boulding[319]

21

Steady Stability

[Christ] gives us increasing steadiness
in the deeper sense of his Presence . . .
an amazing stayedness in him. . . .
We are becoming what Fox calls "established people."

—Thomas Kelly[320]

In the twenty-first century, people often lack the foundation they need to withstand the onslaught of betrayals, assaults, divisiveness, pandemics, and confusion. Because they have no sense of a unifying core—the deep joy and love of Christ—they lack adequate strength to hold everything together, heal, and move on after a tragedy. Chronic anxiety and compulsions can sometimes take over.

Only the primordial Word unifies and heals. If there is no resilient center, no experience-based Word of the mystics, life's fractures and fissures can overwhelm us. The integration of our postmodern world's discordant shards is a tall order—but that is the power of Christ's Real Presence. Christ's Real Presence heals, unifies, and picks up the pieces after trauma. It holds us steady.

Quakers like George Fox and Margaret Fell had vast interior resources to cope with persecution, imprisonment, and abuse of various kinds. These resources came from their interior lives, the Quakers' source of strength.

I wish my friend Brad had discovered and cultivated interior silence and peace. If he had found Christ's Real Presence within, he wouldn't have jumped off a Bangkok skyscraper in 2016. He would have found a way over, under, or through the tragedy, and would have emerged broken but kicking. Then, in time, the Light of the Word would have put him back together again, stronger than before. Despite the pain he suffered, he would have had a source of stability.

The holistic life celebrated by Quakers integrates the various aspects of life from spirituality to career to family. Intimacy with God shows up in business transactions, relationships, and prayer time. It also shows up in composure throughout the IRS audit or the divorce. No matter what life throws at us, somehow, there is an inner calm, even amid the bare-knuckle fights for our lives.

Two of my favorite books are *Hidden Wholeness* by Parker Palmer and *The Wounded Healer* by Henri Nouwen. Throughout Palmer's book, he is candid about his debilitating clinical depression, but by the end of the book, we see how his illness helped to form the integrated spirituality of his life. "My intellect was useless," he wrote; "my emotions were dead; my will was impotent; my ego was shattered. But from time to time, deep in the thickets of my inner wilderness, I could sense the presence of something that knew how to stay alive even when the rest of me wanted to die. That something was my tough and tenacious soul."[321]

Nouwen's book contains a similar paradox: if we come to terms with our wounds in whatever forms, we can help others heal theirs. "When we have found the anchor places for our lives in our own center, we can be free to let others enter into the space created for them and allow them to dance their own dance, sing their own song and speak their own language without fear."[322]

Each of us needs to come home, homecoming parade and all. With our souls anchored in the Divine, we will find deep, unshakable security. Toughness and tenacity will be ours.

Victory in Disaster

We all have our hidden traumas. An individual considered to be a success from a business point of view may have an alcohol problem; their children might not speak to them or a financial mistake could bring their so-called success crashing down. But external success or failure does not define reality.

Caroline Stephen wrote that the evidence of success on the spiritual path is not what we usually think of as success, in terms of tangible achievement, but rather an unshakable reliance on our deepest interior resources. Once we are in a relationship with Christ in the most profound sense, we know solidity and Real Presence. Our inner joy and love are the truth-tellers we rely on, while temptations, snares, and failures no longer define us. Storms may rage all around us, but our inner assurance of Christ's Real Presence triumphs.

This doesn't mean that when we make our way in the Light of Christ—the Light of Quaker mystics—we are guaranteed endless good times. Quite the opposite. If we choose to follow the holistic path of the Quaker mystics, we will still, sooner or later, face colossal upheaval, trauma, and tragedy. We also have our tailor-made crosses, the results of our poor choices and the dysfunctional scripts we've inherited from our families. Nevertheless, the experience of Christ's Real Presence gives us focus, presence, and energy.

We need not be victims of circumstance. We can create new possibilities. We can pause, wait, and trust the Quaker proverb: "A way will open."[323]

Personal responsibility and resilience see us through disaster. And by the end, we may even turn to the dragon that once pinned our head between razor-sharp teeth and say, "Thank you." It may take years of introspection before we can utter those words—but every catastrophe, illness, or toxic person in our lives has something to teach us. As Nietzsche said, "What doesn't kill me makes me stronger."[324]

The cross of Christ demonstrates this. It expresses deep, bitter humility, not the delicious satisfaction of an ego trip. Still, the spiritual journey fulfills us on a level far beyond shallow, materialistic mirages. We learn from Christ's experience that a resurrection is not possible without a tomb.

Consolations When We Suffer

As human beings, we are often quick to condemn and pull away from those whose sins have been exposed for all to see. Christ, however, takes special notice of failures and prodigals. When people fall from grace through addiction, sexual impropriety, failure, or persecution, grace draws near.

Christ always responds to our needs—and the greater the need, the greater the response. According to Thomas Keating, people who suffer traumas or abuse in their lives often experience special consolations in prayer, especially on retreat. To compensate for their suffering, God draws near. This is not mere sentimentality. God responds to us according to our needs, according to our scars.[325]

Those who face the world's disapproval and oppression, as George Fox did, can discover something that exceeds the affections of people and popularity contests. When they find friendship with God, they realize that Divine grace is far greater than human approval. During George Fox's persecutions, his assurance of God's presence and guidance deepened.[326] He had a stability that no human relationship or position could offer.

Built on the Rock

"All that dwell in the light, their habitation is in God," wrote Edward Burrough in the seventeenth century, "and they know a hiding place in the day of storm; and those who dwell in the light, are built upon the rock, and cannot be moved." Burrough's sense of his life being built "upon the rock" of Christ gave him the strength he needed to speak out for justice during Quakerism's early years when they faced oppression and imprisonment.

Burrough was a powerful speaker, but he also used his written words to publish pamphlets that circulated throughout England. This took courage, since Quakers were being imprisoned and even put to death for their faith. Burrough explained the source of his strength: "While waiting upon the Lord in silence . . . we received often the pouring down of the spirit upon us, and the gift of God's holy eternal spirit as in the days of old, and our hearts were made glad."[327]

Burrough died in prison when he was only twenty-nine years old—but like Margaret Fell, George Fox, and so many other heroes in the history of Quakerism's holistic mysticism, Edward Burrough had an interior anchor, a foundation on the Rock, which held him and stabilized him, despite the violence and oppression around him. With the psalmist, he could say, "God alone is my rock and my salvation, my fortress; I shall never be shaken" (Psalm 62:2).

Patient Endurance

The Eastern church's theologians often celebrated the virtue of patient endurance,[328] which is the active expression of the stability we find in holistic mysticism. Rufus Jones called it "patient suffering."

This virtue means that the way to deal with vengeful people full of malice, as well as opportunist control freaks, is not to act on our first angry impulse to get even. Rather, we patiently endure such feelings until they pass. Patience becomes an anchor that holds us stable amid a tossing sea of emotion. This endurance can be applied to exhausting tedium and frustration. When many people would lose their composure and start yelling and throwing things, we take a deep breath, set the centering-prayer app on our phone to seven minutes, and release the tension. Then we pick up the exasperating task again. "Endurance produces character," Paul wrote to the Romans, "and character produces hope, and hope does not disappoint us, because God's love has been poured into our hearts through the Holy Spirit that has been given to us" (5:4).

Patient endurance is one of the keys to the spiritual life. Patient endurance resists both the impulse to despair in our suffering and the compulsion to become reactive or rash. As modern-day Quaker theologian Doug Gwyn wrote, "Patience is an active condition of the Spirit. It can march; it can demonstrate; it can live in jails. It can survive the long haul of transformation. But it is not fed on the bitter fruit of resentment."[329]

Wars, coercion, and fear might bring temporary submission. Still, they cannot effect lasting change that transforms people's hearts. Lasting, earth-moving change is the result of persistent, patient love. We get a sense of this in Peter's relationship with Jesus in the Gospels; although Peter denies and betrays Jesus three times (just when Jesus needs his affirmation most), Jesus patiently endures the betrayals and then reaches out to Peter yet again (John 21:15–19).

Patient acceptance of people, pressure, suffering, and Herculean trials produce something beautiful—even if, as was the case with the Israelites wandering in the desert, it takes forty years. Extraordinary pressures over time form both diamonds and saints.

Patient endurance and self-discipline mean we submit to the present moment as it is, not as we would like it to be. This is easy to say but difficult to practice. It means, moment by moment, we resist daydreams, regrets, and reminiscences about yesterday. Again and again, we bring ourselves back to the present moment as it is. If there is suffering, pain, or regret in the present moment, we accept it. We no longer avoid it or numb it through addictions or fetishes.

Patient endurance also empowers us in the work of justice. As Lucretia Mott wrote, "Those who go forth ministering to the wants and necessities of their fellow beings experience a rich return, their souls being as a watered garden, and a spring that fails not."[330]

Who Was Lucretia Mott?

Born in 1792 to a Quaker family in Massachusetts, Lucretia struggled with a "hasty temper," but she learned to turn to prayer as a source of strength and stability. As she grew into adulthood, she applied that steadiness to the antislavery and women's rights movements. "I have no idea of submitting tamely to injustice inflicted either on me or on the slave," she wrote. "I am no advocate of passivity."[331]

Lucretia's composure remained unruffled, even when she faced audiences that jeered and insulted her. "My convictions led me to adhere to the sufficiency of the Light within us," she said, "resting on truth as authority, rather than 'taking authority for truth.' I searched the Scriptures daily."[332]

Lucretia and her husband opened their home to enslaved people escaping to Canada via the Underground Railroad. After the Civil War, she worked for educational opportunities and voting rights for Blacks. "I do not want to show my faith by my words, or by my Quaker bonnet, I want that we may all show our faith by our works," she wrote, "by our honesty and justice and mercy and love. . . . Let our lives be in accordance with our convictions of right."[333]

In old age, as death drew near, her confidence in her Divine anchor remained firm. "Weep not for me," she told her friends and family. "My work is done. Like a ripe fruit I admit the gathering. . . . I am ready whenever the summons may come."[334] She died of pneumonia at the age of eighty-seven.

Truly Solid

There is a vast difference between people who take their inner lives seriously and those who don't—and that difference shows in our exterior lives. We too, like Edward Burrough and Lucretia Mott, can find in Christ's Real Presence a place of utter security and stability. It is solid beyond the so-called solidity of any other "objective" phenomenon.

The Logos or preexistent Word of John's Gospel, through which all things were made and in whom all things are held steady (Colossians 1:17), can be sought within—but the growth of this Seed requires interior cultivation. Of course, we pay attention to the "husks" of this Seed: clothes, cars, homes, conveniences. But what matters most are the motivations of the hearts of the people who wear the clothes, drive the cars, and dwell in the homes. Yes, we live in this world, so the outer shells are important—but our center of gravity is within. It keeps us stable in a shifting world of upheaval and change.

As we grow older, we find that what we thought was solid is not. Of course, marriage, worship, and fitness are anchors to a vital life. But sometimes, either because of death or divorce, the lifelong relationship turns out not to be lifelong. The security we vested in the church feels misplaced when the politics and infighting behind the scenes combusts. The health we always counted on erodes. Everything changes. Only the uncreated, ever-present inner Presence endures.

Deep inner calm that can still the storms within us—like Jesus calmed the external storm in the Gospels—can take time to cultivate. Once established, however, this primordial peace holds us, caresses our existential anxiety, and bathes us in ancient waters of affirmation and belonging

In silent prayer, when we experience errant thoughts, distractions, and daydreams, endurance gives us the self-discipline to gently guide our mind back to its center, where it is most at peace, most perceptive, and most resourceful. The mind at rest, free from distractions, becomes a reliable ally. Over time, we gain confidence that it will see us through all things. People and external factors may collapse, yet the stable, resilient mind anchors us, holding our lives steady. We no longer have a fretful and tetherless existence.

Consistent contact with the primordial Ground of Our Being instills abiding love and joy, both of which are qualitatively different from the constant ups and downs of conflicting emotions. Our emotions hinge on punishment or reward, gratification or neglect, sensory stimulation or deprivation. Abiding joy, on the other hand, is constant, not dependent on externals.

This joy, built on the ongoing experience of living in connection to that which is truly stable, the Ground of Our Being, is not necessarily bliss or elation but rather a smooth tranquility and serenity. External factors may cloud this sense of peace, but they cannot uproot it once it is established.

Follow steadfastly after all
that is pure and lovely and of good report.
Be prayerful. Be watchful. Be humble.
Let no failure discourage you.
When temptation comes, make it an opportunity
to gain new strength by standing fast,
that you may enter into that life of gladness and victory
to which all are called.

—Ohio Yearly Meeting Book of Discipline, 1992

22

Deep Rest and Peace

In Christ, sit down in life and peace and rest.

—George Fox[335]

True silence is the rest of the mind;
and is to the spirit, what sleep is to the body,
nourishment and refreshment.

—William Penn[336]

Rest, in the deepest sense, eludes many of us. Even when we claim to be resting, our minds obsess about things left to do in the inbox, ponder conversations we had, and think, *Don't forget to take the dog out.* The mind constantly churns.

Even with this background noise, people believe they are at "rest," when really, they've simply become so accustomed to the chaos that they no longer notice it. What they call "rest" is undoubtedly not rest, for true rest, in the deepest sense, lets go of every thought, agenda, desire, intimation, and daydream. Deep rest is to fall, as if through thin air, with nothing to hold on to and no one or nothing to catch us—and to be at peace as we fall. We dispense with all intrigue, deliberation, chatter. We renounce all distortions and frictions in our lives. And to our surprise, we find a more profound rest than we thought possible. There are no words, only spaciousness, primal peace, and deep joy.

"Come to me, all who labor and are heavy laden," said Jesus, "and I will give you rest" (Matthew 11:28). Personally, I find that during centering prayer after a tense day's work, my body unwinds. I feel emptiness and release. Then I am ready for the next day. I let go of the stress. I am again receptive like an empty cup.

Christ knows us better than we know ourselves. In the deep rest of his Presence, he reveals our true selves to us, and then he often underlines his message with words from a concerned friend or a synchronistic event. Deep rest is knowing ourselves the way Christ knows us, in our uncharted depths, before the worlds began, and in our imperfection, seeing our hidden wholeness,[337] divinity, and Light. This Light is not exclusive or the wish-fulfilling whim of a child playing make-believe. It is our birthright—our worthy guide who reveals our ultimate purpose. There, in the Light, our minds finally find complete rest, which is definitive, all-encompassing, absolute.

The Real Presence of Christ doesn't invade our lives, pushing in where we don't want it to go. Instead, Christ comes to our conscience in the form of nudges—and so too his Presence comes to our nervous systems in the form of deep abiding peace and rest. He even speaks to us in our sleep.

The Interior Work of Sleep

Even deeper than thoughts are dreams. As Jungian psychologists state, dreams are doorways from our subconscious mind into our conscious mind.[338]

We can think of the subconscious mind as the lava and magma beneath the volcano. The conscious mind is the earthen volcanic soil above the surface. People are afraid of the subconscious, just as they are afraid of lava and potential volcanic eruptions. Nevertheless, the subconscious is the seat of our primordial creative power—and the courageous probe its riddles for clues about the deeper realities of our lives. Many people, of course, opt to stay on the surface, but I lift my glass to the adventurers who risk the lava, who probe the Mystery of the subconscious mind and its dreams.

Dream interpretation is difficult, but a dream journal is a good way to begin. I need to jot down dreams before doing anything else; otherwise, I forget, and so, as soon as I wake up, I remain horizontal with my eyes closed and try to recall any dreams I had. (Sometimes I'm not able to remember any.) Then I write the dreams in my journal (I use my smartphone's notepad app). As I keep track of my dreams, I begin to see patterns in the riddles, and my dream awareness and interpretation become more accurate. Often my dreams bring intuitive clarity about my life challenges.

The importance of dreams and their interpretation is found throughout the Bible.[339] In the Hebrew scriptures, Joseph, for example, was famous for being able to interpret dreams (Genesis 41:12). In the Gospels, a dream warns the magi to protect the Christ child (Matthew 2:12).

The ancients understood that God speaks subconscious riddles to us. Carl Jung concurred.[340] If we dismiss dreams, perhaps we do so because they require so much protracted patience to decipher. It is like learning Braille. Still, intimacy with our dreams directly connects us with the Seed of Christ. Dreams can be glimpses of God. As the Divine Mystery flits through our subconscious mind, we catch a glimmer of Light.

Some dreams offer us life-defining information. When a friend of mine was applying to be the minister of his first church, he was anxious about the process of choosing between two options, one in California, the other in Washington State. He compared the sensation to walking across a busy street blindfolded: there were so many unknowns. Then he had a crystal-clear dream. (This doesn't happen very often; dreams are usually opaque.) In his dream, he saw an elderly woman with a pot of food. As she motioned for him to take a taste, he noticed she was wearing a sweatshirt with the letters CA emblazoned on it. When he tasted her food, it was rancid, so he walked away. Then he found another elderly woman with a pot of food, and she also motioned for him to try her food. This time, the food was good. Then he saw that her sweatshirt had the letters WA on it. His own brain had told him which church was best for him. And it turned out that the church in Washington was the most joyful and grace-filled community he has known.

Or here's another example: let's say you meet a woman, and that night, she appears to you in a dream, wearing blue-and-white

checkered pants. A reasonable interpretation might come from ana-
lyzing the blue-and-white squares. What do they symbolize? The
blue could indicate she is a Democrat. The white could suggest she
is Caucasian. And the squares could imply that when it comes to her
sexuality, she is square or somewhat prude. The word *pants* might
signify sexual attraction (you are panting with lust). However, ultimately, only you can determine the associations your mind holds
with the colors blue and white, the shape of a square, and the word
pants. There is no single, across-the-board Rosetta Stone we can use
to decipher dreams.[341]

Another less involved dream: you have a graduate record exam
(GRE) in a month, and in a dream, you see yourself as a martial artist,
with a robe and black belt, sitting down to study. A reasonable interpretation might be: passing the GRE requires martial discipline like
a martial arts master. But again, only you can say what the symbols
in your dream mean. As Jungian psychologist Robert Johnson wrote,
"The unconscious has a particular capacity to create images and to use
those images as symbols. It is these symbols that form our dreams, creating a language by which the unconscious communicates its contents
to the conscious mind. . . . As we learn to read those symbols, we gain
the ability to perceive the workings of the unconscious within us."[342]

Everything in dreams, even letters, and numbers are symbols for
interpretation. And some letters and numbers only have significance
for you. For example, the name of the high school bully who tormented
you was Jimmy Tobias. So, if someone named "JT" appears in your
dream, it might be related to the bully. Or, if the date of your marriage
is April 22 and the number 422 comes up in your dream, it could be
related to your marriage.

If we exercise the patience to decode the cipher, dreams impart wisdom from deep within. But a warning from firsthand experience: the wisdom dreams impart is often not practical or valued by the world. With some exceptions, dream wisdom is usually not about mundane concerns such as a paycheck or personal gratification. For example, dream wisdom can decode mysteries of our primal origins and divinity (the interconnectivity of all Creation, which is proven scientifically now). Dreams can also discern national demons and shadows, and recognize painful truths about ourselves and our families of origin. As the psalmist wrote, God provides for us even in our sleep (Psalm 127:2).

Deep Peace

"I told them I live in the virtue of that life and power that took away the occasion of all wars," wrote George Fox, "and I knew from whence all wars did rise, from the lust according to James' doctrine. . . . I told them I was come into the covenant of peace which was before wars and strifes."[343]

Fox spoke these words when the English militia offered him a "get out of jail free card" if he served in a regiment. Fox refused on principle and remained in jail with its rats and gruel. What was the source of Fox's deep conviction? The peace that reigned in his own heart. Those who go into the deep stillness and silence, intimately encounter God, and in the process, they find an ocean of peace.

Long-term meditators experience more than a garden-variety peace, the sort found from a good day at work, a cold beer, and fine conversations with their spouses. The peace I'm talking about here goes far deeper. If cultivated and allowed to ripen, silent prayer invites an all-pervasive natural peace—so powerful it can pull up the roots of war. First, it does so in our hearts, as it did for Fox, and then it does so in our communities. In the case of Fox, that natural peace began the process of pulling up the roots of oppression and war in England.

The deep rest and peace we find in the Real Presence always move from our interior lives into our exterior. The eighteenth-century Eastern mystic Seraphim of Sarov wrote, "Acquire inward peace, and thousands around you will find their salvation."[344] This expresses the idea that if we find the Light within ourselves, this Light will find its way into our lives, relationships, writing, and work.

Elizabeth Fry, who suffered from a "nervous, fearful nature," said that she had found a way to overcome her emotions by trusting God to bring her "into that state where peace flows as a river." No matter how deeply upset she might be, she wrote, "the confidence has never left that . . . if not in time, in eternity, the end would be peace."[345]

Another Quaker woman, Elise Boulding, also discovered the power of peace. "Peace cultures thrive on and are nourished by visions of how things might be," she wrote, "in a world where sharing and caring are part of the accepted lifeways for everyone. . . . There is no time left for anything but to make peace work a dimension of our every waking activity."[346]

Christ is no longer welcoming the lepers and poor along the streets of Galilee, as he was two thousand years ago—but he continues to bring peace to the disenfranchised and marginal in our world. He invites the bullied adolescent to share his peace. He offers his peace to the man with his face in his hands after his marriage went sideways. Christ accepts everything we are. This is where peace begins.

Who Was Elise Boulding?

Born in Norway in 1920, Elise immigrated with her parents to the United States in 1923. In college, she converted to Quakerism. Her marriage to Kenneth Boulding, a well-known Quaker economist and poet, further deepened her commitment to the Friends.

Elise described the challenges of being a young mother. "I am too tired to be patient," she wrote, "too tired to pray, too tired to make our home a place of friendliness, refreshment and peace." But, in the demands of family life, Elise eventually learned the secret of deep inner peace—and she used that knowledge to bring positive change to the global community, both among her fellow Quakers and in society at large. "I have long been convinced," she said, "that families are the primary agents of social change in any society."[347]

Decades into their marriage, she and her husband ran into differences of opinion that led to them living apart for several years. After they reunited, Elise applied what she had learned in her marriage to her larger work of peace-building. Peace between individuals, she believed, flows out from deep interior peace, and the same principles and strategies that build peace in intimate relationships can also be used in the larger world. Elise died at the age of eighty-nine. Today, she is known as the Mother of Peace and Conflict Studies.

Acceptance

As Christ accepts us, holistic mysticism requires that we too accept reality as it is. Once we reconcile ourselves to every aspect of our lives, we experience peace; we rest in the confidence that no matter the hellacious curveballs, we can work through them. This peace relies on the wholehearted acceptance of both the cross and the resurrection in Christ's life and ours. We surrender everything we have—and in return, we bask in the Real Presence of Christ.

Christ is no longer a symbol from the distant past we worship. Now, Christ's Real Presence, at once messy and perfect, at once human and Divine, is the Source of deep peace and rest. And, as Elise Boulding discovered, the serenity we find in Christ becomes the nurturing ground for our true purpose and identity.

*Practically, peace culture values and practices
motivate us to keep trying, to keep learning,
to keep developing new skills that will help us deal with
greed-generated violence, impatience,
and the desire for power over others. . . .
Social compassion begins in the small, the local,
but it never ends there—
it only opens the path to the greater whole.*

—Elise Boulding[348]

23

Purpose and Identity

What is it we were born to do;
for what mission came we into the world . . . ?
[A]n unceasing effort to put love and truth
into circulation in the currents of human life . . .
by self-giving, adventurous, sacrificial love,
that never lets go, never fails,
but bears and endures all things to the end. . . .
There is no way to find yourself
until you discover how utterly to lose yourself.

—Rufus Jones[349]

In the depths of our inner life, Christ's Real Presence gently prompts us. This life is not subject to simplistic control freaks and bullies, nor subject to reductionist interpretations. Inner prompts of the Spirit come from a subconscious repository that makes holistic sense of the zigzags of our lives. It sees everything as a whole. Over time it convinces us that everything belongs. It answers our deepest questions, including questions about our own identities.

Exquisite intelligence beyond our imagination gives us insight into the inner workings of our lives and relationships. This gift allows us true understanding, not as an outsider looking in, but as an insider who sees the clock's inner cogs and workings. Along with the psalmist, we too can exclaim, "Such knowledge is too wonderful for me; it is too high. I cannot attain it" (139:6).

Unlike some of the people in our lives, God does not pigeonhole, belittle, or minimize our struggles. Divinity is perfectly comfortable with complexity, ambiguity, and colossal messes—the real-life stuff we all experience. God joins us in the circumstances of our lives, whatever they may be, and amid it all, we receive a Word to dispel the darkness. This Word seldom comes in a formal way, with worldly pomp; instead, God gives us a brilliant outline scrawled on a paper napkin in the nick of time. We receive confidence that it's time to zig and not zag. Our dreams reveal something we haven't faced or an opportunity we might otherwise have overlooked.

Discovering Life's Meaning

As a teenager, Emilia Fogelklou suffered from bouts of depression that became worse as she grew older. She had a degree in theology and taught religious education to young people—but all the while, her fruitless search for meaning filled her with despair. In her journal, she wrote that she felt like "just a shell, a shell empty of life."[350] She longed for Divine Reality and yearned to have a sense of purpose, and yet both seemed impossible to grasp. At the age of twenty-three, she was on the point of suicide.

But then, on a sunny spring day while she sat outside preparing for a class, everything changed. "Quietly, invisibly, there occurred the central event of her whole life. Without visions or the sound of speech or human mediation, in exceptionally wide-awake consciousness, she experienced the great releasing inward wonder. It was as if the 'empty shell' burst. All the weight and agony, all the feeling of unreality dropped away. She perceived living goodness, joy, light like a clear, irradiating, uplifting, enfolding, unequivocal reality from deep inside."[351]

This, she realized, was God—and nothing else was so *real* as the Divine. "The child who had cried out in anguish and been silenced had now come inside the gates of Light. She had been delivered by a love that is greater than any human love. Struck dumb, amazed, she went quietly to her class, wondering that no one noticed that something had happened to her."

Rooted now in her new identity, Boulding had a sense of purpose and calling. She worked with the international peace effort, contributed to the workers' education movement, wrote books, and traveled the world, lecturing on theology, feminism, and pacifism.

Who Was Emilia Fogelklou?

As a child, Emilia Fogelklou (born in Sweden in 1878) was already a holistic mystic. She sensed the Spirit within all things—but when she tried to describe her experiences to the adults in her life, they accused her of lying. This rupture between her inner perceptions and the perspectives of the people around her made her seek the "really real."

Finally, in Quakerism, Emilia discovered her spiritual home. "Views and opinions were no longer of concern," she wrote. "Now it was the reality behind the interpretation, and the radiance that came from that reality, which really mattered."[352]

Emilia suffered heartbreaks and disappointment, as we all do. Her happy marriage ended after only seven years when her husband died of tuberculosis. Throughout her professional life, she was very conscious of being a woman struggling to have a voice in a male-dominated world. And yet, through it all, she never lost the sense of identity and meaning she had discovered when she found God "without the wrapping paper." When she encountered obstacles, she was empowered to "go right on through" difficult circumstances.[353]

When Emilia died in 1972, these words were carved on her gravestone: *There is light still.*

Called to an Individual Mission

At some point, we too will experience something similar to what Emilia Fogelklou did: the direction of our lives will become clear and focused. We will know what we are called to do. The date and time often stand in high relief. That calling is one of the fruits of holistic mysticism, the radiant ground from which authentic ministry flows. When we feel called to a particular mission, our lives sharply focus; all the cylinders fire.

This idea is central to Quakerism. Rufus Jones emphasized the many "calls" recorded in the Bible, and he understood modern-day callings to be the core of Quaker faith. This is the contemporary vision quest for postmodern people—the rite of passage when we ask the nodal questions: *What are we on earth to do? What are we here for? Is there something we do, that when we do it, we think to ourselves, "This is why I have come into the world. This is where my gifts meet the world's need"?*

When calling is clarified, we find meaning and purpose. We are re-formed, remade. That purpose shapes our calendars, free time, checkbooks, and relationships.

Teleological Transformation

Teleology has to do with something's purpose or its goal. A fork's purpose, for example, is to hold food and transport it into our mouths. A car's purpose is to carry people from one place to another. The fork's purpose is essential to its existence, as is the car's. We don't keep either forks or cars around as pure decoration. Their purposes are built into their very shape, their construction.

The human brain is also wired to have a purpose, an end goal. Like a rocket with preprogrammed coordinates that determine its destination, we too are constructed with a built-in sense of direction. As we connect to the Inner Light, we discover a "target" that maximizes our energy and focuses our minds. We cannot act boldly, with a firm resolve, unless we have a clear sense of objective about what we are called to do.

This teleology is liberated and illuminated during times of centered-down silence and centering prayer. It is the fruit of settling and waiting in silence. "Only wait to know that wherein God appears in your heart," wrote Isaac Penington, "that may be discerned, distinguished, and have scope in you, that it may spring up in your heart, and live in you, and gather you into itself, and leaven you all over with its nature; that you may be a new lump, and may walk before God, not in the oldness of your own literal knowledge or apprehensions of things, but in the newness of God's Spirit."[354]

When Penington spoke of becoming a "new lump," he was referring to a lump of bread dough that is transformed by the presence of leaven—yeast—a material that works from within to change the very nature of the dough. As we go inward, connecting ever more deeply with the Light within us, who we are, in the most profound sense, is transformed by the leaven of the Spirit, making us into God's image. We "put off the old man/woman," and we are remade (Ephesians 4:22), discovering the teleological meaning of our identities. The Divine *I AM* reveals not only God's identity but also our deepest selves.

A sobering realization of my life was how little my sermons changed people in the congregations I served. I concluded that good sermons are fine support on the spiritual path—but they are not the leaven people need to be transformed. Transformation is not a spectator sport. It doesn't happen from simply listening to a good message or reading a meaningful book. We need to have skin in the game—and this comes only when we no longer have wiggle room to evade our Divine purpose. We need total commitment.

Meditation in the latter stages of our practice demands everything from us. If realized, the final aspiration is the great hope of the human family—to realize our God-given potential, heal our nervous systems, and awaken. To become nothing so we can discover who we are, so that no matter what besets us, from cancer to bankruptcy to tornado, we navigate the turbulence. We can limp away from the wreckage and courageously begin again, because our ultimate sense of purpose remains steady.

Purity of Heart

"Daring greatly" requires nothing less than a cleansing of the heart—or what the Desert Elders called "purity of heart."[355] My best stab at what they meant by this is what I call *wholeheartedness*. This means we are "all in." We no longer hold anything back. We can contrast "all in" with "half-hearted." Purity of heart is unwavering commitment and resolve, void of duplicity.

Purity of heart characterizes holistic mysticism. If we emulate the Quaker mystics, we commit to a relationship with Christ through prayer. We don't just talk about it. We get serious about our mission.

Conviction is the taproot of purity of heart. Belief alone is not enough, for beliefs—what George Fox called *notions*—are merely mental constructs that live within our minds. "Not the holding of notions but an inward transforming experience of God, is George Fox's word of life," wrote Rufus Jones.[356] Conviction carries us from our inner worlds out into the external world.

Convictions often require sacrifice. Opinions and beliefs have little staying power, especially under persecution. Only full-bodied convictions—integrated into our minds, hearts, and souls—lead us to our teleological essence. This level of commitment ran deep in the early church. As a result, early Christians did not renounce their principles, even under the pain of death.

Divine Integration

Recently, when I entered a restaurant with my wife, I noticed that at least a third of the people sitting at the tables were on electronic devices. They were not talking to each other; they were not even looking at each other. Although sharing a table, each person was isolated in their own small world.

The tragedy of our times is fragmentation, lack of cohesion, and polarization on every level of society.[357] We are addicted to electronic screens, and meanwhile, we are losing the social skills required for face-to-face human interaction. Even before our age of social media and online entertainment, as Thomas Kelly noted, "our surface potentialities are for selfishness and greed, for tooth and claw."[358]

But this is not our true, Divinely intended nature. "Deep within," wrote Kelly, "in the whispers of the heart, is the surging call of the Eternal Christ, hidden within us all. By an inner isthmus, we connect with the mainland of the Eternal Love. Surface living has brought on the world's tragedy." We do not have to remain in this state of tragic fragmentation. "Deeper living leads us to the Eternal Christ, hidden in us all," Kelly said. "Absolute loyalty to this inner Christ is the only hope of a new humanity. In the clamour and din of the day, the press of Eternity's warm love still whispers in each of us, as our truest selves."[359]

Kelly's words deliver me from fragmented madness and bring me home to the soul's playground. The Divine Presence—the Eternal Christ within us—integrates and synthesizes. It pulls together the fragments, not only within our society but also within our own hearts and lives, and gives us absolute assurance that everything belongs, everything fits together, even the messes. Put more succinctly: nothing is broken. Nothing is finished. Everything is still being transformed into its true, God-given nature

Recently, I went to Kalaloch on the Olympic Peninsula in Washington to see the Big Cedar, the third-largest red cedar in the world. Amazingly, part of the tree was felled in a coastal storm, yet it survived. The two words that occurred to me as I looked at the tree were *resilience* and *emergence*.

Nothing is ultimately broken. Everything is emerging, and to some extent, everything is redeemable. The truth of these words reverberates through living systems. When we closely observe natural processes and ecosystems, we see that everything is in process. No system fits into neat linear labels. Everything is emerging and evolving.

And yet many people get to the end of life and find themselves agreeing with the U2 lyrics: "I still haven't found what I'm looking for."[360] What a shame to go through most of life and end up still seeking. At some point, the seeker should find, the pilgrim should arrive. Then, when we do find the inexplicable radical simplicity at the Center, we say to ourselves, *This is what I am created for. This experience of Divine Union is all in all.*

Even after experiences of unification, we will still have fragmented moments, hours, and days. Now, however, experiences of alienation and disillusionment are counterbalanced with delicious moments of union. Moments of union inoculate us from the poisons of dysfunctional, fragmented people and disjointed twenty-first-century life. The poisons are still there, but they lose their unbearable and sometimes lethal sting. We taste wholeness and integration that heal and revitalize the nervous system and bless us with energy and purpose.

Daggers of personal failures and divisive bullies may lunge and jab with thoughts of suicide, revenge, chemical escape, or whatever— but now, we have a shield of unification and integrity to deflect the daggers. The Source of Life is our refuge and shield (Psalm 18:2). We are freed to live out our deepest purpose, secure in our identity, rooted in our relationship with God in Christ. We have come home.

Life is meant to be lived from a Center, a divine Center . . .
a life of unhurried peace and power.
It is simple. It is serene. It is amazing. It is triumphant.
It is radiant. It takes no time, but it occupies all our time.
And it makes our life programs new and overcoming.
We need not get frantic. God is at the helm.

—Thomas Kelly[361]

Conclusion

Homecoming

All that dwell in the light, their habitation is in God,
and they know a hiding place in the day of storm.

—Edward Burrough[362]

In the Gospel of Luke, Jesus tells the story of the Prodigal Son—a young man who leaves home, searching for fame and fortune, only to find himself desperate, starving, and homesick. When he finally returns home, ready to beg to be allowed in as a servant, his father welcomes him with open arms. The young man's homecoming is celebrated with a feast of joy.

Our True Home

We too, like the Prodigal Son, wander far from our true home, seeking satisfaction from things that leave us empty and yearning. Ultimately, the journey of holistic mysticism is one of homecoming. In silence, in centering, we return to our home, where God welcomes us with open arms.

The world has become too complex and fragmented to take away any satisfying holistic peace. Polarized newscasts and ever more polarized social media and fake news send us reeling. Everywhere, divisions and strife threaten families, communities, and nations. This division feeds inherent insecurity; homelessness becomes rampant in the human soul.

The cure for our deep-seated ailments and pervasive anxieties is homecoming in the most profound sense. It is the realization that God is with us—that we belong to the Divine. The deep experience of the hidden pervasive unity at the core of every cell and galaxy inoculates us further. Now, no matter what happens, we are less prone to debilitating anxiety, depression, or self-sabotage. As Thomas Kelly wrote, "Heaven-led souls are not 'seekers' alone, but 'finders,' finders who have been found by the Father of all the world's prodigals. . . . How different is the experience of life . . . when the Eternal Presence suffuses it!"[363]

The journey of holistic mysticism brings us home to what Kelly calls the "recreating Center of eternal peace and joy,"[364] a place of eternal safety. Kelly's descriptors—peace and joy—are more than mere emotions; instead, they are sovereign and constant, available no matter the external push and pull of life. This vital experience may not come to us early in life, as it did for many of the holistic mystics we've described in this book, but it's never too late to acclimatize the mind to Real Presence and pervasive unity.

In the fourth century, Saint Basil wrote: "When the intellect is no longer dissipated among external things or dispersed across the world through the senses, it returns to itself; and by means of itself it ascends to the thought of God."[365] This is what it means to come home.

Finding a Spiritual Foundation

On some level, conscious or not, we all seek ultimate meaning and purpose, a solid rock on which to build our lives. We want to experience the foundation Jesus described: "The rain fell, the floods came, and the winds blew and beat on that house, but it did not fall, because it had been founded on rock" (Matthew 7:25). We yearn for a solid and unshakeable place to build our spiritual homes.

When we do, what we experience is not some narrow sense of homecoming, like securing membership at the country club or attending a class reunion. It's a homecoming that transcends and includes all preceding layers on the evolutionary ladder of our lives. Every layer matters and contributes to a profound depth and breadth.

When we have truly come home, we can experience our Divine Source in prayer—in surges of intimacy, immensity, and intensity. This creative foundation of life already flows through our spines and the vertebrae of all creatures, but now we are aware of it.

On some level, we always yearn to go back to our Source, to our origin, where it all began. We knew this Source in our mother's womb, but after birth, we soon forgot. We are mystical as children, but then, as life puts more demands on us, we begin to suppress this ability in exchange for learning the skills taught in classrooms. But as I said already, it's never too late to go home. Something as simple as seeing the forest at sunrise can remind us of the multilayered Mystery that is also our Source.

Our conscious and subconscious minds are anxious and on edge whenever we lose touch with our Source. The dualistic, rational mind only gets in the way. All we can do is return again and again to stillness and silence, bypassing reason and binaries. "And as you have intervals from your lawful occasions," wrote William Penn, "delight to step home (within yourselves, I mean), commune with your own hearts and be still."[366]

Spiritual commitment requires a profound dynamism where we wait in silence and in complete submission on the one hand—and on the other hand, we exercise the iron will to fulfill our mission despite the obstacles. The first movement is entirely passive, and the second is fully active. There is the Christ of the cross—and then, there is the Christ of the resurrection. Our spiritual homecoming is the holistic balance between the cross and the resurrection, left and right brain, passivity and action, nondual and dual. To have one of these pairs without the other would be reductionist, limiting our perception of the greater Reality.

This holistic synergy is the contemplative journey. The Real Presence of Christ holds the tension between the extremes. It unites all apparent dichotomies, including that between time and eternity.

Eternity

People who have a firm conviction of eternity do not take refuge in the barren corridors of existentialism and cling desperately to the fleeting moment. Unfortunately, today, in a world of disaster, violence, and political upheaval, too many of us have lost the knowledge of eternity and the vision of paradise. We have forgotten our true home.

We so easily lose sight of eternity in the pressure of today. But that way of thinking rises out of the false duality of time and eternity. We live in eternity now; we do not have to wait until we die to "go home." The daily demands on our time need not come between us and eternity, for everything in our lives—going to work, caring for a family, running a household, participating in community events—already partakes of eternity.

We become more and more aware of this Reality as we practice silent prayer. The contemplative mind doesn't somehow access another dimension; it is, rather, a natural phenomenon, not ethereal, not from some higher plane. The contemplative mind is of this world, reflecting the synergistic whole of Nature.

The Realm of God, which Jesus referenced again and again in the Gospels, is not some inaccessible heaven. It is the Unity embodied in the symbiotic relationships of the natural world and expressed in the relationships of the Trinity. It is here, now.

What Next?

I don't advocate that people drop their faith tradition and convert to Quakerism. Still, if you yearn to ground Christian mysticism within a particular tradition, then you need look no further. The fertile sacred silences of George Fox and the Quakers can be a tradition within a tradition for you. You can find ways to integrate waiting worship/ sacred silence into your journey of faith. (For example, you can be a friend [lowercase] while retaining your current church membership.) You can be a member of the Society of Friends, and you can continue to be a member of your own faith tradition. I have a "Neo-Quaker Anglican" friend who reflects this gestalt.

Ultimately, Quakerism is not about external appearances, titles, and the brick-and-mortar of Meeting Houses. Its true foundation—the rock upon which Quakers have built their lives—is sacred silence and interior transformation, no matter the outer garments and street address.

My favorite analogy of a seasoned Friend or Quaker elder is a geode. A geode is dull on the surface, not much to see. Geodes are often passed over as plain rocks. They don't dazzle or demand attention; they are inconspicuous, homely, humble, unassuming— and yet at the same time, grace-filled and extraordinary, for beneath the surface layer of rock are rows of colorful crystals that gloriously refract light. The "human geodes" in plain clothing drew me to seek Quaker membership decades ago, and the many Quaker "geodes" I have encountered through the years compel me to celebrate both their quiet inner work and their outer work in solidarity with marginalized people.

We contemplatives have not inherited a spirit of timidity and skepticism, but of boldness and strength of purpose (2 Timothy 1:7). We are confident in our forms of silent prayer, which have ignited the missions of Apostles before us. And we are forthright in the Light of Christ, called to shine in our lives and common work, destined to integrate the many branches of the one Vine (John 15:5).

And so, may we fan the flames of that calling in formal and informal ways, with both Friends and friends. Together, may we cultivate Christ's Real Presence within and make our home there. May that Light shine forth from us, bringing transformation, purpose, and zeal to individuals and communities.

Deep within us all
there is an amazing inner sanctuary of the soul,
a holy place, a Divine Centre, a speaking voice,
to which we may continuously return.
Eternity is at our hearts, pressing upon our time-torn lives,
warming us with intimations of an astounding destiny,
calling us home unto itself . . .
the Light, the Seed, the Sanctuary.

—Thomas Kelly[367]

Acknowledgments

I thank all who have believed in my writing and who've encouraged me to write. Specifically, I thank the Recover Christianity's Mystic Roots network; Rich Lewis and I have worked together and known a synergy greater than we could achieve individually. I give thanks for David Sanford, my cheerleader from the start, a selfless networking genius who passed last year. Thanks to Margery Post Abbott, a contemplative artist, for her eloquent and intimate foreword to this book. Margery has contributed to many Quaker publications through the years, and I am a fan of her writing, especially her open forthright words on Quaker mysticism. Thanks also to Max Carter, for writing his foreword. Max went through the early manuscript chapter by chapter, then emailed his feedback. During our correspondence, Max introduced me to relevant books, videos, online resources, and people, who enliven the manuscript. Thanks to my friend Bill Ehri, who is a lifelong Quaker and co-clerk of a Friends Meeting in Washington State. Bill was a reader of an early draft of my manuscript.

Many thanks to my wife, Trees, for revising multiple drafts and overhauling the citations. She was a tireless enthusiast for the work and brought needed clarity to the book's scholarship. Trees celebrates our Quaker friends and community.

I give a special thank-you to my publisher, Anamchara Books. I appreciate executive editor Ellyn Sanna's down-to-earth, no-nonsense approach and her dedication to mystical works.

I thank my community of contemplatives, my Friends, my Quaker Meeting. I feel their support in the background and their complimentary dedication to the inner life, as opposed to outward appearances. Their numerous examples of patience, integrity, and service light my path. They humble and deepen my spirit.

Appendix

Quaker History, Terminology, and Modern-Day Forms

The term *Quaker* was originally used derisively by critics. According to George Fox's autobiography,[368] the word *Quaker* came about when he was brought to court on a charge of religious blasphemy; the magistrate used the term, said Fox, "because I bade them tremble at the word of the Lord" (referring, perhaps, to Isaiah 66:2 and Ezra 9:4). Many early Friends did in fact tremble in their Meetings and showed other physical manifestations of spiritual experience.[369] Although *Quaker* was originally used in a derogatory way, the community accepted it as their own.

George Fox and his wife Margaret Fell Fox and other early Quakers embodied the resounding rhythms of the Protestant Reformation, including Martin Luther's "priesthood of all believers."[370] Since then, Quakers have continued to emphasize individual conscience and personal experience, rather than mediated or secondhand experiences. No intermediary is required to commune with the Divine.

Terms

- *Friends* are formal members of the Religious Society of Friends (Quakers).

- *friends* (lowercase) are people who are not Quaker members but who identify with Quakerism's essence, which informs their faith. These are neo-Quakers, informal friends, or friends by association.

- *Seasoned Friends* or *weighty Friends* are wise people who have been Quakers for years, but not necessarily in any formal capacity. Quaker "elders" often have formal responsibilities that go with this title.

Four Forms of Modern Quakerism

- Friends General Conference (FGC)

- Friends United Meeting (FUM)

- Evangelical Friends International (EFI)

- Conservative Friends.[371]

There is no need to go into particulars about these four Quaker denominations, except to say that Unprogrammed denominations (FGC and Conservative Friends) emphasize extended collective silences and waiting worship, while the Programmed branches (FUM and EFI) have a worship style comparable to other mainline Protestant denominations. Many FUM and EFI worshiping communities honor varying degrees of worshipful silence, such as silent pauses during worship, and centering prayer groups. For our purposes, when I refer to Quakerism, my affinity is with the Unprogrammed branches (while wholeheartedly affirming our Programmed sisters and brothers in faith, which, in the spirit of George Fox, have a great deal to teach about evangelism). There is much diversity among Friends within the context of a larger unity.

Convergent Friends

Some upstarts who seek to build bridges between the denominations are referred to as *Convergent Friends*. Convergent Friends are interested in open dialogue assisted by the internet. They interact between the various branches of Friends, which stretch across numerous divergent traditions, theologies, and polity. Convergent Friends have the courage to hold creative tension and stretch the comfort zone of dialogue. In other words, Convergent Friends are a community formed more by dialogue than common understanding, more interested in conversation than in conclusions. They practice Quakerism in dialogue with divergent elements of the tradition and with high-tech postmodern culture.

Notes

Author Disclaimer

1. Thomas Kelly, "The Gathered Meeting," *Quaker Spirituality: Selected Writings*, Douglas V. Steere, ed. (Mahwah, NJ: Paulist Press, 1984), 313.

Introduction

2. Richard Rohr, "Mysticism in Religion: Three Ways to View the Sunset," *HuffPost* (February 11, 2011), https://www.huffpost.com/.

3. Harvey D. Egan, *What Are They Saying About Mysticism* (Eugene, OR: Wipf and Stock, 2021), 2.

4. Pew Research Center, "In U.S., Church Attendance Is Declining," *Pew Research Center* (October 16, 2019), https://www.pewresearch.org/fact-tank/.

5. Russell Heimlich, "Mystical Experiences," *Pew Research Center* (December 29, 2009), https://www.pewresearch.org/fact-tank/. Researchers are also now investigating mysticism as a legitimate area of scientific study from various perspectives, including psychological, neurological, and quantum physical (see John Hurgan's "Rational Mysticism" in the *New York Times*, March 23, 2003, https://www.nytimes.com/).

6. This is my paraphrase of Rahner's quote: "The devout Christian of the future will either be a 'mystic,' one who has experienced 'something,' or he will cease to be anything at all." See Mary Steinmetz, "Thoughts

on the Experience of God in the Theology of Karl Rahner: Gifts and Implications," *Lumen et Vita* 12 (1: 2012), 1; also, Karl Rahner, *Theological Investigations VII*, David Bourke, trans. (New York: Herder and Herder, 1971), 15.

7. Thomas Merton is often credited with initiating this change, particularly in American Christianity, with his interest in Eastern religions (see Egan, p. 61). The *New York Times* noted this trend in a 1977 article, "Neglected and Forgotten Spiritual Traditions Are Being Restored" by Kenneth A. Briggs, available from the *Times'* online archive, https://www.nytimes.com/1977/12/04/archives/.

8. While may people are familiar with individual mystics such as Julian of Norwich, Meister Eckhart, and Hildegard of Bingen, community mysticism is often overlooked. Quakers are not the only society of mystics in Western Christian tradition (the authors of *The Philokalia* are one such community, the Desert Fathers and Mothers a second, the Beguines of medieval Europe are a third, and there are others), but few such societies within Protestant tradition come close to the numbers, longevity, and well-defined mystical theology of the Quakers.

9. This collective waiting on the Light should be differentiated from Eastern meditation. Informed Quakers I have talked to, such as Max Carter who wrote a foreword for this book, understand the aim of Quakers' corporate waiting worship to be "a single dialogue between Creator and community." This is in contrast to Eastern meditation, such as Goenka-style Vipassana, which is understood as individual, even when meditation is practiced in the presence of others.

10. Quakers often use the phrase "silent worship" to characterize their form of worship, which they practice on Sunday mornings at silent Meetings for Worship. The phrases "expectant worship" and "waiting worship" are also used. See *Quaker Faith and Practice,* 5th edition (London: Religious Society of Friends, 2015), 26, 29, and 31. See also Caroline Stephen, *Quaker Strongholds* (Wallingford, PA: Pendle Hill, 1951), 56–57.

11. With only marginal numbers, Quakers brought about sweeping prison reforms in the UK, women's rights to vote and the abolition of slavery in the U.S., and advances in nonviolence, conflict mediation, and the disarmament of nuclear weapons. They also promoted education for those on the margins, including people with disabilities and minorities. Of course, reformers never get it all right. For example, solitary confinement was a Quaker prison reform. The intentions behind the reform were good but when implemented, proved psychologically

disastrous. (For a good reference on English Quaker prison reform, see Robert Alan Cooper, "The English Quakers and Prison Reform 1809–23," *Quaker History* 68 (1: 1979).)

12. These guidelines, as well as the other information in this section, are provided by the organization that Father Keating founded, Contemplative Outreach, https://www.contemplativeoutreach.org/history-of-centering-prayer/.

13. Pink Dandelion, *The Quakers: A Very Short Introduction* (Oxford, UK: Oxford University Press, 2008), 48.

14. Dan Wilson, *Promise of Deliverance* (Wallingford, PA: Pendle Hill, 1951), 17.

15. Rupert Jones in *Quaker Faith and Practice,* 44.

Chapter 1: Holy Silence

16. J. Brent Bill, *Holy Silence: The Gift of Quaker Spirituality* (Grand Rapids, MI: Eerdmans, 2016), xvi.

17. "Noise Pollution," *National Geographic,* https://education.nationalgeographic.org/resource/noise-pollution/.

18. Quentin Bell, *Virginia Woolf: A Biography* (New York: Harcourt, Brace, Jovanovich, 1974), 6.

19. Caroline Stephen, *Quaker Strongholds* (Wallingford, PA: Pendle Hill, 1951), 4.

20. Ibid., 93.

21. Ibid., 144.

22. Alison M. Lewis, "A Quaker Influence on Modern English Literature: Caroline Stephen and Her Niece, Virginia Woolf," *Type and Shadows* (September 2002), https://quaker.org/legacy/fqa/types/t21-woolf.html.

23. I took silent retreats at Benedict's Monastery in Snowmass, Colorado; Guadalupe Monastery in Lafayette, Oregon; and the Desert House of Prayer in Tucson, Arizona.

24. Thomas Keating, *Invitation to Love: The Way of Christian Contemplation* (New York: Continuum, 2000), 90. Silence being God's first language is also a concept found centuries ago in the writings of both Gregory the Great and John of the Cross.

25. The ancient English monastic text titled *The Cloud of Unknowing* is the basis of the contemporary centering prayer movement embodied by Thomas Keating and Contemplative Outreach, Ltd. *The Cloud of Unknowing* was essentialized by Benedictine Monk William Menninger and popularized by Benedictine Monks Basil Pennington and Thomas Keating.

26. Thomas R. Kelly, *A Testament of Devotion* (New York: HarperOne, 1996), 118–119.

27. The word "discipline" and the word "disciple" have the same root.

28. J. Brent Bill, *Holy Silence: The Gift of Quaker Spirituality* (Grand Rapids, MI: Eerdmans, 2016), 6.

29. Of course, the decision to be inner directed as opposed to outer directed is not the abandonment of all outward laws. It is simply a reorientation toward Divine inner-direction.

30. Stephen, 20.

31. William Penn, *Advice of William Penn to His Children* (Philadelphia: Franklin Roberts, 1881), available online at http://www.qhpress.org/quakerpages/qwhp/advice2.htm.

32. Stephen, 144.

Chapter 2: Settling into Silence

33. William Penn, *Selected Works of William Penn, Volume 3* (London: William Phillips and George Yard, 1825), 461.

34. Elizabeth Gilbert, *Eat, Pray, Love: One Woman's Search for Everything* (New York: Penguin, 2007), 138. For more on this topic, see Jennifer Shannon's *Don't Feed the Monkey Mind: How to Stop the Cycle of Anxiety, Fear, and Worry* (New York: New Harbinger, 2017).

35. Søren Kierkegaard, *Purity of Heart Is to Will One Thing* (New York: Simon & Schuster, 2012).

36. William Johnston, *Christian Zen: A Way of Meditation* (New York: Fordham University Press, 1997), 111.

37. Caroline Stephen, *Light Arising: Thoughts on the Central Radiance* (London: Heffer & Sons, 1908), 66–67.

38. Stephen, *Light Arising*, 22.

39. Davide Melodia, "The Lord of Silence," Simon Grant, trans. (1992), available online at http://www.simongrant.org/quaker/melodia/silence/. Melodia was an Italian Quaker who died in 2006.

Chapter 3: Waiting and Listening

40. George Fox, *George Fox: The Journal* (New York: Penguin, 1999), 79.

41. Ben Handy, "The Importance of Noise During Silent Worship," *Friends Journal* (February 1, 2020), https://www.friendsjournal.org/.

42. Traditionally, Quakers talked about "waiting on the Lord." There is a diversity of theologies among Quakers. So, many would phrase this differently today. Some wait on the Spirit and others wait in the silence without identifying any particular theology, just trusting in the waiting worship in stillness and silence.

43. Francis Howgill, *Observations on the Operation of the Holy Spirit upon the Mind of Man* (Hobart, NY: James Ross, 1834), 16.

44. Thomas R. Kelly, *A Testament of Devotion* (New York: HarperOne, 1996), 91, 92

45. Advent is the four weeks/Sundays of waiting in the liturgical church calendar year that precede Christmas Day.

46. Søren Kierkegaard, *Christian Discourses,* Walter Lowrie, trans. (New York: Oxford University Press, 1940), 4.

47. Søren Kierkegaard, *Kierkegaard for the Church: Essays and Sermons,* ed. Ronald F. Marshall, ed. (Eugene, OR: Wipf & Stock, 2013), 229. This quotation appears in various forms and translations; I have adapted this one slightly for clarity.

48. Kelly, 85–86.

49. This story can be traced back to the Buddha. See *The Śūrangama Sūtra: A New Translation with Excerpts from the Commentary by the Venerable Master Hsüan Hua* (Ukiah, CA: Buddhist Text Translation Society, 2009), Kindle locations 1542–1548.

50. *George Fox: The Journal*, 17.

51. Ibid., 83.

52. Ibid.

53. D. Elton Trueblood. "A Radical Experiment" (Philadelphia: William

Penn Lecture, 1947).

54. William Penn, *A Brief Account of the Rise and Progress of the People Called Quakers* (Philadelphia: Solomon W. Conrad, 1803), 61.

55. William Charles Braithwaite, *Spiritual Guidance in the Experience of the Society of Friends* (London: Swarthmore Lecture, 1909).

56. Dandelion, 53.

57. Trueblood.

58. Stephen, *Quaker Strongholds*, 55.

Chapter 4: Words into the Silence

59. Noah Baker Merrill, *Prophets, Midwives, and Thieves: Reclaiming the Ministry of the Whole* (Melbourne Beach, FL: Southeastern Yearly Meeting Publications, 2013).

60. These words were recorded by Margaret Fell after George Fox had visited her church; *Faith & Practice*, 19.07. I have "modernized" the archaic pronouns and verb forms here and also in many other seventeenth-century quotes throughout this book.

Chapter 5: Built on Love

61. Rufus Jones, *The Inner Life* (New York: Macmillan, 1916), 68.

62. Jones, *Finding the Trail of Life* (Tamil Nadu, India: Isha Books, 2013), 120–123.

63. Jones, *Social Law in the Spiritual World: Studies in Human and Divine Interrelationship* (New York: Swarthmore Press, 1904).

64. Jones, *Pathways to the Reality of God* (New York: Macmillan, 1931), 48–49.

65. Jones, *A Dynamic Faith* (London: Headley, 1901).

66. Jones, *Social Law in the Spiritual World*, 167–168. Jones acknowledged that "the term 'Inner Light' is older than Quakerism, and the idea which is thus named was not new when George Fox began to preach it. But this idea received a meaning and an emphasis from the Quakers which make it their own peculiar principle and their distinct contribution to religious thought."

67. Information about volunteering with the AFSC is posted at http://

www.afsc.org/jobs/ht/d/sp/i/46346/pid/46346/TPL/Jobs/displaytype/ raw. The Friends Committee on National Legislation needs volunteers to make phone calls to activists in important congressional districts; you can join their list of volunteers by sending an email to field@fcnl. org or going to http://fcnl.org/about/jobs/volunteer/. To find out about other opportunities for service through Quaker organizations, go to the Quaker Information Center, https://quakerinfo.org/service/volunteer. Other Quaker organizations, including the Friends Committee on National Legislation and the Friends Disaster Service, also carry out the Quaker expression of holistic mysticism. And you do not have to be a Quaker to volunteer with these organizations! There are many books that emphasize the service arm of the Quakers, but the unique angle of this book is the contemplation and mysticism. This aspect is often misunderstood and sidelined as impractical, yet without it, social servants court burnout and may end up going through the motions. Without the inspiration of deep interior work, activists lack the wisdom and courage to make substantial systemic changes.

68. Jones, *Rufus Jones Speaks* (Brooklyn, NY: Leonard S. Kenworthy, 1951), 4.

Chapter 6: The Seed of Christ

69. *George Fox Journal*, 367.

70. This is a phrase used throughout Margaret Fell's letters. See Elsa F. Glines, ed., *Undaunted Zeal: The Letters of Margaret Fell* (Richmond, IN: Friends United Press, 2003).

71. Isaac Penington, *The Works of Isaac Penington Vol. 3* (Philadelphia, PA: Friends Book Store, 1863), 485.

72. In the Eastern church silent prayer is most often referred to as *hesychia*, which is translated as inner stillness, quiet, tranquility, and watchfulness. Sometimes *Philokalia* authors refer to hesychia as "blessed stillness" (see, for example, *Philokalia vol. II*, 317).

73. *Philokalia vol. I*, 194 and 303; *vol. II*, 169, 245, and 381; *vol. III*, 314.

74. Quoted from Fox's journal in *The Story of George Fox* by Rufus Jones (New York: Macmillan, 1922), 37.

75. Donald X. Burt, *Day by Day with Saint Augustine* (Collegeville, MN: Liturgical Press, 2006), 27–28.

76. Meister Eckhart, *The Complete Mystical Works of Meister Eckhart*,

translated by Maurice O'Connell. Walshe (Chestnut Ridge, PA: Crossroad: 2009), 310.

77. This is another term Margaret Fell frequently used in her letters.

78. Isaac Penington, *Memoirs of the Life of Isaac Penington* (Philadelphia, PA: Kite, 1831), 32. (I have replaced archaic pronouns and verb forms with their modern versions.)

79. Ibid.

80. Our integrity may not always measure up to external standards. Yet, when we come to terms with ourselves, we know the nature of the curveballs thrown at us and what we have had to contend with. Our conscience and our intimacy with God have the last word, not sometimes-arbitrary external authorities.

81. Epistle 181 (1659) found in Steere, *Quaker Spirituality*, 132.

82. Penington, 148.

83. Ibid.

84. Abraham J. Heschel, "The Older Person and the Family in Perspective," in *Aging and the Human Spirit: A Reader in Religion and Gerontology*, edited by C. LeFevre and P. LeFevre (Chicago: Exploration Press, 1985), 42.

85. An example of a holon sequence would be: electron, atom, molecule, cell, tissue, organ, system, body, family, local community, county, state, nation, continent, Planet Earth, Milky Way galaxy, universe. For more on holons, see Ken Wilbur. *A Brief History of Everything* (Shambhala, 2000), 23–24.

86. Carol Reilley Ulmer in *Faith and Practice* (2018 version), 170.

87. Jens Soering, "Fighting for the Light in the Darkest Places: A Personal Vision Statement," *Scribd, Jens Soering Media Kit*, https://www.scribd.com/document/337610745/Jens-Soering-Media-Kit#.

88. *Thomas Keating: Rising Tide of Silence*, directed by Elena Mannes and Peter C. Jones (Syndicado: 2013).

89. Quoted in *Faith and Practice* (London: Yearly Meeting, 1995).

90. Anna-Teresa Tymienniecka, ed., *Analecta Husserliana: The Yearbook of Phenomenological Research, Volume LIII* (New York: Springer Science, 1994), 313.

91. Blaise Pascal, *Pensées* (New York: E. P. Dutton, 1958), 425.

92. Thomas Kelly, *The Eternal Promise* (Richmond, IN: Friends United Press, 2008), 55.

93. Robert McAfee Brown, *The Bible Speaks to You* (Louisville, KY: Westminster John Knox, 1955), 9. Editor's note: For some reason, this quote is commonly attributed to Thomas Merton, but as best we can determine, this is the actual source.

94. The Song of Songs is a book in the Hebrew scriptures that equates the search for God to a romantic courting and erotic intimacy. Christian mystics through the ages have seen their spiritual journey mirrored in its prose. I recommend *The Song of Songs: A New Translation* by Marcia Falk (Harper San Francisco, 1993).

95. Ayesha Clark-Halkin Imani, *Faith and Practice,* Philadelphia Yearly Meeting, 2018.

96. Robert Barclay, *The True Christian Divinity* (Manchester, UK: William Irwin, 1850), 175.

97. Penington, 185.

Chapter 7: Real Presence

98. Keri Weems, *Rhythms of Grace: Discovering God's Tempo for Your Life* (Grand Rapids, MI: Zondervan, 2014), 119.

99. Kelly, *The Eternal Promise,* 39.

100. Quakers had two objections to paying government taxes (tithes) to support an institutional church whose faith and practice conflicted with their own. First, they objected to being forced to support a church structure not of their own choice. Second, they recognized that the institution put individuals in the clergy who had no authentic call to or gifts for ministry. These individuals claimed an exclusive qualification for the ministry that Quakers rejected.

101. Margaret Fell Fox, *Undaunted Zeal: The Letters of Margaret Fell*, Elsa F. Glines, ed. (Richmond, IN: Friends United Press, 2003).

102. For more information see "Free Ministry," in *Quaker Strongholds* by Caroline Stephen, 93: "At the root of our abstinence from all these generally accepted practices [including paid clergy], there lies the one conviction of the all-sufficiency of individual and immediate communication with the Father of our spirits." A frequent criticism of

paid clergy was that they were "professors" rather than "possessors" of what they preached. In other words, they professed the Word but did not own it for themselves. They had not internalized the Word. They held the Word at a more or less academic arm's length.

103. Kelly, 8.

104. See Thomas Kelly, "Holy Obedience" (Philadelphia: William Penn Lecture, 1939).

105. If I were to summarize the Christian spiritual journey it is to move from self-centered and self-absorbed to Christ-centered.

106. William Taber, *Four Doors to Meeting for Worship* (Wallingford, PA: Pendle Hill Pamphlets, 1992), introduction.

107. Thomas Keating, "Talk One: The Divine Economy," *Unity in Contemplation: Talks on the Spiritual Journey* (Austin, TX: Contemplative Outreach, February 20–21, 2009), https://www.youtube.com/watch?v=H4JseJyKI50.

108. Kallistos Ware, *The Orthodox Way* (Yonkers, NY: St. Vladimir's Press, 1995), 47–48.

109. This is sometimes referred to as the Taborian Light, the "uncreated light" that enveloped Jesus at his transfiguration on Mount Tabor, which is recorded in the Gospels (Matthew 17:1–13, Mark 9:2–30).

110. See McGinn, "The God Beyond God," *The Essential Writings of Christian Mysticism* (New York: Modern Library, 2006).

111. Kelly, *The Eternal Promise*, 40.

112. Jones, *Finding The Trail of Life*, 18–19.

113. This reverberation may not conform to the standards of our society. And we may have profound personal faults and failures yet we still embody what the Bible refers to as "integrity of heart" (Psalm 78:72). This phrase was used to describe King David, who had many personal failures (2 Samuel 11); nonetheless, he had symmetry with God's heart.

114. Of course we work toward the life we want and set goals to get there. Yet, we also must humbly accept our life as it is in this moment, no matter the circumstances.

115. Oliver Clement, *The Roots of Christian Mysticism* (Hyde Park, NY: New City Press, 1993), 116.

116. Kelly, 117

117. Claire Buchanan, "A Water Quality Binning Method to Infer Phytoplankton Community Structure and Function." *Estuaries and Coasts*, 43, no. 4 (2020): 661–679. See also "Save the Plankton, Breathe Freely," National Geographic Resource Library.

118. Kelly, 3.

Chapter 8: Group Mysticism

119. Kelly, *The Eternal Promise,* 64, 66–67.

120. Howard Brinton, *Quaker Journals: Varieties of Religious Experiences Among Friends* (New York: Church Publishing, 1983), 11.

121. Ursula Jane O'Shea in *Faith and Practice* (Philadelphia, PA: Friends Publications, 2018), VI Extracts from the Writings of Friends.

122. Kelly, *Reality of the Spiritual World and the Gathered Meeting* (London: Quaker Home Service, 1996), 12.

123. William Taber, *Four Doors to Meeting for Worship* (Wallingford, PA: Pendle Hill Pamphlets, 1992).

124. Kelly, *The Eternal Promise,* 44.

125. Marcelle Martin, *Our Life Is Love: The Quaker Spiritual Journey* (San Francisco, CA: Inner Light, 2016) and *A Guide to Faithfulness in Groups* (San Francisco, CA: Inner Light, 2019).

126. Thomas Jeavons in *Faith and Practice* (Philadelphia, PA: 2017), 99.

127. Parker Palmer, *A Hidden Wholeness: The Journey Toward an Undivided Live* (New York: Wiley, 2022), 55.

128. Palmer, *A Place Called Community* (Wallingford, PA: Pendle Hill, 1977), 27.

129. Martin Buber, *I and Thou* (New York: Charles Scribner's Sons, 1970), 11–19.

130. Marcelle Martin, "A Community Formed for Faithfulness," *Friends Journal* (September 1, 2017), https://www.friendsjournal.org/.

131. Martin, *A Whole Heart* (blog, 2012), https://awholeheart.com/about/.

132. Ibid.

133. Rufus Jones, *Finding the Trail of Life* (London: George Allen & Unwin, 1926), 89.

134. Calvin Keene, *Daily Readings from Quaker Writings,* Linda Hill Renfer (Perth, Australia: Serenity Press, 1989), 5th month, 3.

135. *Tao Ching.* The word Lao-Tzu used for "Way" was Tao, the path that leads to harmony, the guiding principle of all reality. Compare to Jesus' words in John 14:6: "I am the way, the truth, and the light."

136. Howard Brinton, *Reaching Decisions: The Quaker Method* (Wallingford, PA: Pendle Hill, 1952), 18.

137. Of course, there are many others who I will not name here for the fear of leaving any out, yet we have to start somewhere, and these four are the best start I know.

138. The saying didn't originate with Newton. Before Newton, the twelfth-century theologian and author John of Salisbury wrote, "We are like dwarfs sitting on the shoulders of giants. We see more, and things that are more distant, than they did, not because our sight is superior or because we are taller than they, but because they raise us up, and by their great stature add to ours." See Gary Martin, *The Phrase Finder,* https://www.phrases.org.uk/meanings/268025.html.

139. Parker J. Palmer in *Faith and Practice: A Book of Christian Discipline* (Philadelphia, PA: Friends Publications, 1997), 105.

Chapter 9: Original Blessing

140. Jones, *Faith and Practice of the Quakers,* 44.

141. Augustine, *City of God* (Liverpool, UK: Liverpool University Press, 2014), see chapters 2.3 and 6.4.

142. John Calvin expanded upon Augustine's doctrine; see John Calvin, *Institutes of Christian Religion,* translated by Henry Beveridge (Peabody, MA: Hendrickson, 2009), xv. Even so, the more moderate in Christian tradition, specifically the Orthodox, have always maintained that yes, the Divine image in people was obscured but not obliterated.

143. The Greeks called the Word the *Logos.* The Logos was the self-organizing principle of creation and the cosmos.

144. Hannah Whitall Smith, *The Christian's Secret of a Happy Life* (Chicago: Fleming Revell, 1883), 49.

145. Ibid., 168.

146. Smith, *My Spiritual Biography: How I Discovered the Unselfishness of God* (Chicago: Revell, 1903), 214.

147. *Secret of a Happy Life,* 42.

148. Portions of Hannah's letters are recorded in Kent Brandenburg's *Hannah Whitall Smith: Quaker and Universalist,* published online by *Faith Saves* (accessed August 19, 2023), https://faithsaves.net/.

149. Uncreated Light of Christ is referred to as Taborian Light or the Light of Tabor. It is so named because the essence of God is Light and is uncreated. When Jesus was transfigured in the Gospels, that Light shone from Mount Tabor (Matthew 17:1–9, Mark 9:2–8, Luke 9:28–36). Taborian Light underpins the theology of the Eastern church, and it is this Light that blinded Saint Paul and threw him from his high horse. In the Eastern church in the tenth century, this Light also transformed Simeon the New Theologian in a vision. Many other saints and prophets through the ages have seen and been changed by the Uncreated Light.

150. Danielle Shroyer, *Original Blessing: Putting Sin in Its Rightful Place* (Minneapolis, MN: Fortress Press, 2016), xi.

Chapter 10: Scripture and the Spirit

151. Elton Trueblood in *Quaker Quotations on Faith and Practice,* edited by Leonard S. Kenworth (Kennett Square, PA: Quaker Publications, 1983), 37.

152. Calvin Keene, *God in Thought and Experience* (Newberg, OR: Quaker Theological Discussion Group, 1981), 17.

153. Howard Brinton quoted in *Howard and Anna Brinton: Re-inventors of Quakerism In the Twentieth Century, An Interpretive Biography* by Anthony Manousos (Philadelphia, PA: FGC Quaker Books, 2013).

154. Brinton, "The Place of Quakerism in Modern Christian Thought," *Friends Journal* (January 10, 1959).

155. Brinton, *The Nature of Quakerism* (Wallingford, PA: Pendle Hill, 1949), pamphlet no. 47.

156. Stephen, *Quaker Strongholds*, 28.

157. Ibid., 171–173, 186–187.

158. *George Fox Journal*, 200.

159. *George Fox Journal*, 17 and Epistle 197 (1660) found in Steere, *Quaker Spirituality*, 132.

160. Quoted in *Elias Hicks: Quaker Liberal* by Bliss Forbush (New York: Columbia University Press, 1956).

161. *George Fox Journal*, 136.

162. The root word of Bible is *biblio,* referring to a library of many scrolls; the early church eventually merged all the scrolls into a single book—today's Bible.

163. *George Fox Journal*, 34.

164. I expand on the important role of stillness and silence in the Bible in my book *Be Still and Listen* (Paraclete Press, 2018).

165. This is recorded in George Fox's *Journal,* xl. Margaret Fell later became George Fox's wife.

166. It would be easier on our minds to cancel out some portions of scripture, like Martin Luther attempted to do when he wrote that the Book of James is an "epistle of straw" and even advocated for its removal from the cannon. For more on this, see Brian Johnston, *The Book of James: Epistles of Straw?* (Swindon, UK: Hayes Press, 2014).

167. *George Fox Journal*, 136.

168. Bernard McGinn, *The Essential Writings of Christian Mysticism* (New York: Modern Library, 2006), 3.

169. Jones, *Faith and Practice of the Quakers,* 43.

170. Epistle 65 (1654) found in Steere, *Quaker Spirituality*, 130.

Chapter 11: Mystery and the Nature of God

171. Jonathan Hewett, "Embracing Uncertainty," *The Friend* (1990), 757.

172. Yukio Irie, "The Way of Divine Mystery," in *Pilgrimage Toward the Fountainhead: Quakerism and Zen Buddhism Today* (Toorak, Australia: Religious Society of Friends, 1973), 27.

173. Irie in *Quaker Faith & Practice*, 5th edition (London: Religious Society of Friends, 2023), 27.09.

174. Irie, *Emerson and Quakerism* (Wallingford, PA: Pendle Hill, 1957).

175. Ibid., 29–30.

176. The four letters, YHWH, are referred to as the Tetragrammaton.

177. For more on this, see: E. C. B. MacLaurin, "YHWH, the Origin of the Tetragrammaton," *Vetus Testamentum 12* (4: 1962), 439–463; Raymond Abba, "The Divine Name Yahweh," *Journal of Biblical Literature 80* (4: 1961), 320–328; Robert D. Miller, *Yahweh: Origin of a Desert God* (Gottingen, Germany: Vandenhoeck & Ruprecht, 2021); Harold Bloom, *Jesus and Yahweh: The Names Divine* (New York: Riverhead, 2011).

178. Rex Ambler, *The Quaker Way: A Rediscovery* (Winchester, UK: John Hunt, 2013), n.p.

179. Elizabeth Watson, "Your Good Is Too Small" (1996), https://quaker.org/legacy/quakernature/Qvisionsquotes.html.

180. This phrase originated with Gregory of Nyssa, the fourth-century church father. In Gregory's *The Life of Moses,* he wrote about the encounter with the mystery of God as three stages: light, cloud, and darkness. Great mystics like Moses and John the Revelator penetrate "the luminous darkness," yet "no one has ever seen God "(John 1:18).

181. Faith & Play Working Group (Philadelphia: Philadelphia Yearly Meeting, 2008).

182. Irwin Abrams, *Daily Readings from Quaker Writings,* 1st Month, 3, https://www.quakercloud.org/.

183. Irie, "The Way of Divine Mystery," 30.

Chapter 12: Mindfulness and Inward Focus

184. Teresa of Avila, *The Collected Work of St. Teresa of Avila, Vol. 2* (Washington, DC: Institute of Carmelite Studies, 1976), 303.

185. Robert Griswold, *Faith and Practice* (Corvallis, OR: Friends Bulletin, 2018), 34.

186. Ana Smiljanic, trans., *Our Thoughts Determine Our Lives: The Life and Teachings of Elder Thaddeus of Vitovnica* (Platina, CA: St. Herman of Alaska Brotherhood, 2012).

187. Gil Scott-Heron, "The Revolution Will Not Be Televised" on *Small Talk at 125th and Lennox* (Flying Dutchman, 1970).

188. Elfrida Vipont Foulds, *Elfrida Vipont Foulds Speaks* (Philadelphia, PA: Quaker Press, 1982).

189. Foulds, *Faith and Practice* (2018), VI Extracts, 54.

190. *Elfrida Vipont Foulds Speaks.*

191. Christopher Holdsworth, *Daily Readings from the Quaker Writings* (Quote of the Week 07/14/19), https://www.quakercloud.org/.

192. Brother Lawrence, *Brother Lawrence: A Christian Zen Master* (Vestal, NY: Anamchara Books, 2016), 18, 36.

193. Ibid., 35.

194. Kelly, *A Testament of Devotion*, 95.

195. Heraclitus (535 to 475 BCE), *On Nature*, Fragment 91.

196. Josephine Duveneck, *Faith and Practice* (Corvallis, OR: Friends Bulletin, 2018), 36–37.

197. Brother Lawrence, 37.

Chapter 13: Silent Prayer

198. Thomas Kelly, *Reality of the Spiritual World* (Philadelphia, PA: Friends Home Service Committee, 1948), 53

199. *Faith and Practice* (Corvallis, OR: Friends Bulletin, 2018), 35.

200. *George Fox Journal*, 40–41, 221, and 310–311.

201. Ibid., xxvii and xliv.

202. *George Fox Journal*, xliv.

203. Teresa of Avila, *The Collected Works Volume One* (Washington, DC: Institute of Carmelite Studies, 1976), 194, 95.

204. Thomas Keating, *Open Mind, Open Heart: The Contemplative Dimension of the Gospel* (London: A&C Black, 2002), 44.

205. Ibid.

206. Keating, *Fruits and Gifts of the Spirit* (New York: Lantern, 2014), 5.

207. Neurologists used to speak of the three layers of our brains: the brainstem (reptilian brain), limbic system (emotions), and the cortex (complicated thoughts). However, modern neuroscience research has demonstrated that the triune brain theory does not accurately explain how the brain functions in everyday life or during the stress response. "Specifically, emotion and cognition are interdependent and work

together, the limbic system is not a purely emotional center nor are there purely emotional circuits in the brain, and the cortex is not a purely cognitive center nor are there purely cognitive circuits in the brain" (Patrick R. Steffen, Dawson Hedges, Rebekka Matheson, "The Brain Is Adaptive Not Triune," *Frontiers in Psychiatry 1* (April 2022), https://www.frontiersin.org/articles/10.3389/fpsyt.2022.802606/full. The metaphor of the reptilian brain remains a useful one, however, for helping us to better understand our reactions.

208. Kelly, *A Testament of Devotion*, 35.

209. Look online, and you'll find a host of silent retreat opportunities. Sites like this one (https://bookretreats.com/s/yoga-retreats/silent-retreats) list silent retreats from around the world, with various focuses. Remember, though, a silent retreat need not be expensive, nor does it need to be taken in some exotic location. The structure of a retreat house can be helpful, but with intention and discipline (and some help from friends and family), you might even go on a silent retreat in your own home.

210. Kelly, *The Eternal Promise*, 74.

211. Kelly, *A Testament of Devotion*, 36.

212. My use of the phrase *absolute consciousness* is very similar if not identical to Meister Eckhart's phrase, "Absolute Unity." See B. McGinn, "The God Beyond God," *The Essential Writings of Christian Mysticism*.

213. Holy people are important in many traditions, especially in the beginning and middle stages of spiritual development. It is the overreach of a holy person and over-reliance on a holy person, which inhibits self-reliance. And of this I am wary and skeptical.

214. In other words, Keating emphasized centering prayer within the context of contemplative Christianity in general, not Catholicism or monasticism in particular.

215. Athanasius, *The Life of Anthony* (Pickerington, OH: Beloved Publishing, 2015).

216. *Deification* is an Eastern Orthodox and Oriental Orthodox term, which basically asserts that God became human so that humans can become Divine. A synonym of deification is Christification, which means to become like Christ.

217. Kelly, *A Testament of Devotion*, 34.

218. Keating, *Centering Prayer in Daily Life and Ministry* (New York: Bloomsbury, 1997), 125.

Chapter 14: Persistence and Steadiness

219. Denis Waitley, *The Winner's Edge* (New York: Berkley, 1986), 13.

220. Thomas Kelly, *A Testament of Devotion,* 42.

221. Ibid.

222. Palmer, et al, *The Philokalia, Vol. 2,* 60, 81, 234, 258, 271, 320, 328, 329, and 349.

223. See, for example, Revelation 2:2 and 1 Peter 2:20.

224. Rachel R. Cadbury, *The Choice Before Us,* quoted in *Quaker Quotations on Faith and Practice,* 95.

225. *George Fox Journal,* 510.

226. Ibid., viii.

227. Ibid., 570.

228. Ibid., quoted in *Quaker Faith & Practice* (London, 2023), 20.23.

229. John Woolman, *John Woolman Journal* (New York: Houghton Mifflin, 1884), 172.

230. Tertullian, *Apologeticus* (Cambridge, UK : Cambridge University Press, 2012), L.13.

231. M. K. Gandhi, *The Power of Nonviolent Resistance (*New York: Penguin Classics, 2019).

232. Garrett A. Sullivan Jr., Alan Stewart, Rebecca Lemon, eds. *The Encyclopedia of English Renaissance Literature, Vol. 1 (*New York: Wiley, 2012), 336.

233. Henri Nouwen, *The Road to Daybreak* (New York: Doubleday, 1990).

234. Isaac Penington, *Memoirs of the Life of Isaac Penington* (London: Harvey and Darton, 1830), 58.

235. Elizabeth Gray Vining, *The World in Tune,* quoted in *Quaker Quotations on Faith and Practice,* 95.

Chapter 15: Deepening Self-Surrender

236. Rufus Jones, "The Vital Cell," (Philadelphia, PA: William Penn Lecture, 1949), available on line at https://quaker.org/legacy/pamphlets/wpl1941a.html.

237. Quoted in *Writings of Thomas Kelly*, Keith Beaseley-Topliffe, ed. (Nashville, TN: Upper Room, 2017), introduction.

238. Ibid. For this background on Thomas R. Kelly, I am indebted to both Beaseley-Topfliffe's biography and email conversations with Max Carter, who wrote part of this book's foreword.

239. William Blake, *Complete Writings* (London: Oxford University Press, 1966), 151.

240. Fox's letter to Lady Claypool, quoted in Rex Ambler's *Light to Live By: An Exploration of Quaker Spirituality* (Ypsilanti, MI: Quaker Books, 2011), 20.

241. Penington, *The Works of Isaac Penington, Vol. II* (Glenside, PA: Quaker Heritage Press, 1997), 297.

242. Kelly, *A Testament of Devotion*, 30.

243. Ibid., 45.

244. Rufus Jones, *The Inner Life* (New York: Macmillan, 1916), 12.

245. Kelly, *The Eternal Promise*, 18.

Chapter 16: Taking a Stand

246. *George Fox Journal*, 1.

247. Let us clarify that our society is in regression, and dysfunction is everywhere. The author Roberta Gilbert wrote about this with research to back it up. See Roberta Gilbert, *The Eight Concepts of Bowen Theory: A New Way of Thinking About the Individual and the Group* (Leading Systems Press, 2006).

248. Cynthia Bourgeault, *The Wisdom Jesus* (New York: Penguin, 2008), 30.

249. *Seasoned Friends* is a phrase that refers to long-standing members of Quaker Meetings. They are Friends who have been seasoned with experience and time.

250. Epistle 319 (1675) found in Steere, *Quaker Spirituality*, 135.

251. See also *George Fox Journal*, 35, 263, and 699–700.

252. This idea is also explored at length by Paul Tillich. See F. Forrester Church, *The Essential Tillich* (Chicago: University of Chicago Press, 1999), 50; and Paul Tillich, *Biblical Religion and the Search for Ultimate Reality* (Chicago: University of Chicago Press, 1964), 51 and 74.

253. Stephen Mitchell, ed., *The Enlightened Heart: An Anthology of Sacred Poetry* (New York: Harper & Row, 1989), 100.

254. Stephen, *Quaker Strongholds*, 136.

255. Jane Addams, "A Book That Changed My Life," *The Christian Century* 44 (Oct. 13, 1927), 1196.

256. Ann W. Duncan, "The Impossibility of Complacency: Scripture in the Life and Work of Jane Addams," *The Journal of Scriptural Reasoning 14* (2: 2015). Brandon Harnish also discusses this connection to the Social Gospel and Progressive movements and contrasts it to the Catholicism of the time in his article "Jane Addams's Social Gospel Synthesis and the Catholic Response," *The Independent Review* 16 (1: Summer 2011), 93–100.

257. Quoted in Victoria Bissell Brown, *The Education of Jane Addams* (Philadelphia: University of Pennsylvania Press, 2004), 250.

258. Addams, *The Excellent Becomes the Permanent* (Freeport, NY: Books for Libraries Press, 2008).

259. Duncan.

260. Addams, "A Book That Changed My Life."

261. Anne Firor Scott, *Making the Invisible Woman Visible* (Champagne: University of Illinois Press, 1984), 111.

262. Ibid.

263. Elizabeth Fry, *Elizabeth Fry Speaks* (Brooklyn, NY: Leonard Kenworthy, 1950), 6.

264. Ibid.

265. The foundational book, *Servant Leadership,* by Robert Greenleaf, emphasizes the genuine motivation of service instead of self-interest and self-promotion (Greenleaf Center, 2002).

266. William Penn, *No Cross, No Crown* (Shippensburg, PA: Destiny Image, 2001), 42.

Chapter 17: Quaker Nonviolence

267. *George Fox Journal*, 400–402.

268. See Rita Nakashima and Gabriella Lettini, *Soul Repair: Recovering from Moral Injury After War* (Boston: Beacon Press, 2013). In *War Is a Force That Gives Us Meaning* (Public Affairs, 2014), Chris Hedges make a strong argument for why war is hell. He bases his argument upon direct observations on the front lines of war-torn areas when he was a war correspondent.

269. Hoffman, "Compassionate Listening—First Step to Reconciliation?" talk give on November 25, 1997 at University of California, Santa Barbara. The quotes throughout this chapter are from this speech.

270. Quoted in "Gene Hoffman, Quaker Peace Activist, Rests in Peace," *LA Quaker* (July 23, 2010), http://laquaker.blogspot.com/2010/07/gene-hoffman-quaker-peace-activist.html.

271. To find out more, see https://www.compassionatelistening.org.

272. *George Fox Journal*, 406–407, 572.

273. Quaker Horace Alexander (1889–1989) worked with the British government and Gandhi in 1928 and 1930, serving as an intermediary for the transfer of power from the British government to the independent powers of India and Pakistan. For more information see Alexander's Pendle Hill pamphlet 165, "Gandhi Remembered" (1969).

274. Epistle 177 (1659) found in Steere, *Quaker Spirituality*, 132.

275. Early-church leader Tertullian forbade Christian soldiers to fight in war. The distortions and machinations of the ultraviolent Roman Empire changed this principle when, as Phyllis Tickle has said, the church first got in bed with government when the Emperor Constantine made Christianity legal in 313 CE.

276. Walter Wink, *Jesus and Nonviolence: A Third Way* (Minneapolis, MN: Fortress Press, 2003), 12.

277. One of the seminal books that exposed the conditions of farm animals in the United States is *Diet for a New America* by John Robbins (New York: Stillpoint, 1987).

278. Jeremy L. Conkle, Del Valle Christian D Báez, and Jeffrey W. Turner, "Are We Underestimating Microplastic Contamination in Aquatic Environments?" *Environmental Management 61* (1: 2018), 1–8.

279. Christina Gerhardt, "Pacific and Plastic: Midway Atoll, Plastiglomerate, and Love of Place," *Mosaic: A Journal for the Interdisciplinary Study of Literature 51* (3: 2018), 123–140.

280. The American Friends Service Committee (AFSC), brain child of Quaker mystic Rufus Jones, focuses on peace and justice, realizing that many of these issues are interconnected with environmental concerns. For more information, see wwwAFSC.org.

281. *George Fox Journal,* 2

282. Elise Boulding in an interview with Alan AtKisson, "Concentrating on Essence," *What Is Enough?* (Langley, WA: Context Institute, 1990), 52.

283. John Vidal, "'Environmental Taliban' Is the Latest in a Series of Insults Aimed at the Greens," *The Guardian* (October 19, 2022).

284. Carl G. Jung, *Man and His Symbols* (New York: Random House, 1964), 110.

285. Jung, *Aion: Researches into the Phenomenology of Self* (New York: Routledge, 2014 [reprint]), 9.

286. See D.G. Tendulkar, *Mahatma, Vol. 8, 1947–1948* (New Delhi: Government of India, 1954), 5, online at www.mkgandhi.org. For more information on this aspect of Gandhi's Satyagrahi philosophy, see Eknath Easwaran, *Gandhi the Man,* "The Way of Love" (Tomale, CA: Nilgiri Press, 1978), 39–102.

287. For more on the issue of scapegoating, see René Girard, *The Scapegoat* (Baltimore, MD: John Hopkins University Press, 1986).

288. Jones, *Faith and Practice of the Quakers,* 108–109.

289. William Penn, *Selected Works of William Penn* (London: William Phillips, 1825), 391.

Chapter 18: Integrity and Simplicity

290. Wilmer Cooper, *The Testimony of Integrity* (Wallingford, PA: Pendle Hill, 1991).

291. Quakers use *query* to refer to a question or series of questions used for spiritual reflection. Queries are tools that offer spiritual challenges; they often take the form of a collection of themed questions that are read at the beginning of a time of worship or reflection.

292. Elizabeth Watson, "Sexuality: A Part of Wholeness," conference

sponsored by the Family Relations Committee of Philadelphia Yearly Meeting (November 13, 1982); available online at https://quaker.org/legacy/sexuality/files/Watson-Wholeness.pdf.

293. Elizabeth Watson, in *Each of Us Inevitable,* Robert Leuze, ed. (New York: Friends for Lesbian, Gay, Bisexual, Transgender, and Queer Concerns, 2003), 4. This was taken from Watson's keynote address on February 20, 1977, at the gathering of the Friends Committee for Gay Concerns in New York City.

294. Fred Bratman, "A Daughter's Death, A Mother's Faith," *New York Times* (December 30, 1979), https://www.nytimes.com/. Implied in all the Quaker authors I have read is that every Quaker has a ministry or mission. A call to ministry is not reserved to clergy only; as with Watson, it extends to all members of the Society.

295. Stephen, *Quaker Strongholds,* 150–151.

296. One nice thing about writing is that a writer can never have a captive audience. Readers can stop reading at any moment. It is entirely consensual.

297. *George Fox Journal,* 1.

298. Ibid., 28.

299. Jones, *The Faith and Practice of the Quakers* (Kingsley, AU: Left Of Brain Onboarding Pty Limited, 2021), 92.

300. Stephen, *Quaker Strongholds,* 144.

301. Nicholas Burton and Mai Chi Vu, "Moral Identity and the Quaker Tradition: Moral Dissonance Negotiation in the Work Place," *Journal of Business Ethics 174* (1: 2021), 127–141.

302. Jones, *The Faith and Practice of the Quakers,* 90.

303. Watson, "Sexuality: A Part of Wholeness."

304. Cooper, *The Testimony of Integrity.*

Chapter 19: Courageous Love

305. Cecil Eugene Henshaw, *The Light Within as Redemptive Power* (Philadelphia, PA: Young Friends Movement, 1945), 29.

306. Elizabeth Fry, *Elizabeth Fry Speaks,* 2.

307. Ibid.

308. June Rose, *The Story of Elizabeth Fry* (Kendal, UK: Quaker Tapestry, 1994), 30.

309. Elizabeth Fry, *Memoir of the Life of Elizabeth Fry* (London: Charles Gilpin, 1847), 86.

310. The famous poem, "Footprints in the Sand," originally written by Mary Stevenson in 1939, comes to mind here.

311. *George Fox Journal*, 10.

312. *Elizabeth Fry Speaks*, 4.

313. John Woolman, *The Journal and Major Essays of John Woolman* (Richmond, IN: Friends United Press, 1989), 240.

Chapter 20: Abiding Joy

314. Kelly, *A Testament of Devotion*, 99.

315. Ibid., 267. I chose to change the spelling of principalities to modern English.

316. Glines, ed., *Undaunted Zeal*, 98–99.

317. Glines, ed., *Undaunted Zeal*, 4.

318. Marjon Ames, *Margaret Fell, Letters, and the Making of Quakerism* (London, UK: Routledge, 2017), 4.

319. Elise Boulding, "The Joy That Is Set Before Us," (Philadelphia, PA: William Penn Lecture, 1956), https://quaker.org/legacy/pamphlets/wpl1956a.html.

Chapter 21: Steady Stability

320. Kelly, *A Testament of Devotion*, 42

321. Parker Palmer, *A Hidden Wholeness: The Journey Toward an Undivided Life* (New York: Wiley, 2022), 58.

322. Henri Nouwen, *The Wounded Healer: Ministry in Contemporary Society* (New York: Crown, 1979), 91.

323. This concept is part of the known Quaker process, which harkens back to Stephen, *Quaker Strongholds*, 4.

324. Friedrich Nietzsche, *Twilight of the Idols* (Oxford, UK: Oxford University Press, 2008), 10.

325. See Thomas Keating. *The Spiritual Journey* (Snowmass, CO: Contemplative Outreach, 1992), transcript.

326. *George Fox Journal*, 10.

327. Edward Burrough, "Epistle to the Reader," in *The Works of George Fox, Vol. III* (Philadelphia: Marcus T. C. Gould, 1831), 13.

328. Palmer, et al, *The Philokalia Vol. 2*, 60, 81, 234, 258, 271, 320, 328, 329, and 349.

329. Doug Gwyn, "Qualities of Quaker Witness," *FGC*, https://www.fgcquaker.org/.

330. Lucretia Mott, quoted in Margaret Hope Bacon's *Valiant Friend: The Life of Lucretia Mott* (Philadelphia, PA: Quaker Press: 1999/1850).

331. Mott, speech given at the Seneca Falls Convention, 1848.

332. Mott in *Woman's Record, Or, Sketches of All Distinguished Women From the Creation to A.D. 1854: Arranged in Four Eras: with Selections from Female Writers of Every Age*, Sarah Josepha Buell Hale, ed. (New York: Harper, 1855), 752.

333. Mott, *Lucretia Mott Speaks: The Essential Speeches and Sermons* (Champagne: University of Illinois Press, 2017).

334. Quoted in "Friendly Voices," *Friends General Conference*, https://www.fgcquaker.org/exercises/friendly-voices/.

335. Epistle 194 (1660) found in Steere, *Quaker Spirituality*, 132.

Chapter 22: Deep Rest and Peace

336. William Penn, *William Penn's Advice to His Children,* chapter 2, http://www.qhpress.org/quakerpages/qwhp/advice2.htm.

337. Parker J. Palmer, *A Hidden Wholeness: The Journey Toward an Undivided Life* (Hoboken, NJ: Jossey-Bass, 2004).

338. "His [Jung's] overwhelming contribution to psychological understanding is his concept of the unconscious—not merely a sort of glory-hole of repressed desires, but a world that is just as much a vital and real part of the life of an individual as the conscious, 'cogitating' world of the ego, and infinitely wider and richer. The language and the 'people' of the unconscious are symbols, and the means of communications dreams." Carl Jung, *Man and His Symbols* (New York: Dell, 1968), viii. This is one of Jung's foundational pieces on dream work.

339. Through the Bible, dreams are sighted as warnings and communications from God. Twenty-one dreams are recorded in the Bible. Some of my favorites: Genesis 28:12, 37:1–10, 41; 1 Kings 3:5–15; Daniel 2; Matthew 1:18–24, 2, 27:19.

340. "Unfortunately, dreams are difficult to understand. As I have already pointed out, a dream is quite unlike a story told by the conscious mind ... dreams have a different texture. ... They do not make sense in terms of his normal walking experience, and he therefore is inclined either to disregard them or to confess that they baffle him." Jung, *Man and His Symbols*, 27.

341. If you are interested in reading a more thorough description of dream interpretation, Robert Johnson's *Inner Work: Using Dreams and Active Imagination for Personal Growth* (San Francisco, CA: HarperCollins, 2010) is an excellent resource.

342. Johnson, 2.

343. *George Fox Journal*, 64.

344. Seraphim of Sarov, "Concerning the Aim of the Christian Life," *Life and Teaching of Saint Seraphim of Sarov* (The Hague: Gozalov Books, 2014), 56, 58.

345. *Elizabeth Fry Speaks*, 2.

346. Boulding, *Cultures of Peace: The Hidden Side of History* (Syracuse, NY: Syracuse University Press, 2000), 29.

347. Boulding, *The Family as a Way Into the Future* (Wallingham, PA: Pendle Hill, 1978), pamphlet.

348. Boulding, 2.

Chapter 23: Purpose and Identity

349. Rufus Jones, "The Vital Cell," William Penn Lecture 1941, https://quaker. org/legacy/pamphlets/wpl1941a.html.

350. Emilia Fogelklou, *Reality and Radiance: Selected Autobiographical Works of Emilia Fogelklou,* Howard T. Lutz, trans. (Richmond, IN: Friends United Press, 1985); also quoted in *Quaker Faith & Practice*, 5th edition, 26.01, https://qfp.quaker.org.uk/chapter/26/. All quotations in this section are from Fogelklou's journal. (Note that she speaks of herself in the third person.)

351. Ibid.

352. Ibid.

353. Ibid.

354. Isaac Penington, *The Works of the Long Mournful And Sorely Distressed Isaac Penington Whom the Lord in His Tender Mercy, at Length Visited and Relieved by the Ministry of That Despised People Called Quakers and in the Springings of That Light, Life, and Holy Power in Him, Which They Had Truly and Faithfully Testified of, and Directed His Mind To, Were These Things Written and Are Now Published as a Thankful Testimony of the Goodness of the Lord unto Him, and for the Benefit of Others* (Farmington, ME: Quaker Heritage Press, 1995), 32, available online at http://www.qhpress.org/texts/penington/letter114.html/

355. Palmer, et al, *The Philokalia Vol. 1*, 95.

356. Jones, *Faith and Practice of the Quakers*, 45.

357. For more on this see the Netflix documentary directed by Jeff Orlowski, *The Social Dilemma* (Argent Pictures, 2020).

358. Thomas Kelly, *The Eternal Purpose* (Richmond, IN: Friends United Press, 1988), 53.

359. Ibid.

360. U2, "I Still Haven't Found What I'm Looking For," *The Joshua Tree* (Island Records, 1987).

361. Kelly, *Testament of Devotion*, 117.

Conclusion: Homecoming

362. Edward Burrough, *Quaker Center*, http://www.quakercenter.org/programs/quaker-quote-archive/.

363. Kelly, *The Eternal Promise*, 22.

364. Kelly, *A Testament of Devotion*, 74.

365. Saint Basil, Letter 2, Roy Deferrari (New York: Putnam, 1926). 12–14.

366. William Penn, *William Penn's Advice to His Children*, 2.1, available online at http://www.qhpress.org/quakerpages/qwhp/qwhp.htm.

367. Kelly, *A Testament of Devotion*, 3, 11.

Appendix: Quaker History, Terminology, and Modern-Day Forms

368. Fox's autobiography is available online at https://web.archive.org/web/20070926224431/http://www.strecorsoc.org/gfox/title.html.

369. Scott Martin. "'The Power,' Quaking, and the Rediscovery of Primitive Quakerism." *Friends Journal* (May 2001). When involuntary bodily tremors and even convulsions sometimes happen during centering prayer, Thomas Keating and contemporary centering prayer practitioners refer to the phenomena as "unloading." Unloading happens when in the silence and stillness we reach a higher degree of relaxation than what is possible during sleep. In the context of that deep relaxation the nervous system sometimes evacuates bodily tensions, and tremors are the side-effects. See Keating, *Invitation to Love*, 148.

370. Martin Luther (1483–1546) used the well-known phrase, "the priesthood of all believers" throughout the Protestant Reformation. Roland H. Bainton. *Christianity* (New York: Houghton, 1992), 253. See also 1 Peter 2:4–5.

371. FGC and Conservative Friends are closest to the Quakerism, and silent Meetings for Worship in particular, that George Fox practiced. For more on the history of the Branches of Friends see "A Brief History of the Branches of Friends" at http://www.quakerinfo.org/quakerism/branches/history. This article only scratches the surface, however; for a deeper dive, *The Oxford Handbook of Quaker Studies* is a good place to start.

Reading List

Jane Addams, *Democracy and Social Ethics* (New York: Macmillan, 1902).

———, *The Selected Papers of Jane Addams, Vol. 1: Preparing to Lead, 1860–81,* Mary Lynne McCree Bryan, Barbara Bair and Maree de Angury, eds. (Urbana: University of Illinois Press, 2003).

Rex Ambler, *The Quaker Way: A Rediscovery* (Winchester, UK: John Hunt, 2013).

Stephen W. Angell and Pink Dandelion, eds., *The Oxford Handbook of Quaker Studies.* (New York: Oxford University Press, 2015).

Margaret Hope Bacon, *The Quiet Rebels: The Story of the Quakers in America* (Wallingford, PA: Pendle Hill, 1999).

Robert Barclay, *The True Christian Divinity* (Manchester, UK: William Irwin, 1850).

Keith Beaseley-Topliffe, ed., *Writings of Thomas Kelly* (Nashville, TN: Upper Room, 2017).

J. Brent Bill, *Holy Silence: The Gift of Quaker Spirituality* (Grand Rapids, MI: Eerdmans, 2016).

Harold Bloom, *Jesus and Yahweh: The Names Divine* (New York: Riverhead, 2011).

Cynthia Bourgeault, *The Wisdom Jesus* (New York: Penguin, 2008).

William Charles Braithwaite, *Spiritual Guidance in the Experience of the Society of Friends* (London: Swarthmore Lecture, 1909).

Howard Brinton, *The Nature of Quakerism* (Wallingford, PA: Pendle Hill, 1949).

———, *Quaker Journals: Varieties of Religious Experiences Among Friends* (New York: Church Publishing, 1983).

———, *Reaching Decisions: The Quaker Method* (Wallingford, PA: Pendle Hill, 1952).

Rita Brock and Gabriella Lettini, *Soul Repair: Recovering from Moral Injury after War* (Boston: Beacon Press, 2013).

Brené Brown, *The Gifts of Imperfection: Let Go of Who You Think You're Supposed to Be and Embrace Who You Are* (Center City, MN: Hazelden, 2010).

Victoria Bissell Brown, *The Education of Jane Addams* (Philadelphia: University of Pennsylvania Press, 2004).

Martin Buber, *I and Thou* (New York: Charles Scribner's Sons, 1970).

Nicolas Cabasilas, *The Life in Christ*, Carmino J. de Catazaro, trans. (Yonkers, NY: St. Vladimer's Press, 1974).

John Calvin, *Institutes of Christian Religion*, Henry Beveridge, trans. (Peabody, MA: Hendrickson, 2009).

F. Forrester Church, *The Essential Tillich* (Chicago: University of Chicago Press, 1999).

Oliver Clement, *The Roots of Christian Mysticism* (Hyde Park, NY: New City Press, 1993).

Carol Conti-Entin, *Improvisation & Spiritual Disciplines: Continuing the Divine-Human Duet* (Wallingford, PA: Pendle Hill, 1989).

Wilmer Cooper, *The Testimony of Integrity* (Wallingford, PA: Pendle Hill, 1991).

Pink Dandelion, *The Quakers: A Very Short Introduction* (Oxford, UK: Oxford University Press, 2008).

Eknath Easwaran, *Gandhi the Man* (Tomale, CA: Nilgiri Press, 1978).

Meister Eckhart, *The Complete Mystical Works of Meister Eckhart*, Maurice O'Connell Walshe, trans. (Chestnut Ridge, PA: Crossroad,f 2009).

Harvey D. Egan, *What Are They Saying About Mysticism* (Eugene, OR: Wipf and Stock, 2021).

Bliss Forbush, *Elias Hicks: Quaker Liberal* (New York: Columbia University Press, 1956).

Elfrida Vipont Foulds, *Elfrida Vipont Foulds Speaks* (Philadelphia: Quaker Press, 1982).

George Fox, *George Fox: The Journal* (New York: Penguin, 1999).

Mahatma Gandhi, *The Power of Nonviolent Resistance* (New York: Penguin Classics, 2019).

Francis Howgill, *Observations on the Operation of the Holy Spirit upon the Mind of Man* (Hobart, NY: James Ross, 1834).

Brian Johnston, *The Book of James: Epistles of Straw?* (Swindon, UK: Hayes Press, 2014).

Rufus Jones, *A Dynamic Faith* (London: Headley, 1901).

———, *The Faith and Practice of the Quakers* (Kingsley, AU: Left Of Brain Onboarding Pty Limited, 2021).

———, *Finding The Trail of Life* (Tamil Nadu, India: Isha Books, 2013).

———, *The Inner Life* (New York: Macmillan, 1916).

———, *Pathways to the Reality of God* (New York: Macmillan, 1931).

———, *Rufus Jones Speaks* (Brooklyn, NY: Leonard S. Kenworthy, 1951).

———, *Social Law in the Spiritual World: Studies in Human and Divine Interrelationship* (New York: Swarthmore Press, 1904).

———, *The Story of George Fox* (New York: Macmillan, 1922).

Carl G. Jung, *Aion: Researches into the Phenomenology of Self* (New York: Routledge, 2014 [reprint]).

———, *Man and His Symbols* (New York: Random House, 1964).

Thomas Keating, *Centering Prayer in Daily Life and Ministry* (New York: Bloomsbury, 1997).

———, *Fruits and Gifts of the Spirit* (New York: Lantern, 2014).

———, *Invitation to Love: The Way of Christian Contemplation* (New York: Continuum, 2000).

————, *Open Mind, Open Heart: The Contemplative Dimension of the Gospel* (London: A&C Black, 2002).

————, *The Spiritual Journey* (Snowmass, CO: Contemplative Outreach, 1992).

Calvin Keene, *God in Thought and Experience* (Newberg, OR: Quaker Theological Discussion Group, 1981).

Thomas R. Kelly, *A Testament of Devotion* (New York: HarperOne, 1996).

————, *Reality of the Spiritual World and the Gathered Meeting* (London: Quaker Home Service, 1996).

Leonard S. Kenworth, ed., *Quaker Quotations on Faith and Practice* (Kennett Square, PA: Quaker Publications, 1983).

Søren Kierkegaard, *Christian Discourses,* Walter Lowrie, trans. (New York: Oxford University Press, 1940).

————, *Kierkegaard for the Church: Essays and Sermons,* Ronald F. Marshall, ed. (Eugene, OR: Wipf & Stock, 2013).

Ernest Kurtz and Katherine Ketcham, *The Spirituality of Imperfection: Storytelling and the Search for Meaning* (New York: Bantam, 2002).

Brother Lawrence, *Brother Lawrence: A Christian Zen Master,* Ellyn Sanna, ed. (Vestal, NY: Anamchara Books, 2016).

Rich Lewis, *Sitting with God: A Journey to Your True Self Through Centering Prayer* (Vestal, NY: Anamchara Books, 2020).

Anthony Manousos, *Howard and Anna Brinton: Re-inventors of Quakerism in the Twentieth Century, An Interpretive Biography* (Philadelphia, PA: FGC Quaker Books, 2013).

Marcelle Martin, *A Guide to Faithfulness in Groups* (San Francisco, CA: Inner Light, 2019).

————, *Our Life Is Love: The Quaker Spiritual Journey* (San Francisco, CA: Inner Light, 2016).

Bernard McGinn, *The Essential Writings of Christian Mysticism* (New York: Modern Library, 2006).

Noah Baker Merrill, *Prophets, Midwives, and Thieves: Reclaiming the Ministry of the Whole* (Melbourne Beach, FL: Southeastern Yearly Meeting Publications, 2013).

Robert D. Miller, *Yahweh: Origin of a Desert God* (Gottingen, Germany: Vandenhoeck & Ruprecht, 2021).

Stephen Mitchell, ed., *The Enlightened Heart: An Anthology of Sacred Poetry* (New York: Harper & Row, 1989).

———, trans., *Tao Ching: A New English Version* (New York: Harper & Row, 1988).

Rosemary Moore, *The Light in Their Consciences: The Early Quakers in Britain, 1646–1666* (State College, PA: Penn State University Press, 2011).

Rita Nakashima and Gabriella Lettini, *Soul Repair: Recovering from Moral Injury after War* (Boston: Beacon Press, 2013).

Henri Nouwen, *The Road to Daybreak* (New York: Doubleday, 1990).

———, *The Wounded Healer* (Image Books, 1979).

Parker Palmer, *A Hidden Wholeness: The Journey Toward an Undivided Live* (New York: Wiley, 2022).

———, *A Place Called Community* (Wallingford, PA: Pendle Hill, 1977).

Isaac Penington, *The Works of Isaac Penington* (Philadelphia, PA: Friends Book Store, 1863).

William Penn, *Advice of William Penn to His Children* (Philadelphia: Franklin Roberts, 1881).

———, *A Brief Account of the Rise and Progress of the People Called Quakers* (Philadelphia: Solomon W. Conrad, 1803).

———, *No Cross, No Crown* (Shippensburg, PA: Destiny Image, 2001).

———, *Selected Works of William Penn* (London: William Phillips and George Yard, 1825).

———, *Memoirs of the Life of Isaac Penington* (Philadelphia, PA: Kite, 1831).

The Philokalia, G. E. H. Palmer, Philip Sherrard, and Kallistos Ware, trans. (New York: Farrar, Straus and Giroux, 1983).

John Punshon, *Encounter with Silence: Reflections from the Quaker Tradition* (Richmond, IN: Friends United Press, 2006).

Linda Hill Renfer, ed., *Daily Readings from Quaker Writings* (Perth, Australia: Serenity Press, 1989).

Charles River, ed., *The Quakers: The History and Legacy of the Religious Society of Friends* (Scotts Valley, CA: CreateSpace, 2017).

Clive Sansom, *Faith and Practice* (Philadelphia, PA: Friends Publishing, 1962).

Anne Firor Scott, *Making the Invisible Woman Visible* (Champagne: University of Illinois Press, 1984).

Danielle Shroyer, *Original Blessing: Putting Sin in Its Rightful Place* (Minneapolis, MN: Fortress Press, 2016).

Ana Smiljanic, trans., *Our Thoughts Determine Our Lives: The Life and Teachings of Elder Thaddeus of Vitovnica* (Platina, CA: St. Herman of Alaska Brotherhood, 2012).

Amos Smith, *Be Still and Listen: Experience the Presence of God in Your Life* (Brewster, MA: Paraclete Press, 2018).

———, *Healing the Divide: Recovering Christianity's Mystic Roots* (Eugene, OR: Wipf & Stock, 2013).

Jens Soering, *The Way of the Prisoner: Breaking the Chains of Self through Centering Prayer and Centering Prayer Practice* (New York: Lantern Books, 2003).

Douglas V. Steere, ed., *Quaker Spirituality: Selective Writings* (Mahwah, NJ: Paulist Press, 1984).

Caroline Stephen, *Quaker Strongholds* (Wallingford, PA: Pendle Hill, 1951).

Garrett A. Sullivan Jr., Alan Stewart, Rebecca Lemon, eds., *The Encyclopedia of English Renaissance Literature*, Vol. 1 (New York: Wiley, 2012).

William Taber, *Four Doors to Meeting for Worship,* Pendle Hill Pamphlet #306 (Wallingford, PA: Pendle Hill, 1992).

D.G. Tendulkar, *Mahatma, Vol. 8, 1947–1948* (New Delhi: Government of India, 1954).

Teresa of Avila, *The Collected Work of St. Teresa of Avila* (Washington, DC: Institute of Carmelite Studies, 1976).

D. Elton Trueblood, *The Life We Prize* (New York: Harper, 1951).

———. *Your Other Vocation* (New York: Harper, 1952).

Kallistos Ware, *The Orthodox Way* (Yonkers, NY: St. Vladimir's Press, 1995).

Dan Wilson, *Promise of Deliverance* (Wallingford, PA: Pendle Hill, 1951).

Walter Wink, *Jesus and Nonviolence: A Third Way* (Minneapolis, MN: Fortress Press, 2003).

John Woolman, *John Woolman Journal* (New York: Houghton Mifflin, 1884).

Index

Scripture Index

Sitting with God

A Journey to Your True Self
Through Centering Prayer

"Lewis presents an intimate view of his centering prayer journey. He helps us discover the contemplative life and who we are in the deepest sense, made in God's image."

— Fr. Carl Arico, founding member of Contemplative Outreach Ltd., and author of *A Taste of Silence*

"This work offers a friendly and accessible approach to centering prayer that will be of great benefit to those new to the practice. Rich has a lovely way of inviting the reader in through honest reflections on his own experience, both struggles and graces. These stories offer comfort and gentle encouragement on the way."

— Christine Valters Paintner, author of *The Soul of a Pilgrim*

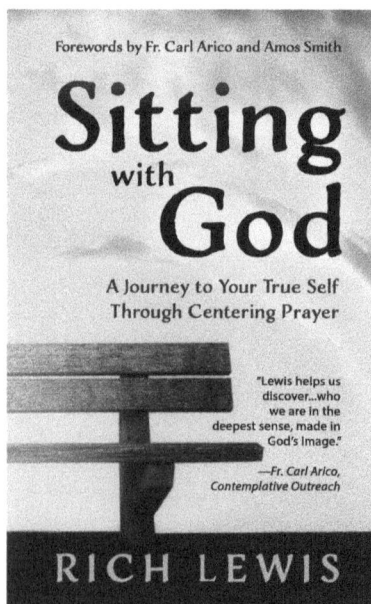

Forewords by Fr. Carl Arico and Amos Smith

Sitting with **God**

A Journey to Your True Self
Through Centering Prayer

"Lewis helps us discover...who we are in the deepest sense, made in God's image."

—Fr. Carl Arico, Contemplative Outreach

RICH LEWIS

Dante's Road
The Journey Home for the Modern Soul

Nautilus Book Awards 2019 Gold Winner

This spiritual guidebook follows in the footsteps of Dante on his journey through the Divine Comedy. A fresh, modern take on this path, the book invites us to explore these questions: what is my hell and how do I move through it? What is my purgatory and what lesson do I need to take away? What is my paradise; how do I get there and how do I stay there? With wisdom distilled from the great myths, scriptures, and the world's mystics, this book is an invitation to ever-greater awakening and wholeness.

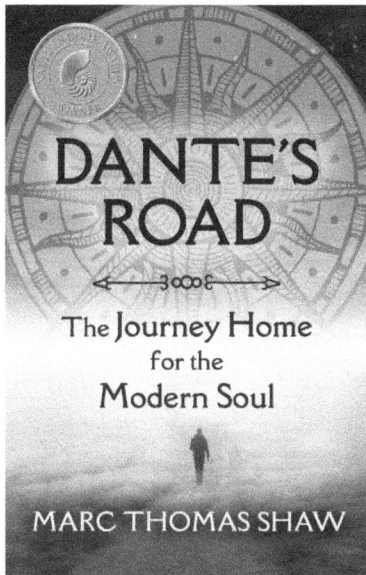

Deeper

Finding the Depth Dimension Beneath the Surface of Life

"Written with the clear thinking of a physicist, this inspiring book uses fresh language and creative metaphors to guide the reader on a deepening contemplative journey. . . . The author offers a sense of reassuring companionship for what can sometimes be a lonely inner pilgrimage."

— Father Richard Rohr

"Here is a book that is worth reading and meditating slowly. Sharon bites on what it is to be human, on how the life of the spirit gets to work within genuine anthropological and psychological reflection. The result is a slow narrative that takes the reader deeper and deeper, but cumulatively, without ever losing its way."

— James Alison, author of *Faith beyond Resentment* and *Undergoing God*

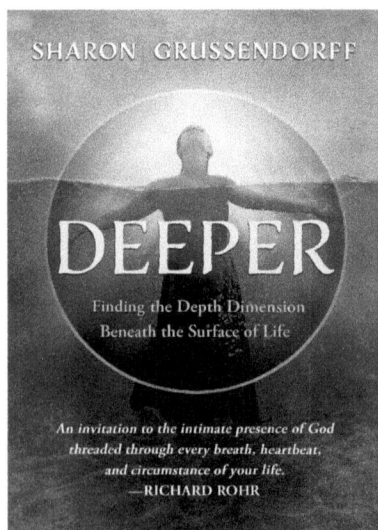

SHARON GRUSSENDORFF

DEEPER

Finding the Depth Dimension
Beneath the Surface of Life

An invitation to the intimate presence of God
threaded through every breath, heartbeat,
and circumstance of your life.
—RICHARD ROHR

Discovering the Essence

How to Grow a Spiritual Practice When Your Religion Is Cracking Apart

If you're feeling disillusioned with organized religion, this book is for you. With Jeff Campbell as your tour guide, you can embark on your own personal journey to discover the essence of spirituality.

"Many of us can identify with Jeff Campbell's experience of being disenchanted with religion, leaving church, learning from the spiritual disciplines of others, and finding his way back to a vitality he'd sought all along. His path and his book are punctuated with deceptively simple, but life-changing practices. They offer hope for those seeking an authentic encounter with the Holy."

— Belden C. Lane, author of *Backpacking with the Saints: Wilderness Hiking as Spiritual Practice*

www.ingramcontent.com/pod-product-compliance
Ingram Content Group UK Ltd.
Pitfield, Milton Keynes, MK11 3LW, UK
UKHW011328220525
6044UKWH00006B/15

9 781625 249029